MANAGING RADICAL CHANGE

Managing Radical Change

WHAT INDIAN COMPANIES MUST DO
TO BECOME WORLD-CLASS

SUMANTRA GHOSHAL
GITA PIRAMAL
CHRISTOPHER A. BARTLETT

Field research by Sudeep Budhiraja

VIKING

VIKING

Penguin Books India (P) Ltd., 11 Community Centre, Panchsheel Park, New Delhi 110 017, India
Penguin Books Ltd., 27 Wrights Lane, London W8 5TZ, UK
Penguin Putnam Inc., 375 Hudson Street, New York, NY 10014, USA
Penguin Books Australia Ltd., Ringwood, Victoria, Australia
Penguin Books Canada Ltd., 10 Alcorn Avenue, Suite 300, Toronto, Ontario, M4V 3B2, Canada
Penguin Books (NZ) Ltd., Cnr Rosedale and Airborne Roads, Albany, Auckland, New Zealand

First published in Viking by Penguin Books India 2000

10 9 8 7 6 5 4 3 2

Typeset in *Sabon Roman* by SÜRYA, New Delhi
Printed at Rekha Printers Pvt. Ltd., New Delhi

We dedicate this book to Susmita Ghoshal, wife of one of us but friend of all three

CONTENTS

PREFACE

This book has a long and somewhat tortuous history, in the course of which many people have contributed to it in diverse ways. While the rest of the book is written in a plural voice, reflecting its joint authorship, I chose to write this preface in the first person singular because of this history, since the contributions of many have come to the book via their associations with me.

The foundation stone for this project was laid over ten years ago when the Indian Institute of Foreign Trade in Delhi offered me the Unilever Visiting Chair to spend a few months in India. This gave me the opportunity to visit a number of Indian companies such as Maruti Udyog, Bajaj Auto, ICICI, Tata Sons, Reliance, Thermax, Hindustan Lever and Bharat Forge. Up to that time, my academic work had been limited to studying North American, European and Japanese companies, and this first research link with a few remarkable Indian companies and managers created the germ of an idea: wouldn't it be fun to do a proper study and write a book focused on the management challenges facing Indian companies?

I must highlight the contributions of a few individuals in creating this desire in my mind. First, I was deeply influenced by my meeting with the late Rohinton Aga at Thermax. His personal values, his beliefs about management and his overwhelming gentleness and kindness had a very important and durable impact on me. Second, it was at this time that I got to know Sushim Dutta and the top management team at Hindustan Lever, and the sheer quality and enthusiasm of that team helped me understand just how good a good Indian management team could be. I had, by then, become quite familiar with the management processes of some of the high-profile global corporations: General Electric, Unilever, Philips, Matsushita, NEC, Procter and Gamble, and so on—and the people I met at HLL were as good as the best I had seen anywhere. Third, both Tarun Das of CII and N. Vagul of ICICI made this overall experience possible because, without their support, I could not get access to the companies and managers I met.

The idea lay dormant, however, for a few years. The initial flush of enthusiasm subsided after I returned to INSEAD, the French business school where I then taught. The day-to-day pressures of my normal teaching, research, writing and consulting pushed aside the dream of what, by then, I had come to call the 'India Book'.

The next boost came in 1992, when Professor J. Ramachandran of the Indian Institute of Management, Bangalore, came to INSEAD for a year, as a visiting scholar. He instantly became a friend, and together we revived the idea of a book on Indian management.

He and I worked together on two cases—one on Reliance, where Ram had excellent access, having worked for a while with Anil Ambani, and the other on Wipro, for whom I had done some consulting work. Again, these two cases, and the managers we met in the course of our field work, left some very durable impressions on me and those impressions have significantly influenced the content and tone of this book.

Having worked in a large Indian public sector company for over twelve years before retiring into academe, I could not believe what I saw in Reliance. Like other Indians, I had read about Reliance in the business press—both good and bad—but seeing the company from inside was a unique experience. In interview after interview with Reliance managers, I heard the same tales of breathtaking ambition and extraordinary speed. That is where the concept of radical performance improvement first entered our lexicon—just imagine what other Indian companies could do, if only they could capture a bit of the Reliance spirit!

At Wipro, Azim Premji provided a complete counterpoint. His absolute commitment to a set of values, particularly to complete and total integrity, was as novel in the Indian corporate context as Dhirubhai Ambani's sense of ambition and dedication to growth. If Premji could build a successful business in India on the strength of those values, why couldn't others? Another important piece of the overall argument we present in this book had fallen in place.

Ram and I planned to continue the work after his return to Bangalore. But, alas, that did not happen. I got busy writing a book with Chris Bartlett, and Ram had to take on a senior administrative role at IIM Bangalore. So, the 'India Book' once again found itself on the backburner.

It is a pity, because it would have been wonderful to have Ram as a co-author of this book. For me, working with him was a very satisfying experience. He challenged much of my thinking, and that has undoubtedly influenced the ideas in this book in ways that I may not even be consciously aware of. I believe there is also an issue here that the directors and governing boards of Indian business schools may need to consider. Are they eating their young? Among the faculty in these schools there are many Rams, with the intellectual capacity to be world-class scholars. Yet, heavy teaching and administrative responsibilities early in their careers are preventing them from achieving their potential. Somehow, people like Ram must be given the time and the resources to research and write, for they are capable of producing outstanding work.

In 1994, I moved from INSEAD to the London Business School, and my contact with Indian managers broadened almost immediately. For many Indian business families, London serves as the second home. As a result, I gradually become acquainted with quite a few of them—Dr Parvinder Singh of Ranbaxy, Ajay Piramal of Nicholas Piramal, and Rahul Bajaj, among others. The growing Indian contingent at Davos provided another opportunity for at least once-a-year connections. Over the next two years, I did some brief consulting work with some of them, and followed that up with research and case writing. It was through this process that the Ranbaxy, Indian Oxygen and Infosys cases came into being. While I was still far away from the 'India book', the raw materials were slowly being assembled.

Once again, both Ranbaxy and Infosys appeared to be very antithetical to the classic systems of Indian business and management I had experienced over the 1970s, as a junior manager in Indian Oil. At Ranbaxy, Dr Parvinder Singh demonstrated that wealthy family owners of successful businesses did not have to be feudal and authoritarian in their style. His commitment to internationalization was an eye-opener, as was his unwavering dedication to R&D. At Infosys, N.R. Narayana Murthy demonstrated an even more extreme form of the same characteristics. The clarity of his thoughts, the courtesy he extended to everyone, the simplicity of his lifestyle—indeed everything about him contradicted my caricature view of the billionaire owner-CEO of Indian companies. Dr Singh and Narayana Murthy are the originators of many of the ideas we present in this book—we are largely the tellers of their tale.

In 1997, three things happened simultaneously which, together, converted the vague aspiration of writing an 'India Book' into a concrete project.

First, Sudeep Budhiraja gave me a ring from Malaysia. We did not know each other, but I knew his father, Mr S.B. Budhiraja, who was my boss in Indian Oil. After completing his

MBA at Michigan, Sudeep had joined Citibank, rising to a senior middle management position. As he neared forty, he wanted to take a breather—a break for a year, to rethink his life and his career. Could he use this year to do some research work with me?

Second, I met Gita Piramal. I had, of course, heard about her because of the success of *Business Maharajas*, but an accidental meeting with her soon led to a strong and durable family friendship.

Third, Kumarmangalam Birla, an alumni of the London Business School, sponsored the Aditya V. Birla India Centre at LBS and—simply because of the lack of any alternative—I took over as its temporary director.

Suddenly, there was momentum. The India Centre was created to facilitate and support research relevant to Indian management, and some serious work had to begin. Gita knew everyone in India, so company access was not a problem. Sudeep had taken his sabbatical leave from Citibank and was willing to start work immediately. We launched the India project.

I cannot adequately convey my gratitude to Kumarmangalam Birla and to Santrupt Mishra, our immediate contact in his organization. The A.V. Birla India Centre at LBS has the potential of creating an enormous amount of value for Indian companies and for India. Already, over the last two years, its activities have raised the visibility of Indian companies and managers within LBS and its support community that includes numerous industrialists and senior managers in the UK. Thanks to the resources provided by Kumar, the centre is supporting the dissertation research of more than twenty-five Ph.D. students in Indian business schools. Over time, it can create a two-way channel of communication between Indian and foreign managers that is of great benefit to both. It was the centre that provided the final impetus for launching our project and I hope this book will be seen as a worthy, if small, first step in pursuing the vision that the London Business School and Kumarmangalam Birla shared when they jointly set it up.

Over 1998 and 1999, Sudeep, Gita and I spent a lot of time together, visiting companies, conducting interviews and gathering data. Not all the case studies we started came to successful completion—in some instances, there was no story to tell, in others, top-level managers declined to release the cases for public use. But, finally, we had some of the most interesting stories we tell in this book—cases on Hero Honda, Bajaj Auto, HDFC, Zee Telefilms and Hindustan Lever. Ajay Piramal's nephew was a student at LBS, and his project on Nicholas Piramal added one more example. That was enough: we now had a sufficient variety of cases to start the real work of writing a book.

The dozen cases that provide the contextual grounding of this book are based on interviews with hundreds of managers at all levels of the companies. All of these managers gave us freely of their time. More than that, a vast majority of them talked to us openly and with candour, and we learnt a great deal from those conversations. While it is impossible to thank each of them individually, the book owes them an enormous debt of gratitude, for without their cooperation nothing else we did would have mattered.

The actual grind of writing the book started in April 1999. At this point, Sudeep dropped out, and that is the second regret I have about the authorship of this book. He should have had his name on the cover; he deserved it and the book undoubtedly would have been the better for it. But, the challenge of simultaneously building two homes left Sudeep with little time. Also, coordination between Gita at Mumbai and me in London was difficult enough, and a third ongoing link with Sudeep in Chandigarh proved impossible to maintain. So, while Sudeep is a co-author of the accompanying case book, I must specially acknowledge his role in the fieldwork phase, without which this book might never have come into being. I understand that

Sudeep may stay on in India, and I hope that we will soon start on another project together. Like a tiger that has tasted blood, Sudeep has tasted the joys of research and writing, and I am sure he will soon return to it. I will eagerly wait for that to happen.

Until Gita and I finished the actual writing of this book, we had no idea that Chris Bartlett was our co-author. It was only when we read the completed manuscript that we realized that his thumbprints were all over it. Chris and I have worked together for nearly twenty years; we have written three books together, and over two dozen articles. That joint work has shaped the way I look at the world of business and management.

So, I have looked at the Indian data through the same lens. Given the extent of that influence—indeed a number of chapters in this book bear close resemblance to ideas Chris and I presented in the *Individualized Corporation*, our last book—an acknowledgement would not be enough. So, having finished the book, we added Chris's name on the cover because, unknown to both him and us, he was writing it with us, all along.

Beyond Chris, a few of my academic colleagues have also had some significant influence on this book. Of them, I must particularly emphasize the roles of C.K Prahalad and Nitin Nohria.

While Chris has been my partner, C.K is my guru. It has been a bit like the Dronacharya–Ekalavya situation: we have had little direct connection. He and I have never written anything together, nor have we done much joint teaching or consulting, except for a brief stint in a major European company. But, every time I have met him, in every conversation I have had with him—at work, in his home or in mine—I have learnt something. That is C.K. He has an amazing intellectual breadth, and a profound capacity to conceptualize without becoming abstract. Many, many ideas and phrases we have used in this book have their origin in conversations with C.K. It is simply not possible for me to identify all of them, so as to acknowledge his specific contributions, because they have become so much a part of me that I cannot distinctly see their sources any more. The only way to address this deficiency, of not concretely assigning to C.K some of the thoughts that came from him, is to acknowledge that the overall perspective of the book—the belief in radical performance improvement—came to me from him. He is there everywhere in this book, and I do not feel apologetic about that in any way because it is a sishya's right to appropriate the wisdom of his guru.

Nitin is perhaps the closest to what I consider to be my family, outside of my immediate family. He and I have taught a course together, covering some of the concepts that are contained in this book. Once again, undoubtedly, his voice hides in many chapters, impossible to pinpoint because it has so inextricably become a part of mine.

I must also acknowledge here the role of Sharon Wilson, my secretary, not only for all the work she put in on this book—from managing all the administrative and travel logistics at the time of the fieldwork to typing up the whole manuscript— but also for the way she organizes my life, without which I would not have had the time to do either the research or the writing. Having used Sharon's help in numerous ways, I am sure that Gita will add her voice to mine in thanking Sharon not only for doing what she has done but also for being who she is. At Gita's end, Marie Pinto, her secretary, deserves similar thanks.

Finally, while it is not customary to express gratitude to a co-author, this quick history of the intellectual journey behind this book will remain incomplete without a clarification of Gita's role.

Beyond her wide network that opened doors everywhere, Gita brought to this work her outstanding story-telling ability and her gift for jargon-free, easy-to-read writing. She also brought her intimate understanding of Indian business and businessmen. Given her own personal background, she could interpret the actions of the companies we studied, and the statements of their managers, with a level of richness that was totally beyond me. And writing can be dreary work—long hours spent in isolation, with little to show for it at the end. She brought joy to the whole project, maintaining balance and good humour, while adding ideas and insights.

London   **Sumantra Ghoshal**
17 March 2000

I

THE CHALLENGE OF RADICAL
PERFORMANCE IMPROVEMENT

1

RADICAL PERFORMANCE
IMPROVEMENT IS POSSIBLE

We learnt more about corporate leadership and change management in a single morning in February 1989 than it is possible to learn from reading any number of books and articles.

The top management group of a multi-billion dollar European giant—let us call it Semco—had gathered for their annual two-day retreat. The retreat, held every year in the same location, was an opportunity for the seniormost fifty people, including the CEO and all board members, to catch up with one another, and to take stock of the overall situation of the company. One of the two mornings had been scheduled for a review of the company's strategy, and one of us had been asked to facilitate discussions in that session. Indeed, the HR director of Semco had been very specific in his brief: 'No lectures, please—just help us think about our overall corporate strategy.'

How can you review the 'overall corporate strategy' of a company that operates in over ten distinctly different businesses, with over 3000 products produced and sold in 100 countries around the world, in one brief morning session?

After considerable thought, we had settled on a very simple—to our mind, almost simplistic—way to begin the discussions. We compared Semco's performance in the preceding year with that of two roughly comparable companies, General Electric and Matsushita, with whom it competed in several different businesses. Lacking the resources and information for any elaborate or sophisticated benchmarking, we picked the easiest numbers from all three companies' annual reports. The comparisons looked as follows (table 1.1):

Table 1.1: Semco's Relative Performance

	Semco	General Electric	Matsushita
1. Sales per employee	$88,471	$184,534	$215,223
2. Inventory to sales	27.4%	12.4%	14.5%
3. Sales to net fixed assets	3.0%	3.4%	6.7%
4. Operating margin	2.9%	9.5%	7.6%
5. Return on equity	3.9%	18.9%	7.4%

In that memorable morning, we put up this comparison right at the beginning, and said 'Gentlemen,'—all men in the group, no women—'these numbers appear to us to be a good starting point for a review of your corporate strategy. What are you going to do about this situation?'

For us, what followed was education for a lifetime. A long and vigorous argument ensued as to why 'our' numbers were either wrong or irrelevant.

The people in the room were seasoned experts—in their own areas of specialization, they had forgotten more than we could ever hope to learn. So, their arguments were intellectually unassailable. How could we compare their performance with that of Matsushita for a year when, as everyone knew, the yen was severely undervalued and most of the key European currencies including their own were equally severely overvalued? How could their returns be compared with those of an American and a Japanese company when both America and Japan had well-developed and competitive component suppliers while Europe did not, forcing Semco to continue with the capital intensive and low-return component businesses to ensure the reliability and quality of its final products? How could we be so simple-minded as to overlook the dramatic differences in wage rates and labour productivity across the United States, Japan and Europe—and could they, as managers of a European company, do anything about the leisure-loving decadence of European labour? Were the European governments not to blame, rather than corporate managers?

The finance director of a large division of the company made a long speech about accounting norms and standards: 'If you took into account the differences between the Japanese and our methods of accounting, you would see that our ROE, if we accounted like the Japanese, would be closer to 4.3 per cent'!

There were other kinds of arguments, too. Was business all about making money? Did a company not have other responsibilities? Why were we looking at only the simplest financial figures, ignoring all the other priorities? Also, the Japanese were obsessive people. In Europe people were not like that at all. Everything in Europe was at 5 per cent—inflation was 5 per cent, unemployment was 5 per cent, growth was 5 per cent. The implications were that if only we understood Europe better, we would not be wasting their time with such silly numbers.

Some readers may find this story amusing, given the abysmal performance of Semco the numbers reveal, and ask, were those people in the room stupid? Prestigious and established global corporations do not hire stupid people; in fact, they hire the best and the brightest around the world. And then, only the very best of these hires ascend to the top ranks of the hierarchy. There are too many checks and balances in these companies for stupid people to reach the top. There were no stupid people in the room.

Then, why did they react as they did? Why could they not see how poor their performance was, compared to that of their key competitors? Why did they find it so hard to confront that simple reality, without which they could not even begin a discussion on how they could improve that performance?

The Pathology of Satisfactory Underperformance

The answer to these questions, we have since learnt, is very simple. It lies in a corporate disease called satisfactory underperformance. It is a pervasive disease—we have confronted it in companies all over the world. It is a disease that is very easy to catch—indeed, finding a way to avoid it is the difficult part.

Consider the case of Semco. The graph below (figure 1.1) shows its performance in the second half of the 1980s. Our encounter with its senior managers took place in early 1989. At that point, what were these managers seeing?

Figure 1.1: Semco's Profitability

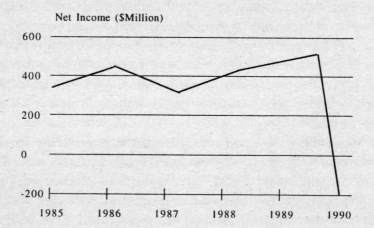

First, they were seeing an annual profit of about $400 million, which is a lot of money. They were not seeing that the profits were a pathetic 4 per cent of equity, nor were they seeing that given their cost of capital of over 11 per cent, at that rate of profit, they were destroying value every year. They were not seeing that their profit margins were worse than practically risk-free bank returns. One does not naturally 'see' these things—they are too intellectual, too abstract, too remote. Besides, they were also seeing that their profits that year were higher than the profits of the preceding year; indeed, higher than their profits for the three preceding years. They were not seeing that in each of those years, and in the three earlier ones, they had been systematically destroying value, which is why their stock prices were doing so badly.

What was even more remarkable for us was the fact that, deep in their hearts, all the fifty managers in the room knew that they were performing very poorly. You could take any one of them aside, on a one-to-one basis, and they would honestly admit that given their strengths in technology, people, brands, distribution, and so on, the results were poor. Yet, they would never acknowledge that reality in any collective forum. Individually, they knew the truth; collectively, they would conspire together to deny the truth.

For established companies, the truth is relatively easy to deny. Often their competitive strengths erode rapidly, as had happened at Semco. But the company continues to make money—because of all the resources it has, in terms of an established customer base, a historically developed distribution channel, strong brands, and so on. All these resources would have been built by earlier generations of managers, yet the incumbent management takes credit for all the returns these resources generate, never asking the question, 'What are we doing to add value?' The crisis ultimately comes, as it did for Semco when it fell off the precipice towards the end of 1989. But, before the crisis hits, there is often a long period when the company can coast along in a state of satisfactory underperformance, assigning all uncomfortable signs to factors in the external environment, beyond management control; and finding rationalizations on the one hand, and reducing ambition on the other hand, so as to maintain satisfaction in the face of declining fortunes.

The Dynamics of Satisfactory Underperformance

There is a highly predictable process through which the pathology of satisfactory underperformance takes hold of a company (see figure 1.2).

Figure 1.2: The Dynamics of Satisfactory Underperformance

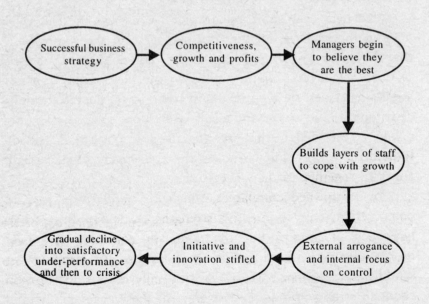

By luck, chance or foresight and courage, a company develops an effective and successful business strategy. The strategy fits the market demands, and matches the company's strengths. As a result, the company becomes highly competitive, with growth and profits as the ensuing rewards.

With growth and profits come recognition and celebration. Top managers of the company start seeing their face on the covers of business journals. The Harvard Business School writes a case on their success. Soon they start believing all that is being said of them—they are the best. It is their brilliance that caused it all. They go on the lecture circuit to tell others how they did it, despite great odds.

With growth comes the perceived need for better control. After all, if they did it all, then they must continue to do it all, to protect the success and build on it. As the company becomes bigger, to do it all they need support to collect all the information, to bring all the important choices and decisions to them. So, they hire layers of staff, as instruments to leverage their own brilliance in the expanded organization. The staff joins the business press in telling them how good they are, and it all becomes a positive reinforcement cycle.

Being the best gives these managers the right to be arrogant, not only with their subordinates, but also with customers and suppliers: 'Why make a fuss if some little thing goes wrong? Don't you understand what a privilege you have, dealing with the best?'

External arrogance and a focus on internal control soon stifle all initiative and enthusiasm at the operating levels of the company. Those who can manage the politics progress, those who side with customers or employees or raise uncomfortable questions are seen as obstacles and are soon sidelined or, better still, pushed overboard. Compliance and fear take over from enthusiasm and passion. Gradually the company slips first into satisfactory underperformance and, finally, into acute crisis.

Satisfactory Underperformance Is Pervasive in India

While there are some exceptions—and this book will tell the tales of some of these exceptional companies—satisfactory underperformance is pervasive in corporate India. We confronted its full force in a senior management programme a few years ago.

In the room were about thirty-five managers from different Indian companies, belonging to both the private and the public sectors. Some were from multinational subsidiaries. All of them occupied very senior positions, including three who were CEOs. A number of them represented organizations that are household names in the country.

'How satisfied do you feel with your company's performance over the last three years?' we asked them. We focused on the word 'satisfied', to tap into their honest feelings. We put up a simple five-point scale, in which 1 represented 'complete dissatisfaction' and 5 indicated 'total satisfaction'. 'Total satisfaction does not mean that everything is perfect and all that needed to be done has been done,' we explained. 'All it means is that the company is dealing with the right issues and making progress in the right direction at the right speed.' Complete dissatisfaction stood for the opposite. We asked all the managers to pick their satisfaction scores—not for the part of the company they worked for, but for the overall company.

The responses followed a predictable near-normal distribution with a skew to the right. Twenty-one managers gave their companies a 3: there were nine 4's, and five 2's. No one rated his or her company either 1 or 5.

'Now,' we asked them, 'what does a 3 mean for you? After all, if 5 is excellent and 1 is abysmal, 3 lies somewhere in the middle—sort of OK performance. What is OK?' We put up a blank chart, with Return on Capital Employed (ROCE) on the horizontal axis, and annual revenue growth on the other. What was 'OK' for each of these two key performance parameters?

The first remarkable discovery was that most of the managers had no clue about their company's ROCE. They knew about their annual profits, but not about either the asset base or the capital employed. These were senior-level managers—typically among the top ten people in their company—and they had no knowledge about their company's ROCE! In fact many had not confronted the term earlier.

Once we got past explaining what ROCE meant, we could get back on track: what was 'OK' ROCE in their minds? With weighted average cost of capital (WACC) varying from 15 per cent to 21 per cent, the different participants suggested numbers between 18 and 30 per cent. Eighteen was the minimum—anything below that would not be 'OK', they felt.

Then we turned to growth: what average rate of annual growth was OK? We emphasized that what we were seeking was their emotional response, not just the intellectual one. 'What growth rate makes you personally feel OK—not great, not lousy, but acceptable?' Influenced by the specifics of their own industries, the different managers came up with different numbers—for some in IT-based industries, for example, 40 per cent growth was OK; for others, it was 15 to 20 per cent. Once again, 15 per cent was the lowest number—anything below that wouldn't do.

We then put up a chart showing the performance of the companies represented in the room—we had worked it out ahead of time (see figure 1.3). We drew thick black lines at 18 per cent for ROCE, and at 15 per cent for growth. Then we shaded the top right-hand box—where performance exceeded the minimum acceptable level for both of these parameters. Anything outside of this box was not OK, according to the participants' own definition of acceptable performance.

There was not a single company in the room whose performance could find a place in that top right-hand box. Not one! There were a few who had grown rapidly, but their returns were relatively poor. There were others whose returns were acceptable, but not growth. And, for a vast majority of companies represented in the room, both growth and returns were below the acceptable minimum.

'How come thirty of you—out of thirty-five—marked your company's performance a 3 or more, i.e., OK or better, when not one of you meet your own criteria for OK performance?' we asked.

Figure 1.3: Performance (1994-97) of Companies Participating in the Senior Management Programme in India

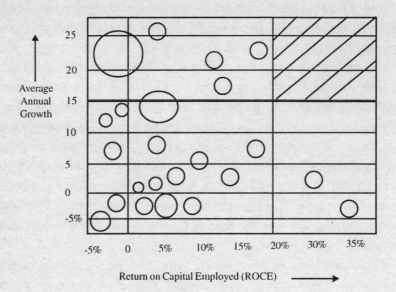

Return on Capital Employed (ROCE) ⟶

The point is simple. While all the thirty-five managers loudly claimed that their companies needed to change, and change quite radically, to respond to the changing economic and competitive situation in India, deep in their hearts none of them felt the urgency they were professing. Without that urgency in their hearts and without their own belief about the possibility of radical change—of radical performance improvement—no one in their organizations was likely to develop that sense of urgency or that belief. People do not listen to what their senior managers say, they look into the eyes of the managers to see the conviction and passion that lie behind the words. Without the energy of their own convictions, what chance did those managers have of leading change in their organizations?

There is something very interesting about the topic of managing change. On the one hand, almost every company in

India is struggling with this issue: what to change to, and how to change. Consulting organizations are enjoying a boom period, helping companies find answers to these questions. Academic seminars on this topic proliferate, with eager participants filling auditoriums to listen to the latest guru-speak on managing change. Everyone is looking for answers, for solutions on how to respond to the radically changing business situation in India.

On the other hand, in every airport bookshop, the largest number of books are on this topic. And, while the language and the examples vary, the basic message in most of those books is similar. They advocate similar actions, often in roughly similar sequence: take the lead, build a case for action, shape a shared vision, mobilize commitment, create actions plans, track progress . . . and so on. And these are good books by competent experts, written on the basis of the experiences of companies around the world. We know a lot about managing change; we know what to do and how.

Why then is something that we know so much about—something that, in this sense, is so easy—so hard to do? Where are the bottlenecks? Where are the barriers?

Bottlenecks tend to be at the top of the bottle. Here too the most critical barrier to change lies at the level of top managers—in their lack of belief in and passion for change. They all say the right words, publish them in the annual reports and in in-house journals, but deep in their hearts, they do not believe what they say. This is why companies find it so hard to manage change. Surely, there are many other barriers and obstacles, but none of them is as debilitating as the mindset of senior managers.

Radical Performance Improvement Is Possible

This is the first and essential prerequisite for creating and managing change: senior managers have to develop the belief that radical change is possible.

That is the fundamental premise behind this book, as well

as its key purpose: to make managers believe—really believe—that radical performance improvement is possible. It is certainly possible for small and medium-sized firms, but it is also possible for large, established companies. And, it is possible to achieve such non-incremental improvements within a reasonably short period of time—not a quarter, or even a year, but not ten years either.

There is a religion in the field of management: it is called incrementalism. It is based on the belief that everything in companies happens slowly and incrementally. It comes with its own rituals and metaphors: like the analogy of supertankers. Supertankers turn slowly, in long turning circles. You cannot jerk them around. Ditto for companies, particularly large companies with thousands of employees: you can't push them too much too fast. You have to have patience, you have to be pragmatic. In big companies, things simply do not happen that quickly.

There are those—Dhirubhai Ambani at Reliance, for example—who have never believed in this religion, but most Indian managers practise it, knowingly or unknowingly. They have been brought up in an era of crippling regulations, bureaucratic dominance, and poor systems and infrastructures when the tenets of this religion tended to be valid most of the time. That is how they got converted to this faith. They continue to maintain that faith. They do not like words like 'radical change'—they find the concept too childish, too unsophisticated, too unIndian. For them, it is difficult to convert once again to the faith of radical performance improvement.

Yet, this is the most important implication of deregulation. In a deregulated, competitive economy driven by the cruel logic of markets, a company that fails to change fast enough can and will die—as is manifest in the slow march to extinction that has already become inevitable for some of India's great old companies. At the same time, in this deregulated market economy, a determined management can transform a company much more quickly and much more effectively than was possible in the past.

International experience clearly shows that radical performance improvement is possible. Motorola had fallen off the precipice in 1985: its profitability had collapsed from 6.3 per cent to 1.3 per cent, a drop of 80 per cent. Competition from Japanese companies had forced Motorola out of the DRAM business. It had slipped from the second to the fifth position as a supplier of semiconductors and was considering a merger—a polite term for divestment—of its semiconductor operations with that of Toshiba. Even in the pagers and cellphone businesses, the Japanese competitors were surging ahead in the battle for miniaturization and featurization, appearing well set to soon capture market leadership.

By 1988, in a mere three years, the position had totally changed. Profitability was back at 5.3 per cent and Motorola had established clear leadership in pagers and cellphones with a slew of innovative and price competitive products. It was back in the DRAM business, and had emerged as a major supplier of semiconductor products to the most demanding customers around the world.

Within these three years, Motorola achieved dramatic improvements in its operations. Development time for new products was shortened from an average of 3 years to 1.8 years. Design improvements led to a fall in the average number of parts per product from 3400 to 630. The order-to-shipment period was cut from thirty to three days. Defects per million fell from 3000 to 200, thanks to the celebrated six-sigma total quality programme.

Motorola is by no means an isolated case. Over the last two decades, many companies around the world have achieved similarly radical performance improvement, shattering the myth of incrementalism. Collectively, their experiences demonstrate some simple truths that most managers, steeped in the tradition of business-as-usual incrementalism, may find hard to believe.

1. High-performance companies exist in 'unattractive' industries

Industry determinism is perhaps the most debilitating of all management beliefs. 'How can I do much better, my industry is in lousy shape.' In India, we have heard it over and over again from executives in consumer durables, electrical machinery, paper, heavy engineering, bulk chemicals and a variety of other businesses. 'Didn't Michael Porter talk about industry attractiveness? Well, mine is a most unattractive industry.'

Here is a quiz. Draw a horizontal line on a piece of paper. On that line, at equal spaces, list some of the major industries: semiconductors, banking, automobiles, petroleum, telecommunication, and so on. Find out the average profitability of each of those industries—the average of all the companies in that business—for a five-year period, and plot these numbers on the vertical axis.

What you will get is a zig-zag curve—some industries, like tobacco, will have a high average industry profitability; others, like semiconductors or airlines, will have low profitability for that particular five-year period. Instead of profitability, you can look at some other performance measure, like shareholder value creation. The same highs and lows will emerge.

Now, check the figures for the best performing company in each industry—not the average, but the best. What do you think the plot of these numbers will look like?

Zero marks for those who think that this plot will parallel average industry profitability. The ups and downs will be much smaller. The performance of the best performers in different businesses are a lot more similar than the average performance of those businesses. Put differently, even in industries that have poor average results, there are individual companies that do very well—almost as well as the best performing companies in any business.

There are those managers who live their lives by the law of industry averages. And then there are those who are inspired by the outliers and have the courage to ask: if one company can do it, why can't we? This is the mindset that is necessary for achieving radical performance improvement—the willingness to benchmark, not against the average or the comparable, but against the best, and drawing both inspiration and learning from those benchmarks to drive oneself forward.

An Indian example? Ispat International N.V. It is registered in Holland and headquartered in London, but Ispat is a very Indian company in its spirit and in its management. Amid the ruins of the steel industry, Lakshmi Niwas Mittal has built one of the most successful Indian-led enterprises by ignoring the law of industry determinism. Read the story of Ispat in chapter 6 of this book, and you will see non-incrementalism in action.

2. A company can achieve outstanding performance even when its industry is shrinking

Historically, Sheffield in England was the source of the world's best cutlery. It was one of the early 'industrial clusters'—like Silicon Valley is today for IT—with a large number of cutlery makers dominating the upper end of the market through their superb workmanship and quality.

Then, in two decades, the industry collapsed. Competition from Hong Kong and other low-cost Asian producers led to absolute catastrophe for the entire industry in Sheffield. Volumes shrank by over 90 per cent—on an indexed basis, production fell from 160 in 1976 to 20 in 1992 (see figure 1.4). A vast majority of the local companies simply went out of business, victims of the industry collapse.

But one company—Richardson Sheffield—went from strength to strength over the same period, defying gravity by growing over 500 per cent.

In India, which industry has shrunk more in size than jute? Drive out on the Grand Trunk Road from Calcutta and you will see the corpses of once thriving jute mills along the road. Yet, in that industry, Hastings Jute Mills is surging forward, growing profitably and investing in new capacity. We will narrate this story in chapter 13, and it is similar to that of Richardson Sheffield: just as the English company defied the rules of the business through innovation and entrepreneurship, by creating the hugely successful 'Laser Knife', for instance, the Kajaria brothers, owners of Hastings Jute Mills since 1994, have made the jute business attractive by transforming the employee–management relationship to radically improve productivity, and by creating innovative new products that find new uses in international markets.

Figure 1.4: Defying Gravity: Richardson Sheffield

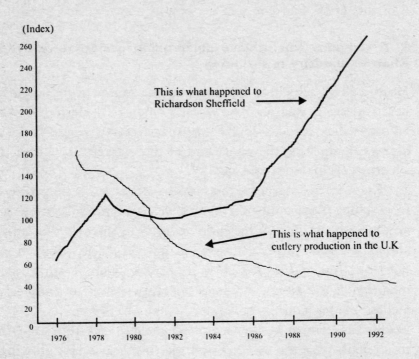

3. Outstanding performance can be achieved even when competitors are much bigger and stronger

In 1975, Xerox enjoyed a staggering 93 per cent share of the worldwide photocopier market. Its technology was guarded by over 500 patents. It had a marketing and support organization of 12,000 sales representatives and 15,000 service people working directly for the Xerox organization in the United States and for the company's joint ventures abroad—Rank Xerox in Europe and Fuji Xerox in Japan. It had a worldwide manufacturing infrastructure, invested more in R&D than the total revenues of most of its competitors, and was one of the few companies whose brand names were indistinguishable from their businesses. Photocopying meant Xeroxing.

When Canon, the little camera company from Japan, jumped into this business in the late 1960s, most observers were sceptical. It was less than a tenth the size of Xerox, and had no sales and service organization to reach the corporate market for copiers. Nor did it have a process technology to bypass Xerox's patents. Reviewing Canon's entry vis-à-vis those of other corporate giants like IBM, Kodak, 3M, Nashua and Smith Corona, who also chose to challenge Xerox around the same time, one investment analyst commented that 'a photocopier is not a large camera'.

Yet, over the next three decades, Canon rewrote the rule book on how copiers were supposed to be produced and sold to build up Rs 300,000 crore in annual revenues in the business, emerging as the second largest global player in terms of sales and surpassing Xerox in the number of units sold. Evidence of this success is visible in the ubiquitous 'Xeroxing by Canon' signs over photocopying shops all over India.

Yes, size matters, but no, size does not determine. While David and Goliath stories may be relatively rare in other aspects of life, they are all too common in the world of business. To those Indian managers who shy away from the aspirations of radical performance improvement on the ground that their ambitions must match the reality of their comparative resources and scale, we say look at the case of Zee TV in chapter 3. Against the Goliaths of Rupert Murdoch and his Star TV, on the one side, and Doordarshan on the other, if Zee could do what it has done, why not you?

4. Radical performance improvement is possible even when you are already very successful

Perhaps the most pervasive myth of all is the belief that truly radical change is possible only when a company is in actual crisis. With crisis comes defreezing, a delegitimization of the existing order that includes the existing power structures, beliefs and processes, and this delegitimization of the old clears the path for the new. 'Fix it while it ain't broken yet' is a fashionable statement but not a very practical one, the belief goes, because people cannot see the need for change when everything is going so well.

Perhaps the strongest evidence against this myth lies in the experience of General Electric over the last twenty years. All over the world, including in India, Jack Welch, GE's formidable CEO, represents the epitome of determined leadership. For good reason. He took over the helm of GE in 1981, when the company's market capitalization was $11 billion. Now, it hovers in the range of $450 billion! You could buy almost all of India's established corporate sector with about a fifth of GE's current value.

This jump in market value has been achieved through change that is spectacular by any measure. As we will describe in chapter 2, over his tenure, Welch has transformed GE's business portfolio, organization, culture and behaviour. Indeed, there is at least some element of truth in the claim made by a Harvard Business School professor that Welch's transformation of GE, with its employee base of over 200,000 people, represents 'one of the biggest planned efforts to alter people's behaviour since the cultural revolution in China'.

All of this, of course, is old hat in India by now. Everyone knows of the GE story. What people tend to forget, however, are the circumstances under which the story began.

When Jack Welch succeeded Reginald Jones in April 1981 as the chairman and CEO of GE, the *Wall Street Journal* claimed that the company was 'replacing a legend with a live wire'. Indeed, in the decade of the 1970s, Jones had doubled GE's sales and tripled its profits. In 1981, GE was the tenth largest industrial corporation in the US and was often referred to as the role model for American management. In a poll of Fortune 500 chief executives in 1981—the year that Welch assumed the leadership role in the company—GE was ranked as the best-managed industrial company in America and Reginald Jones received *Fortune*'s 'CEO of the Decade' award.

In other words, Welch did not inherit a company in crisis, not even a company struggling with satisfactory underperformance. He inherited the best-managed and one of the highest performing industrial companies in the world. And then, again as described by *Fortune*, he seized the company's 'vast bureaucracy by the scruff of the neck and shook it till it saw stars'.

In India, this is precisely what successive generations of top management have done in the perennially successful Hindustan Lever. Sushim Dutta inherited a very successful company from the legendary Ashok Ganguly. And changed the company fundamentally—by merging tea gardens, the food and beverages businesses of Brooke Bond and Lipton, and other units into the big detergents operation—to create an integrated Unilever group of companies, through a spate of acquisitions including Tomco in the detergents business and Kissan in the foods business, and by decentralizing authority down from the chairman's level to the level of the divisional managements. By the time he handed over charge to Keki Dadiseth, he was no less a management legend in India than Reginald Jones was in the US.

But, instead of maintaining the status quo, Keki Dadiseth has once again led a revolution in Hindustan Lever, radically decentralizing the company to create small, highly entrepreneurial businesses. At $4 billion in revenues, Hindustan Lever represents about 5 per cent of Unilever's global turnover; Dadiseth was determined to double it to 10 per cent. 'When we imagined it,' said Dadiseth, 'it was difficult to conceptualize. The key concept here is when there is a huge challenge and people sit down as a team to address it, they may not reach a solution, but the solution comes within sight.' And the solution that came within his sight, as we will describe in chapter 11, was to ignite the entrepreneurial spark plugs in the middle ranks of the company, by creating small profit centres that would help the company retain the aggressiveness and agility of small companies and simultaneously offer personal growth opportunities to a much broader array of young managers.

5. Charismatic leadership is not a prerequisite for radical performance improvement

Last but not least is the myth of charismatic leadership—the belief that only personal charisma at the top can galvanize a company to achieve radical change. Yes, charisma helps. But no, it is not a prerequisite.

'Desi' DeSimone, the CEO of 3M, is not charismatic by any standards. There is an obvious wholesomeness to him, an authenticity that creates trust and confidence, and a genuine love for people that creates the same love in return. But, he is not seven feet tall, nor a great public speaker. He is not the fire that burns with spectacular brightness but only leaves burnt out ash at the end; he is like a gentle stream that cools and comforts people, in a soothing and durable way.

Today, with all the public acclaim creating a halo around him, Infosys' N.R. Narayana Murthy may appear as charismatic, but he too is not seven feet tall. A soft-spoken, conservative and traditional middle-class Indian, he is more courteous than aggressive, more empathetic than evangelical. Yet, he is the soul that has nurtured the body of Infosys, a key attraction why people join and stay in the company, and the primary architect of Infosys' spectacular performance improvement since 1991 that we will review in chapter 5 of this book.

We could list many more examples, but that is not the point. What is not necessary may be interesting, but a far more interesting question is, what does it take? If radical performance improvement is possible, what are its how tos?

A Book of Biases

That is what this book is all about. Over the last twenty years, we have seen—sometimes from the inside and sometimes from the outside—some amazing changes in the fortunes of companies in the United States, Europe and Japan. We have seen a few soar, many more stumble, and some, like Digital Equipment Corporation and Westinghouse, die. Then, over the last five years, we have tried to follow several Indian companies, and here again we have witnessed some, like Reliance, Hindustan Lever and Infosys, go from success to success and seen others, like Indian Oxygen (renamed as BOC India), stumble and struggle. From our interpretations of why their fortunes have changed, we have distilled some biases about how companies can manage radical performance improvement. In this book, we present those biases.

We use the term 'biases' advisedly. We do not know if there are any absolute laws or truths in the field of management. But, if there are, we have no access to them. Our research methods are not amenable to ferreting out truths; all they can lead to are speculations and interpretations, i.e., personal biases. In this book, we present these biases as simply and as directly as we can. The objective is not to provide definitive answers, but to raise issues for thought, discussion and reflection.

In a way, the book is best used as an à la carte menu, rather than as a set lunch. We deliberately do not present an overall conceptual structure, and then elaborate the pieces so as to build up one integrated whole. There is a cohesiveness among the different ideas presented in the book—a cohesiveness that comes from the commonality of the hearts and the minds that have formed these biases—but there is also a deliberate avoidance of presenting a single conceptual framework or theory about performance improvement. Each chapter presents a single idea, in a bite-sized piece, about one issue that we consider to be relevant for radical performance improvement. Each idea is self-standing and can be evaluated for its usefulness or applicability independent of the evaluation of other ideas.

The company stories are an integral part of our argument. Collectively, they provide both illustration and support for the different ideas presented in the book. Clearly, they are oversimplified accounts of complex reality but, taken together, they should enthuse those who believe in our advocacy for radical performance improvement and at least challenge those who do not.

What does it take to achieve radical performance improvement? There is no one answer to that question. It requires the courage of rolling the dice for a big roll, but it also takes the care of managing a lot of small details. History and context matter, so there is no one universal formula applicable to all companies. The case examples provided in the different chapters describe this variety and this multidimensionality of the how tos of achieving outstanding corporate performance.

One of the criticisms about these examples may be that they represent a search for excellence. They are all exceptional cases and, therefore, cannot provide the basis for any generalization.

We disagree. In 'An Observation on Method', Edgar Wind[1] writes: 'It seems to be a lesson of history that the commonplace may be understood as a reduction of the exceptional, but the exceptional cannot be understood by amplifying the commonplace. Both logically and causally the exceptional is crucial because it introduces (however strange it may sound) the more comprehensive category.'

Reliance, Bajaj Auto, Infosys, Ranbaxy, Hero Honda, Zee TV, Hindustan Lever, Wipro, HDFC, Sundram Fasteners—these are all Indian companies and are, therefore, part of the

---

[1]Edgar Wind, *Pagan Mysteries in the Renaissance*. Harmondsworth: Penguin Books, 1967.

comprehensive category of corporate India. What they can do, others can do too. The Indian situation, with all its pathologies and opportunities, is not what is special about them. What is special is their management approach. At least from a normative perspective, they provide a perfectly valid—in fact, indispensable—basis for generalization.

To achieve radical performance improvement, the management of a company will require a sense—a vision, if you will—of the company's destiny. How does one arrive at this sense?

Read each of these case stories. Then try to tell the story of your company's future in the same way. With each case story, you will describe a different future, a different destiny. Try out all the different stories that you can generate in this manner. Mull over these stories—now, not about other companies, but about your own, but told in different ways. Gradually, a special story will emerge—perhaps from just one of the many different stories, or perhaps from a synthesis of some of them. It will be special because it will resonate within you; it will fit something that is inside you, whether you are an individual or a management team. You will feel that resonance because of the flush of energy and excitement it will generate.

Refine that story. Picture—that is what a vision is, a picture—the future state of the company, as it emerges from your special story. Then, have the courage to stand in that future and look at the present from that vantage point. How can you pull the present into that future? Some of the ideas presented in the different chapters may help in identifying some specific actions and processes; other initiatives will emerge from your own experiences and intuition. Have the courage to take those actions to drag your company, 'by the scruff of its neck' if necessary, as Jack Welch did, into that future. You cannot manage from the present to the future—that will inevitably land you into the trap of incrementalism. You will have to manage the present from the future—that is the path and the process for radical improvement.

2

LEARNING TO COOK SWEET AND SOUR

In April 1993, *Business India* hailed Indian Oxygen (later renamed as BOC India) as 'one of the major comeback stories of the Indian corporate arena in recent times'. The company had rationalized its portfolio, selling off the electrodes business; restructured its manufacturing base, closing a number of inefficient plants and replacing them with a few high-scale units with substantially lower cost structures; and reduced its workforce from 5400 in 1989 to 2100 in 1993. As a result of all this rationalization, restructuring and retrenchment, the company's profits had jumped from Rs 25 lakh in 1990 to Rs 705 lakh in 1993, enhancing its market value from Rs 45 crore to a staggering Rs 480 crore.

Five years later, however, the transformation lay in tatters, reflected in a market value that was down again to Rs 191 crore. In the corporate league table, the company had fallen off to a remote 368th position—indeed, a pale shadow of what was once perhaps one of the most visible and prestigious multinational units in the country.

So, what went wrong?

What went wrong was that while the company had learnt

to cut, to restructure, to rationalize, it had not learnt to grow. The management of Indian Oxygen squeezed costs, controlled budgets and improved productivity, but it lacked the energy and the courage required for creating and exploiting new opportunities. As a result, it got caught in a dangerous negative spiral—every cost-cut led to a temporary improvement but ultimately only created the need for another cut.

Indian corporate experience provides examples of the reverse case too—of companies that have tried to achieve spectacular overall performance by focusing on growth alone, without any attention to productivity improvement. Essar is a case in point. Starting from the audacious bet on their sponge iron plant, the Ruia brothers have grown to a Rs 3300-crore conglomerate that lacks underlying competitiveness in many of its core businesses. Here too, after an initial phase of euphoria, performance has plunged, drawing down the group's stock price from a high of Rs 126 in 1994 to Rs 16 in 1998.

The underlying lesson is both simple and universal. Sustained superior corporate performance is based on the ability to manage the tension between two symbiotic forces: the need for ongoing improvement in operational performance and productivity through constant rationalization in existing activities, and the need for growth and expansion through continuous revitalization of strategy, organization and people.

There is nothing new about either of these two needs. The problem is that most managers see the processes of rationalization and revitalization as mutually exclusive. Rationalization is often unpleasant—'sour'. Few managers enjoy closing plants, selling businesses, sacking people. Revitalization, on the other hand, is 'sweet'. Most managers love growth; they love dreaming up a vision and driving their organizations to match their dreams. And, most go for either one or the other, hoping to either cut or grow into the high-performance league.

In contrast, companies that achieve radical performance improvement see these two processes as symbiotic. The continuous rationalization process provides the resources, including money and people, needed for growth, and the continuous revitalization process generates the hope and energy required to sustain the gruelling challenge of relentless productivity improvement (see figure 2.1). Growth without productivity improvement is like building castles on sand—inevitably they collapse under their own weight. An exclusive focus on productivity improvement alone, with no attention to growth, proves to be corrosive, ultimately sapping all the energy and creativity of the organization. In other words, while most companies cook only sour or only sweet, sustained superior performance requires a management that has learnt to do both.

Figure 2.1: The Sweet and Sour Cycle

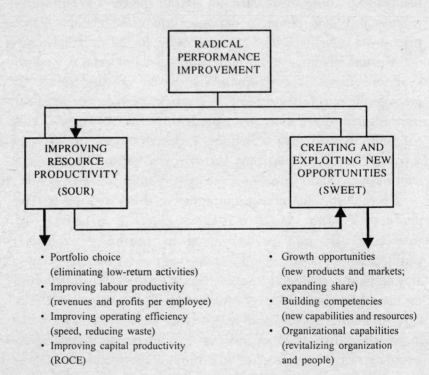

- Portfolio choice
  (eliminating low-return activities)
- Improving labour productivity
  (revenues and profits per employee)
- Improving operating efficiency
  (speed, reducing waste)
- Improving capital productivity
  (ROCE)

- Growth opportunities
  (new products and markets;
  expanding share)
- Building competencies
  (new capabilities and resources)
- Organizational capabilities
  (revitalizing organization
  and people)

Managing Radical Productivity Improvement: Cooking Sour

There is one common feature in each and every instance of truly remarkable performance improvement in an established company: each one of them achieved radical improvements in resource productivity. In each case, efficiency improvements were accompanied by considerable pain, but the management had the courage to cook sour, knowing that it was a precondition for cooking sweet.

In chapter 1, we referred to Jack Welch's remarkable transformation of GE, not from a starting point of weakness but one of great strength and success. The benefits of this transformation began to be publicly visible in terms of improving growth, profits and market capitalization only from about 1986, i.e., a full five years after Welch took over the leadership of the company in 1981. In that intervening period, he laid the foundations of GE's profit and share price growth by driving one of the most dramatic processes of productivity and efficiency improvement ever seen in any established corporation.

An important part of this productivity improvement process lay in restructuring the company's business portfolio. Like many of the large family business groups in India, GE was a conglomerate operating in a highly diverse range of businesses. Welch did not convert GE into a focused single business company, but he radically restructured GE around a clear portfolio logic.

The catchword for Welch's redefinition of GE's portfolio logic was 'number one or number two'. In each business, GE had to be a clear leader. Early in his tenure, he announced to all GE managers:

> To me, quality and excellence means being better than the best
> . . . if we aren't better than the best, we should ask ourselves
> 'What will it take?', then quantify the energy and resources
> required to get there. If the economics, the environment or our
> abilities determine that we can't get there, we must take the
> same spirited action to disengage ourselves from that which
> we can't make better than the best.

What was the rationale behind 'number 1 or number 2'? Was it just a fad, a whim? What's wrong with continuing in a business in which you are number 5 or number 10, but which still makes money?

The answer is simple. As we explained in chapter 1, the best-performing company in a particular business is able to achieve sustainable superior performance even during periods when the overall industry performs poorly. In good times, all or most competitors make money; in bad times, only the best make money. Being better than the best allows a company to control its own destiny, instead of being controlled by the destiny of its industry.

This point is profoundly important for a large number of diversified industrial groups in India. Should they refocus and become a single business company, or can they continue to remain diversified? Most are opting for the second option, and there is nothing wrong with that, as we will argue in chapter 7. There is nothing wrong with diversity, per se, as long as the company can control its own destiny in each of its different businesses. But, when it can't—when it is a rule taker, living at the mercy of business upswings and downswings—then it must radically prune its portfolio, choosing to remain in only those businesses where it has the resources and competencies to set the rules, or at least an opportunity to get there. That is almost the priority number 1 for radical performance improvement.

This process of portfolio pruning will inevitably be difficult and painful. It was no different for Welch, who faced a tidal wave of criticism as he sold over a hundred businesses, worth about $6 billion. Critics characterized him as a heartless, financially-orientated fiend who was trying to achieve his goals and stay one step ahead of foreign competition by giving up on manufacturing businesses that had historically identified the core and essence of GE. We quote at length from Welch's response only because we believe that a large number of managers in India can benefit from its compelling logic.

Housewares and air-conditioning combined in a good year made $20 million, in a bad year they lost $20 million, and their cash flow was about zero. So, they gave us no earnings growth and no cash. When we sold them, we got $400 million of cash to restructure power systems and other strong businesses.

In consumer electronics, we sold our television business. It gave people a lot of grief . . . 'How could you do that?' In the 1980s the consumer electronics business lost $150 million, and used about $170 million in cash. They didn't give cash and they didn't give any earnings. All they did was cause more grief in the stronger businesses.

Power transformers was in the middle of GE's power business. It made everyone feel terrible when we sold power transformers. However, to give you a feeling for the power transformer business, in 1985 its sales were lower than they were in 1970. In thirteen of those fifteen years, it lost money. Cumulatively it lost over $100 million. It didn't belong. It just dragged the whole institution down . . . And, as for hurting people, the employees in those businesses, formerly endangered by being part of an also-ran in a global market, now are part of stronger operations with a reach and volume that gives them a real shot at winning.

Another 'sour' element in Welch's transformation of GE was a substantial downsizing of the company, including a massive series of reductions in personnel. In 1981, when he started, GE employed 411,000 people. Acquisitions brought in an additional 111,150 people into the company, while divestitures took 122,700 people out of it. Of the remaining, 123,400 employees left the company—most as a part of Welch's massive downsizing programme.

This action also led to considerable criticism and, to some detractors, Welch was 'Neutron Jack', the job killer, who was the visible symbol of a new breed of managers driven by greed and contempt for their employees. One publication summarized labour's view of Welch as follows: 'There is not much doubt about what many union members think of him. He is the consummate corporate villain, willing to sacrifice everyone's job to turn a higher profit.'

This issue, too, is of vital relevance for a large number of Indian companies, in both the public and the private sectors, who are clearly overstaffed. The claim that Indian labour rules do not allow them to shed people is simply not true: as we described in the beginning of this chapter, Indian Oxygen reduced its workforce from 5400 in 1989 to 2100 in 1993, and that too in the eastern part of the country, an area notorious for its inflexible labour unions and intensely pro-labour governments. Bajaj Auto reduced employment from 22,000 people to 17,000, despite a Shiv Sena union. Many other Indian companies have similarly reduced employment to improve productivity—all that it takes is investment in VRS, just as improving technical productivity often requires investment in new plant and equipment. A company is morally and legally obliged to treat its people decently, to help them with a soft landing, as indeed GE did, perhaps more generously than any other company in the United States, or as Hastings Jute Mills did in Calcutta. Those who have to leave must also be treated with dignity—a point that managements of both Indian Oxygen and Bajaj Auto took extreme care to ensure. But, it is simply not true that legal restrictions are the primary reason for Indian management's inability to improve labour productivity.

The real reasons lie either in moral objections—some senior managers feel morally obliged not to sack people, even poorly performing people—or a lack of courage and determination. While we will return to the moral and ethical dimensions of this issue further on, here is how Welch responded to these objections:

> We are doing 31 per cent more volume with 31 per cent fewer people. There was no way we could continue doing things the way we used to. We let go of 123,000 people. Assume that the whole mix of all the employees that are gone had an average

salary of $35,000—and that's conservative. If you add benefits to that, you're up close to $50,000. Multiply that by 123,000 people and you get over $6 billion, minus taxes of $2.4 billion, you get a final balance of almost $4 billion. GE's profits today are about $3 billion. We would be losing over a billion dollars now if we were operating the same way we did in 1981. The option is not there to go back to the way we were—the only option is to do it differently.

A focus on portfolio and manpower reductions are the two most contentious elements of cooking sour—but by no means are they the only elements. Radical improvements in operational productivity can contribute as much or more to performance improvement as reductions in headcount. For example, in its hundred years of existence, GE had never achieved more than five inventory turns. In 1991, Welch declared a goal of getting to ten inventory turns. 'We had no idea how to do it,' he said, 'but we announced it to the whole organization, and put it in our annual report.' By 1996, in five years, the company hit the target, releasing well over ten billion dollars in cash for investment in the businesses.

In India, Reliance has built its spectacular rise on a similar commitment to continuous improvements in efficiency and productivity. Everyone knows about the staggering ambition of the Ambanis that has fuelled Reliance's evolution into the largest private sector company in the country. What people are not so familiar with is the relentless focus on cost reduction and productivity growth that equally pervades the company. Reliance's employee cost is 4 per cent of revenues, against 15 to 20 per cent that is the average for all its competitors. Its sales and distribution cost, at 3 per cent of revenues, is about a third of global standards. It has continuously pushed down its cost for energy and utilities—typically a disadvantage for Indian companies—to 3 per cent of revenues, largely through 100 per cent captive power generation that costs the company 4.5 cents per kilowatt-hour, well below Indian utility costs, and about 30 per cent lower than the global average. Similarly, its capital cost is 25 to 30 per cent lower than its international peer group, due largely to its legendary speed in plant commissioning and also its relentless focus on reducing the weighted average cost of capital (WACC) that, at 13 per cent, is the lowest of any major Indian company.

There are two aspects of productivity improvement processes that need to be highlighted. First, this need never goes away. It is not something you do once and then get it over with. To stay ahead of intensifying competition, a company has to work constantly on improving productivity. To remain fit, one has to exercise regularly; similarly, to remain competitive, a company has to improve productivity year upon year. Initially, it feels like a treadmill but, over time and with practice, it becomes a game, a challenge: 'Once you know how to do it, you begin to enjoy it. You realize that the potential is limitless, and it brings out the best in you,' said a GE manager.

The second aspect is a bit of a cliché but no less true because of that: clearly established stretch goals tend to be more effective than small incremental targets. Setting the inventory turn ambition at ten—100 per cent more than the existing level—was more effective in GE than laying down annual 6 per cent improvement budgets. As Welch emphasizes, 'Budgets enervate, stretch energizes.' Setting up bold goals and then allowing people to find their own ways to pursue them is more effective than constantly controlling for small incremental changes in operational efficiency.

CREATING GROWTH OPPORTUNITIES: COOKING SWEET

If one key lesson from corporate experience around the world is that no company can achieve radical performance improvement without transforming resource productivity, the other equally important lesson is that no company can achieve such results only through improvements in operating efficiencies. While 'sour' is necessary, it is not sufficient.

Indeed many companies have over the past decade tried to improve their performance through cutting alone, with predictable and disastrous results. They have got caught in a vicious downward spiral (see figure 2.2).

Figure 2.2: The Downward Spiral of Rationalization

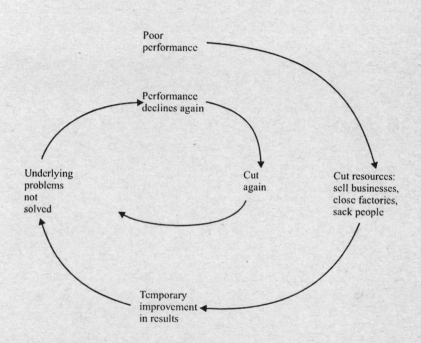

A company's performance drops. To improve profits, the management restructures the portfolio, selling off businesses, and cuts investments in technology, equipment and people. It reduces headcount, cuts inventory and delays supplier payments. As a result, financial results improve, but only for a while. The real underlying problems are not solved through the cuts and performance declines again, triggering off the next turn in the spiral.

Company after company that adopted the mantra of re-engineering in the United States and elsewhere has experienced this negative spiral over the 1990s. In fact, for a period, it had become quite predictable as to which company would launch a major downsizing and rationalizing programme during any particular year—companies that had launched such a programme four years earlier. Every fourth year, they hit the 'cut again' part of the spiral.

This is precisely what happened to Westinghouse, GE's arch-rival for over a hundred years. Like GE, Westinghouse pruned its portfolio, selling off low-growth, low-margin businesses; it drastically reduced employment and instituted tight operating controls. Douglas Danforth, Westinghouse's CEO, famously said, 'I will sack my mother if she did not achieve budget.' But, unlike GE, this is all that Westinghouse did. It pruned and cut, and then pruned again till there was nothing left to prune. Ultimately, the company died when Michael Jordan dismembered it, separating the broadcasting business and selling or closing all the rest.

This, then, is the other key lesson: to achieve radical performance improvement, a company must also learn to create and exploit new growth opportunities. It must learn to cook sweet.

This is what distinguished GE from Westinghouse. While Welch cut and pruned, he also built and grew. While he sold poor performing businesses in which GE could not achieve leadership positions, he used the cash to acquire companies that would further strengthen those businesses that were already strong: CGR for medical equipment and services, Borg-Warner for plastics, Roper for appliances, RCA for broadcasting and aerospace, and so on.

Beyond acquisitions, GE used alliances as another key lever for creating growth opportunities. Significant investments in partnerships with Bosch in Germany, Fuji in Japan and GEC in the UK became key enablers for GE's rapid expansion outside the United States.

The biggest investments were made within the businesses to

drive organic growth—over $2 billion each year, on average. In a single year, in 1988, GE invested $1.8 billion to build a plastics complex in Spain, to exploit growth opportunities in Europe, another $1 billion in GE Financial Services, $1.8 billion on new plant and equipment within the US, and $3.6 billion on R&D.

But, the greatest effort of all on the 'sweet' side lay in building an entrepreneurial culture in GE, to unleash internal creativity. As Welch said:

> As we succeed in ridding our company of the tentacles of ritual and bureaucracy, we are now better able to attack the final, and perhaps the most difficult challenge of all. And that is the empowering of our 300,000 people, the releasing of their creativity and ambition, the direct compiling of their jobs with some positive effect on the quality of a product or service. We want each man and woman in this company to see a connection between what he or she does all day—and winning in the market place . . . Small companies thrive and grow on that sense of contribution and reward. We want it as well . . . to make this $50-billion enterprise as lean, as agile and light on its feet as a small company.

To decentralize entrepreneurial initiatives to lower management levels, Welch first flattened the corporate pyramid, eliminating the sector organizations and reducing the overall hierarchy from nine to four layers of management. At the same time, claiming that 'headquarters can be the bane of corporate America . . . It can strangle, choke, delay and create insecurity', he drastically reduced the size of corporate staff and simultaneously changed their role from 'controllers, checkers and nit-pickers' to 'helpers and supporters of the businesses'.

In the 1990s, Welch pushed the spirit of freedom even lower, to encompass all 300,000 employees of GE, through the 'Work-out' initiative. The central idea was to create a forum where a cross-section of employees could speak their mind about the management of their business without the fear of retribution by their supervisors. More important, it was designed to be a place to get immediate action on their recommendations. 'What do we need to do to make this place better than the best?'—that was the question each employee group confronted. They were encouraged to identify unproductive practices and bureaucratic behaviour that limited their personal effectiveness. Management then had to decide, often on the spot, what could be done to rectify the problems and release the business's performance potential.

In no way has GE been unique in its ability to achieve radical performance improvement through this symbiosis of cooking sweet and sour, nor is this practice limited only to Anglo-Saxon companies. It is precisely the same process that has driven the remarkable achievements of a host of other companies like Intel, ABB, Canon and Kao Corporation.

In the slow-growth electrotechnical business, ABB has doubled its revenues from $17 billion to $35 billion, largely by exploiting new opportunities in emerging businesses such as environmental engineering and integrated plant services, and markets like China, India, Eastern Europe and Latin America. For example, it has built up a 46,000-employee organization in the Asia-Pacific region almost from scratch. At the same time, it has also reduced employment in North America and Western Europe by 54,000 people. It was the hard squeeze in the North and the West that generated the resources to support ABB's massive investments in the East and the South.

In the same year that the Pentium business generated net profit of almost a billion dollars, Intel cut its staff by 22 per cent to improve productivity. It did not sack those people, instead it deployed them to build the next winning product. Canon follows the same practice routinely, cutting in good times, and using the resources to prepare for the next battle.

Kao Corporation—Japan's premier detergents and personal products company—uses the same concept of sweet and sour, but over time, to create a permanent dynamism within the company. In the early 1980s, amid simultaneous roll-out of new products in cosmetics, disposable diapers and floppy disks, Dr Yoshio Maruta, Kao's legendary chairman, inaugurated a major initiative called TCR (Total Cost Reduction), forcing managers to balance their expansionary focus with the discipline of productivity improvement. Four years later, after some major rationalization that significantly improved manufacturing and distribution efficiencies, he changed the same TCR acronym to stand for 'Total Creativity Revolution', refocusing management attention on innovative investments made possible by the savings that were generated by the Total Cost Reduction programme.

COOKING SWEET AND SOUR AT BAJAJ AUTO

In the 1980s, for all its reputation as India's hottest company, Reliance was not the country's fastest growing company. Over this decade, Reliance grew a staggering 1110 per cent, with sales moving up from Rs 200 crore to Rs 1840 crore, yet it trailed behind Bajaj Auto's growth rate of 1852 per cent, from Rs 51.9 crore to Rs 1850 crore. Despite this growth, Bajaj Auto carried practically no debt in its balance sheet. By maintaining an iron-fisted control on costs and by continuously improving productivity to lower the cost per vehicle, Rahul Bajaj funded this growth almost entirely out of internal earnings. As Tarun Das, the director-general of the Confederation of Indian Industries, once said, only partially in jest, 'Bajaj Auto is a professionally managed company but, no one can spend five rupees without Rahul's approval.'

Yet, in the 1990s, with a radical change in the Indian two- and three-wheeler markets, Bajaj Auto missed a step or two. Japanese producers entered the Indian market en masse— Honda set up Kinetic Honda with the Firodias to manufacture scooters, and Hero Honda with the Munjal family to manufacture motorcycles, Suzuki partnered with the TVS group to set up TVS-Suzuki, Piaggio re-entered the scooters market in partnership with LML, and Yamaha tied up with Escorts to make motorcycles. These new entrants had access to new technologies and up-to-date models, courtesy their foreign partners. The proliferation of new models gave consumers the freedom to choose and, despite its low-cost position, Bajaj's overall share of the market dropped from 49.3 per cent in 1994 to 38.9 per cent in 1998, and its share of the scooters market dropped from 74.8 per cent to 64.8 per cent.

After a brief period of hesitation, Bajaj Auto launched a fightback that is a textbook illustration of managing sweet and sour.

At the forefront of the response was the need to engage the company more intimately with the customer. Customer maturity had changed dramatically, in a short period of time, and products seen as 'me-too' were no longer welcome. The challenge was succinctly summarized by Rajiv Bajaj, Rahul's elder son and his anointed successor in the company:

> Consumers want something spicy more frequently. What made a terrific impact on me is when I heard a customer say 'Yes, the Bajaj scooter is the cheapest, but that's what it deserves to be.'

Bajaj Auto had to reclaim its historical share of the customer mind. 'This is directly linked to innovation,' said Rajiv. 'The Bajaj Auto mindset was that once we introduced a product, people would buy in volume.' To reignite growth, the company had to provide more variety, positioning tailored products in each distinct segment of the market. But, with increasing competition and the inherent cost of variety, that could potentially weaken its historical strength in terms of low unit costs. Therefore, radical reduction in costs—in a company that was already the lowest cost producer in the world—was a prerequisite for protecting margins in spite of the added variety, and to fund the investments required for new technology, equipment as well as the enhanced need for marketing and distribution to support the broadened product portfolio.

On the sweet side, Rajiv Bajaj started by scouting for new technologies. In two years, he tied up with a dozen different partners to acquire expertise—with Austria's AVL for technology to improve vehicle emissions and fuel economy, Australia's Orbital engine company for combustion systems, Tokyo R&D for engine design, and so on. As a result, a company that, for almost twenty years, had done minimal upgrades to its single dominant model, the Chetak, announced at the Delhi Auto Fair in January 1998 that it would launch seventeen new models within the next twenty-four months. While externally the new models stemmed market share erosion, internally they acted like adrenaline shots, improving employee morale and excitement.

In 1982, Rahul Bajaj had famously said, 'My marketing department? I don't require it. I have a dispatch department. I don't have to go from house to house to sell.' By 1998, the man and the company had turned around 180 degrees: 'Whatever product or service a company offers, it must meet the customer's wants in the most satisfactory manner. That should be the aim of the company.' This profound change in attitude was reflected in a series of major initiatives to revamp the company's marketing and distribution capabilities.

A company that did not have a marketing department worked long and hard to attract R.L. Ravichandran, perhaps the most reputed marketing person in the industry, the man who had played a key role in raising TVS-Suzuki's market share by 11 per cent, to head its marketing operations. The advertising budget was doubled. A slew of new marketing initiatives were launched to start off and support growth, including a corporate identity and dealer development programme, standardization and modernization of the dealer network, regular dealer conferences for sharing best practices and success stories, and a major offensive for improving after-sales service which was converted from a cost centre to a profit centre in the company's internal classification.

At the same time, while revving up its growth engine, Bajaj Auto initiated a number of programmes for radically reducing its costs. A new agreement with the Shiv Sena-controlled Bharatiya Kamgar Sena Union led to a mutual commitment for 8-10 per cent productivity improvement per annum, in exchange for significant increase in employees' pay and facilities. As many as 5000 people disappeared from the payroll and the remaining 17,000 worked a lot more efficiently. Between 1995 and 1998, the company achieved a remarkable 38 per cent improvement in the number of vehicles produced per employee. As a manager in the Akurdi plant said to us, 'Fewer people made an important difference in cost and quality. The factory was a neater, cleaner and safer place to work.'

To improve agility and speed, which were vital for lowering costs and improving quality and variety, the company fundamentally changed its production methods. On the shop floor, workmen and section managers were grouped into cells. These cell members were guided by a principle called 'visual self-management of quality and productivity for continuous improvement', an elaborate name for a simple but highly effective system for improving operational efficiency. Every aspect of each cell's performance, from man-machine balancing and material handling to preventive maintenance and process control, was monitored through ten charts. A high-speed computer improved information flow across 400 concurrent users at the company's three plants and some key suppliers and distributors, to support the new way of working.

The supply chain provided another source for cutting costs. Historically, about 60 per cent of the value of a Bajaj vehicle was outsourced. This was considerably lower than the 90 per cent figure achieved by Hero Honda. While depending on in-house production had some advantages, rationalization of the supply chain increased outsourcing considerably. The greatest benefit came by way of improvement in speed: 'We used to take 1.9 days to make a scooter. Now, because of increased outsourcing, it has come down to 1.4 days,' said a production executive.

Bajaj Auto took actions to both cut costs and grow, but what made the process 'sweet and sour' was the company's attention to managing the interactions between these two actions. There are inevitable trade-offs between the two. For example, as described by Arvind Gupta, head of manufacturing engineering:

> The new products will be competitively priced because we have been very cost effective in our equipment buying. Overall we paid less because we bought from different manufacturers. We can do this because we have a strong integrating capability in comparison to others. Others may have an advantage in project time, but we are building expertise through the integration process. Yes, this strategy may cost the company more in the long run in terms of time—we could have handed it over as a turnkey job—but the transition might have been difficult and the costs would have been very different.

Perhaps the most important benefit of cooking both the sweet and the sour simultaneously—the key interaction between cost reduction and revenue growth—lay in managing people's emotions and feelings within the company. Rajiv Bajaj captured this emotional aspect most vividly.

> In the future, cost has to be looked at in a different way. The wrong way is to tell people we are cutting costs. People want to come to office eager to work. But, in a meeting if I say that today I want to talk about cost-cutting, I am sure they will do their best but they will not be motivated. I will be talking in isolation. This is especially true in an owner-managed company. Inevitably there is a feeling among executives that the benefits of cost-cutting will go into the owner's pocket. Managers and workers also see cost-cutting as a way to rip them off, and to make them work harder. Outside the company, among vendors and customers, the moment you talk about cost-cutting, people think that the product's quality has gone down. Here

at Bajaj Auto we feel that cost-cutting is all about improving quality at lower cost. That's how profitability improves. That's how customers keep coming back. And that's how everyone in the company benefits.

A Bias for Growth

A simple benchmarking exercise, comparing major Indian companies in key industries with their global competitors, shows that Indian companies are running a major risk. They suffer from a profound bias for growth. There is nothing wrong with this bias, as the Reliance story in this book clearly shows. The problem is that most of them look more like the Ruias than like Reliance. While they love the sweet of growth, they are unwilling to face the sour of productivity improvement.

Nowhere is this more amply borne out than in the consumer goods industry, where the Indian giant Hindustan Lever has consolidated to grow at over 50 per cent while its labour productivity declined by around 6 per cent per annum in the same period. Its strongest competitor, Nirma, also grew at over 25 per cent per annum in revenues, but maintained its labour productivity relatively stable. Unfortunately, however, its return on capital employed (ROCE) suffered by over 17 per cent. In contrast Coca-Cola worldwide grew at around 7 per cent per annum, improved its labour productivity by 20 per cent and its return on capital employed by 6.7 per cent.

The story is similar in the information technology sector where Infosys, NIIT and HCL achieved growth of over 50 per cent, which compares favourably with the world's best IT companies who grew at around 30 per cent in 1994-96. NIIT, for example, strongly believes that growth is an impetus in itself. This focus on growth has helped it double its revenues every two years. Its sister company HCL has been expanding rapidly in overseas markets—often in the saturated and, therefore, low profit markets of Western Europe. Sustaining profitability in the face of such expansion is an extremely challenging task.

In the mid-'90s, Indian infotech companies appeared unable to effectively respond to the challenge. The ROCE for the three Indian majors fell by 7 per cent annually over 1994-96. At the same time, international majors like IBM, Microsoft and SAP managed to improve this ratio by 17 per cent, on average.

There are some exceptions, however, such as the cement industry, which has focused on productivity rather than on growth and has done very well when compared to its global counterparts. While Mexico's Cemex has grown about three times as fast as India's ACC, Indian cement companies have consistently delivered better results, not only on absolute profitability ratios, but also in profitability growth. They achieved a growth of 24 per cent in the return on capital employed while the internationals chalked up only 8.4 per cent. In terms of labour productivity, this industry has done exceptionally well. While overall labour productivity (as measured in revenues per rupee of wages and salaries) fell for most Indian industries over the 1994-96 period, it improved at 2.5 per cent per annum in the cement industry.

The engineering industry also matches up to the performance standards of the biggest and the best in the world. Companies like Cummins (India) (till recently Kirloskar Cummins) have always pushed for growth, as is evidenced by its 27 per cent rate of growth, but not at the cost of present and future profitability. The company achieved a healthy excess of almost 30 per cent over its WACC, displaying great promise for the years to come. BHEL, the public sector giant, has seen similar success and this is reflected in its share price which rose by 25 per cent in this period despite an indecisive Sensex. The only note of caution is on labour productivity. Indian engineering companies have not been able to improve labour productivity over time, while international engineering companies like ABB, Siemens and Cummins Engines have been able to achieve about 13.5 per cent growth in labour productivity per year, on average, over the same period.

The pharmaceuticals industry is where the problems seem to be the worst, with growth being emphasized at the cost of all other performance measures. Companies like Ranbaxy have been growing at over 22 per cent while their returns on capital employed fell at 15.9 per cent per annum, and labour productivity declined at the rate of 7 per cent. Compare this with some of the best pharmaceutical companies of the world— Glaxo-Wellcome, SmithKline Beecham and Pfizer—who have consistently achieved growth of 15 to 20 per cent per annum, while improving returns on capital employed at about 25 per cent and labour productivity at 8 per cent. Ranbaxy is not an exception; the bias for growth at the cost of labour and capital productivity is also manifest in the performances of other Indian pharmaceutical companies. What makes this even worse is the fact that the Indian companies barely manage to cover their cost of capital while their competitors worldwide such as Glaxo Wellcome, SmithKline Beecham and Pfizer earn on average ROCE of 65 per cent.

In the Indian textile industry, Arvind Mills was once the shining star. Like Reliance, it had learnt to cook sweet and sour. Between 1994 and 1996, it grew at an average of 30 per cent per annum to become the world's largest denim producer. At the same time, it also operated a tight ship, improving labour productivity by an impressive 20 per cent per annum. However, despite the excellent performance in the past, there are warning signals for Arvind's future. The excess over the WACC is only 1.5 per cent, thereby implying that it barely manages to satisfy its investors' expectations of returns and does not really have a surplus to reinvest in the business. Apparently, the investors also think so, for Arvind's stock price has been falling since the fourth quarter of 1994 despite such excellent results and, at the end of the first quarter of 1998, stood at less than Rs 70 compared to the Rs 170 at the end of 1994.

Unfortunately, Arvind's deteriorating financial returns over the last few years are also typical of the Indian textile industry. The top three Indian companies actually showed a decline in their return ratios in contrast to the international majors in this industry. Nike, VF Corp and Coats Viyella showed a growth in their returns on capital employed of 6.2 per cent while the ROCE of Grasim and Coats Viyella (India) fell by almost 2 per cent per annum. Even in absolute returns on assets or on capital employed, the Indian companies fared a lot worse than their international counterparts, not only in the United States and Europe but also in China and Brazil. As a result, while the Indian textile companies just about cover their WACC, their international rivals earn about 8 per cent in excess of their cost of capital.

THE VICIOUS SPIRAL OF UNPROFITABLE GROWTH

The consequences of a prolonged period of unprofitable growth are simple, unambiguous and vicious (see figure 2.3).

Profitable growth generates cash, which allows a company to fund further growth without taking on excessive debt or diluting equity too much. As a result, it retains both strategic freedom and investment potential. Rising stock prices support the growth process, both by making acquisitions more feasible and by reducing the cost of capital.

Unprofitable growth leads to exactly the opposite effects. Debts swell, increasing interest costs as well as the overall cost of capital. Gradually, the company loses its ability to pursue growth opportunities because of depressed stock prices and debt capacity externally, and dwindling cash flows and increasing cash demands internally.

The situation faced by the large Korean chaebols post the Asian crisis make the consequences of unprofitable growth abundantly clear.

For almost four decades, since the second world war, the leading Korean chaebols including Samsung, Daewoo, LG and Hyundai have been driven by a passion for growth. And, in this

Figure 2.3: The Virtuous and Vicious Spirals of Growth

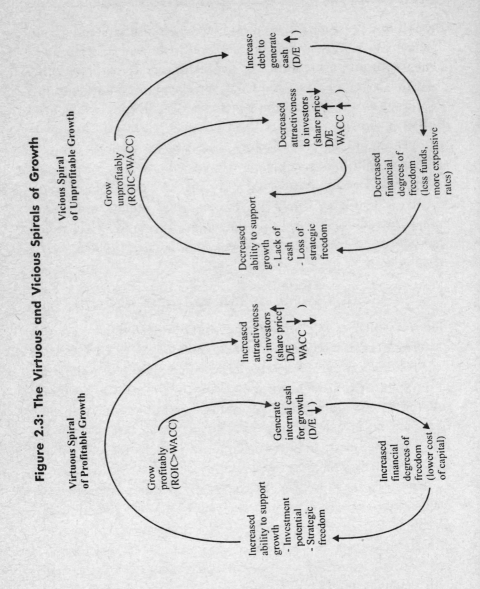

Virtuous Spiral of Profitable Growth

Grow profitably (ROIC>WACC)

Increased attractiveness to investors (share price ↑ D/E → WACC →)

Generate internal cash for growth (D/E ↓)

Increased financial degrees of freedom (lower cost of capital)

Increased ability to support growth
- Investment potential
- Strategic freedom

Vicious Spiral of Unprofitable Growth

Grow unprofitably (ROIC<WACC)

Increase debt to generate cash (D/E ↑)

Decreased attractiveness to investors (share price ↓ D/E ↑ WACC ↑)

Decreased financial degrees of freedom (less funds, more expensive rates)

Decreased ability to support growth
- Lack of cash
- Loss of strategic freedom

measure, they far outclassed both Western and Japanese rivals. While GE has been growing at about 4 per cent per annum in the 1990s and NEC by 6 per cent, Samsung has been growing at an astronomical rate of 25 per cent. As a result, while Samsung was one-third the size of Philips fifteen years ago, in 1998 it was three times as big as Philips.

The problem, however, was that while GE and ABB were achieving a 20 per cent return on equity, LG and Samsung were at 3 to 4 per cent. As a result, the only way they could finance their growth was through debt. By 1998, all of them were carrying debt that was about five times their equity. This was unsustainable and the companies have had to pay a heavy price since 1998. Each of them has been forced to shed businesses and people, and some, like Hanbo, Sammi, Jinro and Kia, have already gone bankrupt. It is not clear that even the big five will all survive their painful and forced restructuring.

This is precisely what will happen to some of India's fastest growing companies of today unless they immediately focus on the productivity side of the equation and learn the art of cooking sweet and sour.

3

INTO THE VALLEY OF DEATH

All our metaphors of transformational change are highly romantic. 'From a caterpillar to a butterfly' sounds and feels so good! From an ugly black caterpillar to a bright, colourful butterfly—the symbol of fantasy, of love, of good cheer! But imagine what is happening to the caterpillar as it goes through this metamorphosis. First it goes blind. Then its arms and legs fall off. Finally, its body splits open, to allow the beautiful wings to emerge. Think of the fear and the pain it goes through. Which caterpillar, willingly and of its own volition, will sign up for the transformation?

Precisely the same is true of corporate transformation. The process of transformational change involves a great deal of fear, and intense pain. That is why it is so much easier to talk about transformation than it is to go through the process.

Top-level managers in many Indian companies have picked up the rhetoric of corporate transformation. Indeed, in the current context of rapid economic, technological and competitive change, more than a few of them do require radical change in strategy, organization and culture to prosper, perhaps even to survive. But, most of these managers have only an intellectual understanding of the changes that are necessary—they have no experience of the emotional roller coaster that such transformational processes involve. To lead such change, they have to manage both the intellectual and the emotional aspects. Of the two, the latter is by far the more difficult and the more draining.

Transformational change is a journey through the valley of death. In different phases of the journey, the organization will experience some very different kinds of emotions—from complacence, denial and resistance through anger and depression to exploration, enthusiasm and commitment (see figure 3.1). To lead a company through this journey, top-level managers must learn to anticipate these emotions and have the courage and the wisdom to cope with them. At each phase, the leadership task is very different and the roles the leaders play must, therefore, radically change in the course of the journey.

Figure 3:1: From a Caterpillar to a Butterfly

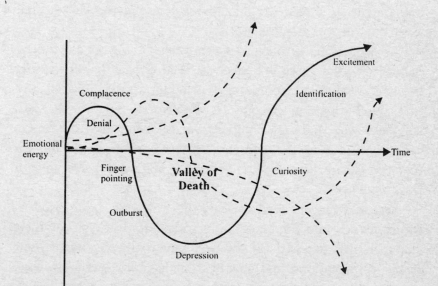

As the discussions about transformational change first enter the agenda of a company, most managers feel energized. General Electric did it, ABB did it, and so shall we! It is a heady feeling of machismo—and the illustrations only add to the excitement. We shall all be like Jack Welch and Percy Barnevik! This is the complacency stage, the euphoria of the ignorant.

Then, as the benchmarking process reveals deep gaps between the company's capabilities and performance and those of its best-in-class rivals, the complacency gradually gives way to rationalization and denial. First, the comparisons are denied, 'the numbers are wrong'. Then, as the truth of the performance gap becomes impossible to deny, valiant rationalization ensues. 'How can you compare our performance with theirs? Our situations are so different.'

As these layers of rationalization gradually melt away and the obvious conclusion of managerial mediocrity stares people in the face, denial gives way to finger-pointing. 'I am doing great, it is all someone else's fault.' Sales is wonderful, manufacturing stinks. Manufacturing is doing the best it can, given the mess that purchase is in.

As deeper analysis begins to show that the gaps are indeed pervasive—sales force effectiveness is abysmal, manufacturing lags well behind key competitors in both cost and quality, and that purchasing enjoys one of the worst reputations with suppliers—the outburst finally happens. 'Who are you to say such things? Has the company lost all respect for human dignity? Where has our civility gone? Why are we doing all this, anyway?'

Senior managers tend to lead this outburst. Long used to the deference and adulation appropriate for the size of their chambers and exposed for the first time to the reality of their feeble contributions and manifest managerial ineffectiveness, anger becomes their sole defence mechanism. Some leave. Others, unable to leave, try to mount a counter-revolution.

Leaders strong enough to push the organization beyond this

stage of outburst finally arrive at the lowest point of the valley—depression. This is when people finally give in and give up. 'I accept that I am terrible. Leave me alone. Let me dig a deep hole and lie down to die.' The toughest phase to plough through, this, however, is also the first sight of the end of the tunnel.

Persist beyond the downing of tools, and you begin to get the first glimpse of exploration, of curiosity, of a sense of possibility. Not everything really is rotten. There are nuggets of high-class resources in the company, of strong competencies and interesting opportunities. As a few instances of successful change begin to filter through, at least some people begin to believe in the promises of a future.

Nurture these beliefs, support and celebrate the successes, and gradually the energy will rise again. Curiosity about the future will lead to commitment and the sense of possibility will expand into the excitement of creation. Gradually, the butterfly will emerge, and will learn to fly.

Change versus Transformation

Not all companies need transformation. In a context of changing economic and social landscapes, most companies must have the capacity to evolve and change. But incremental change is different from transformation. Typically, companies need to realign some aspect of their strategy, organization or culture, while retaining the others. That is change.

Transformation, in contrast, is the systematic and simultaneous attack across many fronts that fundamentally alters the basic rhythm and character of a company. General Electric and Allied Signal have gone through a transformation process. 3M has not. That does not diminish 3M in any way. In fact, it only points to the fact that 3M has benefited from extraordinary and sustained management strength that has helped it renew itself continuously, without the need for disruptive and painful transformation.

Some companies in India are healthy and vigorous enough to need only incremental change and gradual evolution. Infosys, HDFC and Wipro have grown steadily over the years without the cleansing need of tidal waves. In the 1980s Hindustan Lever met the challenge posed by Nirma by introducing a new product, Wheel, through a new organization, Stephen Chemicals. While the experience led to much soul-searching, a lot of learning and some significant change, it did not lead to a fundamental and all-encompassing change in the company's strategy or character. Indeed, such a transformation was not necessary for Hindustan Lever.

At a more extreme level, there are a handful of companies in India that have faced severe crisis and have worked their way out of it. In that process, they have taken a lot of pain, often with great courage and grit. But they too have not had the need to travel through the whole valley of death. Zee provides a good example.

Zee Telefilms

In the mid-'90s, the Zee juggernaut, led by its canny founder, Subhash Chandra, seemed unstoppable. To the delight of viewers and investors, Zee Telefilms was growing at an amazing pace. From next-to-nothing in 1992, the new kid on the block's income doubled from Rs 45.8 crore in FY95 to Rs 88.2 crore in FY96. Viewership was rising steadily at over 10 per cent annually. Exports had moved up from Rs 45 crore in FY95 to Rs 86.5 crore in FY96. Yet Subhash Chandra was a troubled man.

Lurking below the impressive growth figures were dangerous icebergs. To keep viewers happy, boost viewership figures and thereby increase revenues from advertising, Zee had to make substantial additions to its operations: more software, more hardware. In 1995, Zee made major capital investments just as the bottom dropped out of profitability. Their combined effect rattled top management. Swift action was needed. In Zee

Telefilms, for example, profitability dipped from 45 per cent in FY95 to 27 per cent in FY96. Meanwhile, the company's capital expenditure programme jumped from Rs 1.3 crore in FY94 to Rs 5.7 crore in FY95 and Rs 6.4 crore in FY96. The company was caught between two pincers.

'There was a perception in the financial markets that Subhash Chandra was stretching himself too much,' recalled Chandra. 'But I knew where I was going and what resources I had. Our business model was based on suppliers where third parties supply films, etc. At a time when Crest Communications, Plus Channel and others were putting so much money into infrastructure, our capital investment was just Rs 3 crore. Even today, it is Rs 7-8 crore when turnover is Rs 500 crore. But the markets were penalizing Zee and this was getting reflected in stock prices.'

Rupert Murdoch was another factor. Star TV had hired Rathikant Basu, the high-profile head of Doordarshan. According to Chandra, 'They started doing lots of negative things. The attitude was, "Zee has to be weakened and forced to sell to us." So Star TV started Hindi programming and other activities. Internally, it did a lot of damage. Some people started feeling insecure—how will we fight Murdoch?' January 1996 was a particularly difficult month for Subhash Chandra. It was not only the financial pressures. The *Asian Age* front-paged an article that said Zee TV was involved in FERA fraud, an allegation that, in 1999, was still winding its way through the law courts. But more than financial pressures and media witch-hunts, Chandra was unhappy about the complacency which had set in within Zee's management.

When we started, virtually none of us knew what television was. We started from zero base in October 1992 and by 1995 revenue had climbed to Rs 150 crore. All the key people thought they had achieved great things. And each of them believed that he or she was responsible for this great growth, leading to infighting. In December 1994, I brought in S.S.

Sanyal as CEO. He started showing all of them their true faces. People called him the English Jailor, but nobody could find fault with his argument. Digvijay Singh, in fact, said that 'when the whole world tells me how wonderful I am, Sanyal is the only man who tells me how ugly I am'. But what made me stop and think was the 10 per cent projected growth in the 1996 budget. Why should it be only 10 per cent ? The original team had started at zero base and grown. I tried telling them this but then it became clear we would need a new team which would look on Rs 150 crore as zero base.

Samir S. Sanyal, Zee's CEO, had earlier worked at Tractors India Ltd and was 61 years old when he joined Zee. Chandra had heard of him through a manager at Essel Packaging, a sister concern. Two years later, Sanyal left Zee. 'The old team ganged up on Sanyal and forced his exit and then one by one, they left Zee themselves,' remembered Chandra, somewhat bitterly. 'Perhaps some of it was my fault also. I interfered too much. I should have allowed him a free hand but I also was less experienced. I kept getting worried about the pace of change.'

Zee did not have a CEO for the next six months. Eventually Chandra homed in on Vijay Jindal. When Jindal joined as Zee's new CEO in March 1996 he was 38 years old. For the past fifteen years, he had been a director of the Bennett, Coleman group, overseeing the functioning of its flagship, *The Times of India*. While no one explicitly anticipated it in advance, with Jindal's entry, Zee started on the journey through the valley of death.

The initial flush of enthusiasm: One of Jindal's first steps was to call for a review of the past in order to plan the future, as well as to work out objectives, strategy and tactics. He organized a top-management workshop where the most immediate question was 'What business are we in?' Were they in the cable distribution business? Or in the business of creating programmes and software? Or was their main business the studio and hardware business? The company took a step backwards and came to the easy consensus that it was in the media business and that stakeholders obtained value through the creation of media assets.

After more introspection, Zee's top management concluded:

> Every company has a particular currency. For Zee Network the currency of importance is airtime. As a creator or manufacturer of airtime properties, Zee Network views its properties as currency notes. A plug in the airtime by a non-focused or a non-entertainment programme would not only ensure no advertising for the network but would lose viewership and, more important, would leave the slot vacant for any other channel to capture.

Zee's mission statement in 1994 had been: 'To be the leading TV and communications group providing the people of South Asia, wherever they live, with the finest entertainment, information and communications network and to provide a strong medium through which marketing organizations can enhance their business. Through these services we intend to be worthy citizens of this global village. We will be a profitable, dynamic, forward-looking and financially strong organization which cares for the welfare of its people while providing an enjoyable and rewarding work experience.'

After the workshop, the group adopted a new mission statement (1996): 'To be the leading round-the-clock airtime properties provider, delighting the viewers, on the one hand, and providing value to the advertisers for their time and money, on the other. To establish the Company as the creator of entertainment and infotainment products and services to feast the viewers and the advertisers. Through these services, we intend to become an integral part of the global market. As a corporation, we will be profitable, productive, creative, trendsetting and financially rugged with care and concern for all stakeholders.'

As the new mission statement was hammered out, there was much chest-thumping within the top management. The company had reached the first marker on the journey, the point of complacent enthusiasm.

Resignations, finger-pointing and despair: Jindal followed up on the workshop by sending out memos. Over a two-year period, these memos would fill two thick volumes and would become Zee's bible of patchwork corporate transformation. But at the time not everyone was comfortable with the winds of change. Within six months of Jindal's joining, twenty-five senior managers sent in their resignations. 'Employee turnover happens in every industry. People walk in and walk out. I have not sacked anybody,' shrugged Jindal.

Nonetheless, a quick look at the kind of people who left shows the extent and depth of depletion and the inevitable scarring within the company. Notable high profile exits were

- Nitin Keni, who had risen to become the head of Zee Cinema. 'We wanted Keni to be Jindal's deputy but Keni didn't like the idea,' said Chandra.
- Arvind Pandey, celebrated copywriter and specialist in creative advertising, resigned from the position of head of programming.
- Karuna Samtani resigned on the fourth day after the fourth anniversary of Zee TV (October 1996). After Pandey left, she had taken over as the head of programming. But in mid-1996, she had been transferred to the print and publishing department. She resigned two days after Chandraprakash Dwivedi was appointed head of programming.
- Rajat Sharma, anchor of Zee's most popular programme, *Aap ki Adalat*, left amid a storm of media publicity. In a remarkable show of solidarity, forty-three of the forty-eight-member programme team resigned in protest, though eventually twenty-three rejoined the organization.
- Anil Dharker, creative director, resigned in October 1996 but continued as a consultant. His position was filled by Bharatkumar Raut.

- Digvijay Singh escaped the bloodbath—for some time—
  because he was sent off to the UK as Zee's International
  CEO. 'I told him very clearly that he would have to deliver
  the bottom line in London within two years, otherwise he
  would have to go,' said Chandra. 'But the international
  business starting suffering because he and Jindal would not
  talk to each other.'

Some of the high-profile leavers were quoted extensively in
the press. 'When I first joined, Zee netted a revenue of Rs 6
lakh every month,' said Pandey in a newspaper interview, after
giving up his car, his pager, his identity card, his apartment—
and his job. 'Today we make Rs 10 crore. Sure, we had the
advantage of being pioneers who were fortunately unhindered
by bureaucracy of any kind. I have always followed my heart
and success has followed. I have not spoken to Mr Subhash
Chandra as yet, but even if he were to ask me to stay on, I
would not be dissuaded. . . . It is not for me to give my best
to Zee. It is for them to get the best out of me. Why did my
stint at Rediffusion bring out the best in me while that at Grant
and Sista's did not? It is for Zee to create the atmosphere
conducive to creativity, conducive to challenge.' Such statements
from ex-colleagues and seniors caused even more uncertainty
and apprehension among those who chose to stay.

Chandra was unimpressed. 'The team that was there at
start-up had to be replaced, because once the operations are in
place, everybody becomes happy and complacent. They stop
giving their 100 per cent to the job. They stop looking at the
potential.' To put the group back on the right footing, 'the
company needed a new set of horses to start the process'. This
time round, Chandra looked for 'solid' performers who were
professionally ambitious but had no aspirations to star in the
glamorous world of the media. The people Zee had hired in
1992 came from advertising, had degrees from premier institutes
and good track records. Those in 1996 also had degrees from
premier institutes and good track records; in addition they

came from blue-chip companies and, more crucial, 'the new crop had to have earthy common sense and a will to survive in a tough environment'.

According to Jindal, the exodus was not his problem. 'No individual has built Zee TV. In fact Zee TV has established these so-called individuals. Therefore Zee TV has nothing to lose due to the resignation of any individual . . . We need discipline badly. Earlier decisions were made independently and individually. Today matters are being processed at various stages for proper decision making. If you call it bureaucracy, yes, I accept it. What we need is corporate culture. It is healthy.'

Pushing through with fundamental change: Jindal's most immediate concern was to improve profitability. He adopted a two-pronged approach, combining cost-cutting measures with the development of a new business model. As he pointed out, 'We have no capex, no plants, no machines. We have assets which only increase in value—there are no depreciating assets. So design the architecture right and walk away with the profits.'

The group's three channels—Zee TV, Zee Cinema and El TV—were merged into the Zee Network. As Jindal explained, 'Having three independent channels meant three different infrastructures. Networking has proved cost-effective in terms of management and working. Internal rivalry is now curbed due to this decision.' Besides, El TV was not doing well partly because it was a poor clone of Zee TV, without an identity of its own. It was meant to have younger and more adventurous content than Zee but, as Jindal succinctly put it, 'if you use the same kitchen, you will get the same taste'. As much as 90 per cent of the nurturing went to Zee with little left over for El TV. The channel's content was gradually switched away from family entertainment to more news-based programmes.

Zee's relationship with producers and advertisers also underwent a complete strategic shift. But before he set about changing the rules of the game, Chandra examined international benchmarks. He discovered that a programme which cost $100 to make should earn a revenue of 3x that in a free-to-air environment. 'So in Zee we set the benchmark as 3x. Now most of our programmes earn more than 3x. Some earn even 10 to 12 times and, of course, some fall below. But on average we have more above 3x than below,' said Chandra.

Before 1996, Zee was controlled by its suppliers. There were only five or six producers and a handful of available programmes. Whenever a programme succeeded, the producer would hike his price. Another and bigger danger was the threat that they could get together to start their own channel.

Jindal set about nurturing new talent and fresh, untested young producers were commissioned. Bylines were scrapped. Programmes would earlier have a story name linked to the producer. Now they were called the *Zee Horror Show*, *Saturday Suspense* or had advertisers' names tacked on. Competition between suppliers was brought in as Zee commissioned two producers for lookalike programmes. Zee started monitoring every stage of production through several newly appointed 'response' managers. All proposals now had to pass through a formal assessment route and inquiries from 'friends' were frowned upon.

Producers were now treated as 'suppliers'—a status they resented but had to perforce accept—and payment terms were radically changed. Earlier, Zee used to pay after the programme was telecast. After 1996, payment was made as soon as the programme was ready. Initially analysts wondered why Zee was tying up so much money in this manner but the benefits quickly made themselves felt. By breaking the link with telecast, Zee no longer had to issue long-term contracts, yet could build up a library. It could reduce the number of episodes commissioned at a time to thirteen. If a programme did well, Zee would extend it by another thirteen, and so on. 'We created many exit points so that we would not be at the mercy of a producer,' said Jindal.

As Chandra said, Zee now realized that 'programming is more than just buying programmes. It is a marketing weapon. So if you've made the mistake of buying a bad programme, don't make the second one of broadcasting it just because you have paid for it. We turned disorganization into an advantage.' By 1999, Zee was receiving over 500 proposals a year of which about 25 to 30 go on air. Most producers affiliated to Zee made about ten programmes of which maybe one would succeed.

Zee started playing hardball with advertisers also. 'Hindustan Lever was our biggest advertiser,' recalled Jindal. 'Every year, we would go to them and say, please give us advertising, please be kind to us, we are an emerging channel. Even I did this in the first year. But in 1997, I told Hindustan Lever that I wanted to cut their advertising by 30 per cent. It set off alarm bells. Basically we did not want to be in anyone's clutches. We wanted many advertisers, and nobody with more than 2 to 3 per cent of total revenue. Companies threatened to go to other channels. We said fine. Sony's rate card was one-sixth of ours. It would fill in no time leaving Zee in an almost monopoly position. We could then choose our rates and move them upwards.'

To make the pill more palatable, Zee introduced greater transparency by publishing a rate card. It also designed attractive bundles for advertisers, clubbing non-prime time with prime-time slots. Zee's programmes were now spread according to a strategic timetable based on international research and domestic data. A team of Zee professionals conducted an extensive study on viewing habits. Revenue doubled, then tripled. 'Zee was perceived as a desi channel and Star TV as premium. But we didn't want the Nirma market. I am not a volume man but a value man,' said Chandra.

Even as Chandra and Zee tried to shape the external environment, a clean-up was initiated internally. An office at Marol was closed down and the cost of news gathering forced downwards through the closure of select bureaus. Some services were centralized, such as the legal cell—an extremely busy unit because of the various copyrights involved and the fluidity inherent in a business which was still evolving and therefore had few legal precedents—thereby saving on costs. The organization was restructured. 'Too many islands had come up. These islands were demolished. There were fewer teams and smaller teams,' said Chandra.

Profit pools were created by looking at the business differently. Music programming was one such pool. Often it would take as long as five years for a movie to be broadcast on satellite. So Zee tried to match the interest of the viewer and the advertiser by selling the music, not the movie. 'We told film-makers, we will promote your movie by broadcasting songs free of cost. This will boost your sales. In the bargain, we got one hour daily programming free of cost—and it was a win-win situation for everyone: the viewer, us, movie producers. On turnover of Rs 36 crore, our profit was Rs 40 crore,' said Jindal.

Celebrating success: As the Zee Network bootstrapped itself out of the depression and into a positive spiral, it celebrated its success through a generous employee stock option plan. Introduced in January 1999, the scheme overnight made millionaires of its managers. About 450 employees in India and another 450 worldwide benefited. Vijay Jindal's net worth jumped to over Rs 100 crore and Chandra half-jokingly asked him whether he still wanted to work for an owner-promoter when he could easily set up his own rival company. Jindal smiled. During these tough months, his boss had mastered an important lesson which he freely admitted. 'During this difficult period, I needed a fighting team, and the team leader was Jindal, a man who could fight with me. He was bottom-line oriented and a good strategist. Also, from the Sanyal experience, I had learnt to let my CEO be my CEO.'

Instilling discipline, changing the business model, bringing in new people and welding them into a team were all part of the game plan. But, as Jindal pointed out, 'If you break the rules, the market will follow and the benefit of chaos always goes to the leader.' However, another manager suggested that 'the reason this company has been able to succeed is because of the Shiva in it—its ability to destroy and reinvent itself again and again. That is not only the nature of our product, that is also how we run our business.

By 1999, the Shiva within it had served Zee extraordinarily well. In January 2000, the market capitalization of Zee Telefilms hit Rs 390,000 crore, making it one of India's most valuable companies. In FY99 the company booked gross advertisements of Rs 385 crore, earned revenues of Rs 231.7 crore and made a net profit of Rs 61.1 crore. Meanwhile, other parts of the Zee group were busily blueprinting plans to start net-based services, telephony and global satellite communication businesses. The company had walked through the valley of death, emerging at the other end full of excitement, energy and courage.

Leading the Transformation Process

Managers of troubled companies have three alternatives to choose from. First, they can deny the need for transformation and continue with business as usual. At some point, the company will fall off the precipice but this, they hope, will be after their time. Their second option is to gather up the courage to initiate the transformation process and to live through its trauma. Even if they succeed, they will, in all likelihood, be deeply scarred by that experience. Or—the last alternative—they can step out now and allow someone else with more courage and grit than them to take on the mantle of leadership and initiate the journey into the valley of death.

What makes matters even worse is that different key individuals and different parts of the company will go through this emotional journey at different speeds. There will be a few who will avoid the valley and go straight on to excitement and commitment. There will be others who will not recover—they will plunge into despair and the only act of mercy will be to put them out of their misery as gently as possible. Most groups will go through some or all of these phases, but not in sync.

Table 3.1: Leadership Role in Different Phases of the Transformation Process

Phase	Symptoms	Leadership Role
Denial	• Rationalization • Focus on the past • Withdrawal	• Confront with information • Project consequences of 'business as usual' • Provide illustrations
Resistance	• Anger, blame • Downing of tools • The company does not care	• Listen to what is said and not said • Shared mourning • Show personal commitment • Cut losses when unavoidable
Exploration	• Overpreparation • Incoherent energy • Confusion, chaos	• Guide priorities • Educate to improve quality of analysis • Set short-term goals
Commitment	• Cooperation and coordination • Frustration about speed • Looking for new challenges	• Set long-term goals • Celebrate success • Focus on team building • Step back—let the next tier of leadership emerge

At each phase, the task of leadership is very different (see table 3.1). In the early part of the journey—in the complacence and denial phases—leaders must be brutal in their challenge. They must confront with information, project the consequences of business as usual, and provide illustrations of these consequences. This is the phase in which comparative data— competitor benchmarks, internal employee feedbacks, and customer satisfaction surveys, for example—are essential to ruthlessly expose the truth. The task of making a group of complacent managers confront the reality of the company's mediocrity needs a heavy hand. Worst of all, in this phase the leaders must also confront and publicly acknowledge their own failings. After all, they—more than almost anyone else in the company—must take most of the blame for the past inertia that has led to the need for transformation.

In the next phases of anger and depression, however, a heavy hand will merely destroy. The need, in this phase, is for empathy, understanding, and a collective sharing of grief. The leaders must learn to listen, not only to what is being said, but also to what is not being said. They need to show personal commitment. And, of course, this is also the period of mercy killing—they must cut losses when unavoidable.

As the organization turns the corner into the first signs of curiosity and exploration, the symptoms change. Downing the tools gives way to overpreparation; the feeling that the company does not care is replaced by incoherent energy. There is the confusion of multiple initiatives, the chaos of diverse projects and divergent local leaderships. At this stage, the task of top management changes to one of guiding priorities, of educating to improve the quality of analysis, of presenting short-term goals to direct the process.

Finally, as the butterfly emerges, the role of leadership evolves into setting long-term goals and of rebuilding teams and trust. Gradually, those who have led the process so far must step back from the front line, letting others take on visible leadership roles, while they retreat into the background role of embodying and projecting the vision and values of the company, and coaching the new leaders to play their new roles.

II

SHAPING AND MANAGING

THE FUTURE

4

THE THREE STAGES OF COMPETITION

For almost two decades, Indian Petrochemicals Ltd (IPCL) dominated the Indian petrochemicals industry. Its three plants fed half the country's demand from the plastics and textile industries. The remaining 50 per cent was met through imports. In a supply-driven market, managers in its downtown Mumbai marketing office were constantly besieged by hundreds of small plastic processors hungry for raw materials for their factories. For years, IPCL was one of the most successful public sector companies in the country, turning in sturdy profits.

All this changed in the mid-'80s. The Indian petrochemical industry continued to be supply driven, but two factors reversed IPCL's fortunes. The first attack on the government-run monopoly's bottom line was a steady softening in the international prices of petrochemicals. The second was the commissioning of Reliance Industries' cracker at Hazira. IPCL now had local competition. That it came from the private sector made competition all the more interesting.

Reliance is undoubtedly one of India's most interesting companies and its founder, Dhirubhai Ambani, the stuff legends are made of. What is worth noting is that at the time Reliance's

Hazira plant went on-stream, internationally prices of its products had started falling, and locally it had to compete with IPCL's largely depreciated mother plant at Vadodara. The Hazira plant had overshot its budgeted cost more than twice over—partly because the Ambanis were determined to build a world-scale and world-class plant, a gold-plated Rolls-Royce, as a business journalist once described it—and partly because of some unforeseen extras such as a jetty and pipelines which earlier the state government had promised to provide but for which eventually Reliance had to pay. Despite the rocky start, within five years, Reliance overtook IPCL as India's number one petrochemicals company.

The David–Goliath story as played out by Reliance and IPCL is not unique. As we described in chapter 1, over the last two decades, the same story has played itself out on the world stage, with many companies coming from way behind to catch up with or actually surpass much larger global competitors. Many of these new champions used to be purely domestic companies, with no international presence, modest technological capabilities and extremely limited financial resources. Yet, threatened by global competitors in their home markets or simply driven by aggressive strategies of their managements, companies such as Britain's Richardson Sheffield, Finland's Nokia, Mexico's Cemex, Denmark's ISS, Korea's Samsung, Japan's Komatsu, Switzerland's Swatch, and France's Michelin have built similar success stories in businesses as diverse as cutlery, telecommunications, cement, floor cleaning, semiconductors, earthmoving equipment, watches and tyres.

At the risk of gross oversimplification, what these experiences suggest is that to become competitive, Indian companies will need to think about strategy and competition at three very different levels (see figure 4.1). The dynamics and rules are very different for each of these three different kinds of competition, and performance at each level both influences and is influenced by performance at the other stages. To win, companies will have to win at each stage. They will have to win the battle for markets. They will have to win the battle for competencies. And, they will have to win the battle for dreams.

Figure 4.1: The Three Stages of Competition

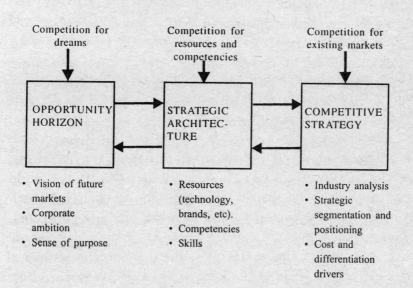

- Vision of future markets
- Corporate ambition
- Sense of purpose

- Resources (technology, brands, etc).
- Competencies
- Skills

- Industry analysis
- Strategic segmentation and positioning
- Cost and differentiation drivers

Competition for Markets

The first challenge is to win the battle for markets. At this stage lies the heart of what is normally referred to as competitive strategy. This is the kind of competition that Michael Porter wrote about[2] and with which many Indian managers are by now very familiar. It starts with a structural analysis of the industry, based on detailed evaluation of the relative powers of suppliers and customers and of the barriers to entry and substitution, to diagnose the dynamics of profitability and to identify the different strategic segments. This analysis, together

---

[2]Michael E. Porter, *Competitive Strategy*, New York: The Free Press, 1980.

with an evaluation of key success factors in each segment and the key strengths and intentions of competitors, leads to a choice of both strategic positioning and competitive posture. The key weapons in this competition for existing markets include market share, scale, a sustainable low-cost position, the ability to differentiate, pre-emption strategies, and so on. To achieve the overall competitive strategy, there is a need to co-align functional strategies: a low-cost strategy, for example, requires a very different approach to manufacturing, marketing and financing than a strategy primarily focused on differentiation.

Consider the case of Reliance. Its many critics argue that Reliance's phenomenal success, particularly in the 1970s and '80s, was substantially on account of some government rules and regulations which seemed to have been designed by Reliance for Reliance. However, there is an old adage that you can take a camel to the water's edge, but you can't make him drink. Reliance wins in the market place every time because customers like to buy its products.

In the textile business, for example, the company won the battle for markets primarily on the strength of a differentiation strategy. Reliance has emerged as India's single largest producer of textiles, but its Naroda complex started modestly in 1966 with just four imported knitting machines. At the time, its entire production was exported. In the early 1970s, the burgeoning demand for polyester fabrics in India caused Reliance to shift its attention to the domestic market. The Vimal brand quickly attained leadership status—customers liked the quality, the designs and the prices of its range of sarees, suitings, shirtings and dress materials.

Unlike other textile mills, Reliance invested heavily in state-of-the-art technology. In 1975 a technical team from the World Bank inspected a number of Indian mills and its report concluded that only Reliance's mill 'could be described as excellent by developed country standards'. In 1977, a *Japan Textile News* reporter was sufficiently taken aback by the design studio facilities to report that 'such a scene is hardly seen even in the highly advanced textile producing countries like Japan'.

Historically the Indian textile market had a three-tier structure: Manufacturer → Wholesaler → Retailer. The market was heavily controlled by the wholesale trade. Dissatisfied with this distribution structure, Reliance opted to bypass the wholesale trade by opening retail showrooms—both its own and franchised, across the country. While Reliance's competitor, Bombay Dyeing, had innovated this practice, it had done so on a relatively modest scale. Reliance executed this strategy on a grand scale— opening one hundred Vimal showrooms on one single day in 1980, for example. By 1980, Reliance fabrics were available all over India through 20 company-owned retail outlets, over 1000 franchised outlets and over 20,000 regular retail stores.

Reliance supported its entry into the domestic market with an unprecedented advertising campaign. Billboards, radio, press and television trumpeted the 'Only Vimal' jingle and the baseline, 'A woman expresses herself in many languages— Vimal is one of them.' In addition to conventional media, the company held fashion shows across the country to add further back-up. Not only did Reliance outspend its competition, its advertising budget was among the highest across product categories—a practice it has maintained since then.

By 1980, sales had jumped to Rs 210 crore and Reliance faced capacity constraints despite continuously upgrading the technology and replacing slower looms with faster ones. It could not install additional looms because of government restrictions. The textile industry, like most other industries, was subject to licensing. The government policy favoured expansion in the small-scale sector—the powerlooms—and sanction of additional loom capacity was hard to come by for larger companies. To overcome this constraint, Reliance started sourcing gray fabrics from powerlooms located in nearby Surat, processing them at its own facility in Naroda and selling the final product under the Vimal brand name. There was no looking back after that. Reliance emerged as the single largest producer of fabrics, a position it retains.

In other words, Reliance differentiated its products, attracted a different set of customers and developed a different business system to meet their different needs. It was a classic differentiation strategy. This is exactly what Nirma did in the Indian detergent market at the cost of Hindustan Lever, what Hero Honda did in the motorcycle market vis-à-vis Bajaj Auto, what Jet Airways did in the airlines business to Indian Airlines, and Zee TV has been trying to do in electronic entertainment to Doordarshan.

If Reliance used the differentiation route to win the textile market, the company won the battle for the petrochemicals market through an aggressive cost leadership strategy based largely on scale and pre-emption. By continuously investing in capacity, often ahead of manifest demand, Reliance not only expanded its market share but also wrested all investment initiative away from its competitors. The net result is that Reliance has come to command between 33 and 80 per cent market share in India for all its key petrochemical products. Coupled with an insistence on always procuring the latest technology, these large capacities and market shares have translated into unbeatable cost advantages that not only make Reliance the most profitable company in its industry during an upswing, but also the most robust in a downswing.

'The fundamental difference between Reliance's approach and that of other companies was that Dhirubhai saw things that were hidden to other companies,' says S.P. Sapra, president of the polyester staple fibre (PSF) business unit, who joined Reliance after a twenty-year career with ICI India (the Indian subsidiary of ICI, UK that had pioneered polyester manufacturing in India twenty years ahead of Reliance). 'The user industry was held back by non-availability of supplies. Other companies would typically do a market survey that would show the current use at, say, 2000 mt. They would project that into the future and arrive at a demand of, say, 5000 mt. They would then set up a 2000 or 3000 mt facility, depending on their projections of their market share. Dhirubhai threw that incrementalist mindset away. He would put up a plant of 100,000 mt, because only at that scale would it be globally competitive in terms of cost and quality. Deep in his heart he believed that India was a big country, with a big potential demand. So, he would create capacity ahead of actual demand and on the basis of the latent demand. Then, he would go about systematically removing the barriers that were constraining the demand.'

How Reliance stimulated demand is typically demonstrated in the methods it used to encourage customers to use its filament yarn. At the time Reliance built its plant, filament yarn was reserved by the government for use by the small-scale weavers in the 'art-silk' industry. Large textile companies could only use cotton. This was the key barrier to consumption. To stimulate demand, Reliance launched a 'buy-back' scheme whereby it sold its Recron brand yarn to the small powerlooms, who then sold the gray cloth back to the company for finishing and eventual sale under the Vimal brand name. 'We gave a fantastic amount of financial support to the little weavers,' says Sapra. 'We gave them ninety days credit to create demand.' Once the positive loop of supply-led demand creation process became fully operational, the company would revert to its tight asset management strategy. 'Today, 90 per cent of our sales is on cash basis. Whatever we ship today, payment is received by 2 p.m. tomorrow.'

This strategy would become vintage Ambani, to be replicated over and over again, in every business Reliance entered. Not only would Reliance enter with a large, world-scale plant far higher in capacity than its domestic rivals, it would also continuously modernize and increase capacity to mop up all incremental market growth to build a position of absolute industry leadership. In 1984, when PSF demand was 45,000 mt, with an installed capacity of 37,000 mt existing within the country, Reliance built a 45,000 tpa plant, which it soon upgraded to 60,000 mt. It was essentially a 'chicken game' that made it hard for Reliance's competitors to challenge the company. If they too created new capacity, the resulting overcapacity would depress prices and no one would make any money. And, given Reliance's reputation of always putting money where its mouth was, the competitors simply couldn't take that risk. Over time, they lost all investment initiative.

Pursuing such a strategy requires supreme confidence. As Sapra points out, 'With low utilization, high capacity can be a millstone round your neck.' In keeping with its strategy of continuous investment in additional capacity, Reliance in a number of cases expanded capacities even as it was installing the originally sanctioned smaller capacities. Further, in each of these businesses, Reliance achieved a level of capacity utilization that was far higher than that of most competitors. For example, the demand for PSF remained sluggish throughout the second half of the 1980s. The domestic industry was plagued with surplus capacity when, in a period of eighteen months, the overall industry capacity went up from 40,000 mt to 250,000 mt because of expansion of capacities by existing players and entry of new players like Reliance.

Realizing that the domestic market could not absorb this volume, Reliance turned to exports. It not only used its scale to advantage, it also upgraded its quality to export a major part of the output. It marketed the product both under its own brand name Recron and through Du Pont who marketed the product worldwide under their own Dacron label. For LAB, too, the company faced a similar situation of overcapacity and responded by exporting nearly 25,000 mt of the product. To support such exports, the company set up Reliance Europe Limited, its wholly owned subsidiary in London. The improvement in quality necessary for export, together with the experience with international customers, in turn reinforced the company's competitive advantage at home.

To pursue its aggressive strategy of demand creation, Reliance often set up special 'business development groups' to create new investment opportunities that would use its own products as feedstock. It provided such services free of cost to potential investors and also used its own network to help these investors secure both funding and distribution. As a result of such 'demand-creation activities' at home and abroad, Reliance was able to achieve 100 per cent capacity utilization in PSF, for example, while most of its competitors struggled to achieve 50 per cent.

For managers used to the more staid approach of large Indian companies, this strategy took some getting used to. K. Ramamurthy, who joined Reliance from the chief operating officer position in Chemplast, once described his feelings. 'Initially I would go to them (Dhirubhai, Mukesh or Anil) with proposals that reflected my conservative market share objectives. And they would say, "Think what a true world-class operation must look like." And my investment objectives would quadruple.'

This continuing capacity growth allowed Reliance to emerge as the lowest cost polyester producer in the world. In 1994, its conversion cost was 18 cents per pound, as against the costs of 34, 29, and 23 cents per pound for West European, North American and Far Eastern producers. But, beyond the cost advantage, capacity was also the company's key instrument for enhancing customer service. As Sapra pointed out, 'Because of our capacity, we could diversify the range of yarns available locally by introducing several new products such as Flat yarns, Bright yarns and Fancy yarns which allowed our customers, in turn, to diversify their product range . . . Also my biggest customer requires 500 mt per month. If my capacity was 2000 mt, I simply could not have given him the service I do. We took the fundamental decisions about capacity strategically, but the benefits came when we exploited the capacity operationally.'

Competition for Competencies

Up to the mid-'80s, the Porterian concept of competitive strategy dominated corporate thinking, particularly in the West. But soon thereafter, its limitations became apparent. Reliance's success in the petrochemicals business could be explained on the grounds of cost leadership, but what was harder to explain was where did that cost leadership come from? Why could their competitors not do what they did? A much more compelling argument was soon offered by C.K. Prahalad and Gary Hamel.[3] Collectively they made the case for a very different kind of competition: the competition for resources and capabilities.

Why was Reliance successful in developing and implementing its strategy? Many other companies, including the public sector giants, also tried to achieve low costs by putting up high-scale plants. Why did they not succeed like Reliance?

Reliance's strategy worked because it was anchored in a set of outstanding competencies. Its project management skills are unsurpassed in India, and among the best anywhere in the world. It pioneered competencies in mobilizing large amounts of low-cost finance. It could manage the regulatory environment, partly through an extensive system for gathering and interpreting information—a key and often overlooked component. And it could move fast. These core competencies allowed Reliance to set up its world-scale plants at the lowest capital costs of any company in India.

'Most traditional economic calculations are wrong because they do not take the cost of time into account,' says Anil Ambani. 'Long before time-based competition became a management hype, we did everything to compress time in both our projects and our operations.'

Reliance had already built up a reputation for setting up projects quickly. It had, for instance, set up its worsted spinning

---

[3]Gary Hamel and C.K. Prahalad, *Competing For the Future*, Boston: Harvard Business School Press, 1994.

plant within eight months of grant of the licence. However, for the PFY plant it outdid even its collaborators by getting it ready in fourteen months—a feat Du Pont, until then, had not managed to achieve anywhere else in the world. Instead of adopting the normal practice of linking the various pieces of equipment through long arrays of pipes (typical for a continuous process plant) after it arrived, Reliance laid scores of kilometres of pipes in advance and cut through them to install the pieces as soon as they landed.

Beyond speeding up commissioning of new projects, this bias for speed also accounted for the company's remarkable operating efficiencies. 'We don't accept a barrier as a barrier,' says Sapra. 'We deal with issues directly. We do not build defences for non-performance.' Another Reliance executive provided a telling example. 'In 1973, the rotary machine at Naroda had broken down on a Friday evening. Import of the component to be replaced would have normally taken two to three months. So I went abroad the same night, bought the component and got it back on Sunday night and the plant was in production from Monday afternoon.'

Perhaps the most dramatic illustration of Reliance's speed came when its Patalganga complex was flooded on the night of 24 July 1989 by flash floods from the nearby 'apology of a river'. Technical experts from Du Pont flown in at considerable cost estimated a minimum period 90 to 100 days before the complex could be operational again. Local newspaper reports, based on the opinions of India's best experts, were even less optimistic, predicting that some of the units would not be operational for at least five months. Reliance had the entire complex fully functional in twenty-one days. K.K. Malhotra, chief of manufacturing operations, provided some details:

> Understand the scale of the havoc . . . After the water receded, we had to remove 50,000 tons of garbage—silt, dead animals, floating junk—before we could get to the actual recovery work. All our sophisticated electronic and electrical equipment

had been under water for hours . . . We set up a control room to connect the site with the outside world. Then we took time to carefully look at the damage and quantify the work. Based on that quantification, we set up objectives, for each plant, when it will be on track . . . Each day at 11 a.m., I would have a meeting for an hour to review . . . on the third day I asked the Du Pont people, 'What do you think?' We had planned to get our two huge compressors ready in fourteen days. They said, 'Out of two, if you can get one ready in a month, you will be lucky.' I phoned Mukesh that evening and said, 'I want these guys out of here. If they say this, it will percolate . . . it will break the will.' We had the compressors one day ahead of schedule, and the whole plant going a week ahead of plan.

The real secret to speed, and to Reliance's core competency in project management, lay in two things: careful planning to quantify tasks and then saturating the tasks with resources. As described by Malhotra: 'Most companies do not quantify the tasks, do not quantify the resources required . . . anyone who says we will do this in twenty-four months has not done a proper estimation for only by accident can the real requirement match such a nice round number . . . we assess the requirement precisely.'

And then, once the plans are done, 'We put in the largest amount of resource that the task can absorb, without people tripping over each other . . . If I had all the time in the world, I would optimize. But given my opportunity cost of lost production, it almost does not matter how much it costs because, if I can get the production going earlier, I always come out ahead . . . only when you put the value of time in the equation do you get sound economics and then saturation almost always makes sense. And finally, we follow a dictum: coordinate horizontally, when in trouble go vertical. That dictum—both parts of it—is also vital for speed.'

Another key element in Reliance's portfolio of core competencies has been its ability to mobilize large amounts of funds at extremely low cost. Between 1977, when Reliance first

went public, and 1993, before the winds of liberalization began
to change the highly regulated and largely government-owned
financial institutions in India, the company's turnover increased
almost forty times, from Rs 120 crore to Rs 4110 crore, with
a staggering increase in its asset base from Rs 31 crore to Rs
4640 crore. To support this growth, the company had to
mobilize Rs 3000 crore from the market. This scale of fund
mobilization was unprecedented in India, and much of Reliance's
spectacular rise came from its superb management of the entire
financial engine during this growth phase (see figure 4.2).[4]

Figure 4.2: Reliance's Financial Engine

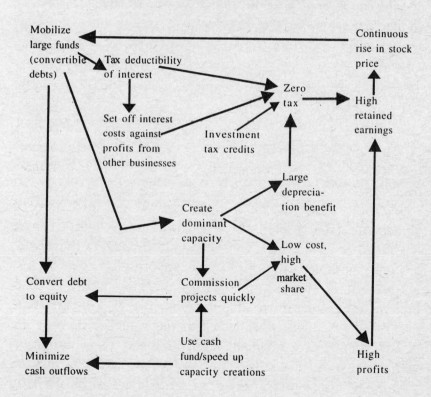

---

[4]We owe this analysis of Reliance's financial strategy to Professor J.
Ramachandran of IIM, Bangalore.

The use of convertible debentures to fund projects—neither the highly expensive debt offered by the public sector institutions, nor immediate equity that, given the growth rate, would have created unacceptable and unsustainable dilution—was perhaps the key innovation in Reliance's financial engine. Convertible debentures created interest costs till they were converted to equity—which was done as soon as the related projects came on-stream. This meant that, for the period of construction, the interest payments were covered by the profits generated from other businesses—with the corresponding benefit of not having to pay tax on those profits—but this cash outflow towards interest expenses was drastically reduced once the project was on line, thereby allowing the resulting profits from the new project to be used for covering interest on the next tranche of debentures. At the same time, the growth in stock price in the intervening period minimized both equity dilution and the dividend outflow.

The whole process was perfectly tailored to make the best use of the Indian taxation rules, as well as the opportunities offered by India's then highly inefficient capital markets. The combination of large depreciation charges and investment tax credits for new investments, together with the profits from other businesses being offset by the interest charges, led to Reliance enjoying—perfectly legally—a zero tax rate. At normal rates of corporate taxes, this essentially meant that the Government of India funded 40 to 45 per cent of Reliance's project costs! At the same time, Reliance avoided the iron cage of bureaucratic government financial institutions—the only source of large-scale debts and equity in India at that time—by directly tapping the household savings of risk-averse Indians. This was done by providing the security of interest together with the lure of significant capital gains on conversion. Large-scale capacity together with quick project commissioning ensured low costs and strong market shares and, therefore, good profits which, together with the advantage of zero taxes, led to high retained earnings and continuously rising share prices—thereby ensuring ever-higher oversubscription for every Reliance debenture offer.

Clearly, Reliance's growth spiral was built on an iterative process. Its competencies in project management, finance mobilization and influencing the regulatory environment supported its high-volume, low-cost strategy of putting up ever-larger scale plants. Each large-scale project, in turn, allowed it to invest more in and deepen those competencies, thus preparing the company for even larger projects and bigger leaps.

While Porter's view of competitive strategy focused on the external world—of industry structure and the strategy of competitors—Prahalad and Hamel focused on the internal world of a company's strategic architecture consisting of all its resources and competencies. At the heart of this new view of strategy lay a profoundly different conceptualization of what constituted a company. In Porter's view of strategy, a company was a portfolio of products and businesses. Prahalad and Hamel saw a company as a portfolio of resources and competencies.

Strategy, then, was not just about finding the best market position. It was about a deep analysis of what a company's competencies really were, and then a creative process of finding external opportunities into which those competencies could be parlayed into competitive advantage. In that process, a static view of competitive positioning also gave way to a more dynamic view of strategy based on two iterative processes manifest in the Reliance story told in this chapter and also in the historical development of Thermax we will describe in chapter 5. The first process was to continuously look for growth by identifying new market opportunities into which the company's existing resources and competencies could be exploited. The second process was to continuously improve on the strategic architecture, both by strengthening existing competencies and also by developing or acquiring new ones.

Competition for Dreams

But this explanation, too, begs a question: what was the engine that was driving Reliance's evolution? Where was the energy coming from?

That question leads to the third stage of competition: the competition for dreams. This is where the power of corporate ambition and human will combines with a vision of future markets to create the exciting sense of purpose that energizes the whole strategic process. The spiralling dynamic of continuously engaging in ever-bigger projects and using the experiences from those projects to deepen its competencies has been powered in Reliance by Dhirubhai's dreams and, later, by the growing ambition of his two sons. This dream has also suggested the kinds of resources and competencies the company needed to build and has been, in turn, shaped and reshaped by the developing strategic architecture.

A retired banker narrated the following story to us:

> One day, Dhirubai came to my office. We had funded his first four looms at Naroda, and he had come to discuss his expansion plans . . . I saw this figure on a piece of paper in his pocketbook . . . it was a schematic of the whole petroleum chain, starting with fabrics at the bottom and moving up through yarn production into bulk intermediates—PTA, PFY—and all the way back into ethylene and propylene . . . to petroleum refining and ending with oil and gas exploration.
>
> He had worked with Shell at Eden. And there he had dreamt of creating a company just like Shell . . .
>
> Imagine that . . . a middle-aged man, with a textile trading business and four looms, carrying around in his head and in his pocketbook the aspiration to set up a fully integrated petroleum chain . . .

As a young yarn trader, waiting in the ante-rooms of Mumbai's mill owners, Dhirubhai would dream of becoming India's largest producer of textiles. As a small-scale weaver, with four looms, he would dream of setting up a great company that would explore for oil, refine it and sell it all over the world. The dreams were never frozen—they evolved as the reality evolved. At least in Dhirubhai's mind, they were always grounded in reality—highly stretched but never a fantasy. 'Growth has no limit in Reliance,' he said. 'I keep revising my vision. A vision has to be within reach, not in the air. It has to be achievable. I believe we can be a $10-billion company by the end of the century.'

What made Dhirubhai's dreams different from the daydreams of many that never get anywhere was the fact that it was backed up with enormous courage and faith—faith in himself and faith in his organization.

In describing his first foray into backward integration from textiles to polyester filament yarn, Dhirubhai said:

> I was a buyer of this product all over the world and I was observing what was going on—not only with the producers in India but also abroad. I went to a major company in the West and saw how inefficient they were . . . people were not working . . . the bosses were not committed . . . and the cost of all these inefficiencies was loaded onto the product and was being passed on to me. I knew that we could manage the business a lot better, make more money than them, and yet supply better and cheaper products from our mills.

It is this heady combination of the courage to aspire and a profound faith in oneself and in the institution that Dhirubhai has passed on to the whole Reliance organization. Anil and Mukesh Ambani are visible carriers of that aspiration, faith and confidence: 'As two well-educated young Indians, without the historical baggage—of saying we are a great multinational company, or with a 100-year family history—we have a fire in our belly,' said Mukesh. 'Kuch karke dikhana hai (we have to achieve something special). That is what keeps driving us.' But, well beyond the two direct inheritors of Dhirubhai's mantle, his vision to undertake 'only extraordinary things' imbues the entire company, and this institutionalized courage to dream is

the source of the energy and passion that continues to drive the
Reliance growth engine.

From Framework to Action

Some managers and strategy analysts make the mistake of
thinking about the three stages of competition in either/or
terms. The notion of core competencies and strategic architecture
is seen as a replacement of the old and outdated concepts of
competitive strategy. A far more appropriate approach is to
think of them as the layers of an iceberg.

The concepts of competitive strategy remain as valid today
as they were when Michael Porter wrote his famous book in
1980. Careful analysis of cost structures and of customer needs
remain vital to arrive at cost leadership or differentiation to
win in the market. But they form the visible tip of the iceberg.
Competitive strategy is supported by the bulk of the strategic
architecture that lies submerged under water—deeply ingrained
within the company, invisible to the outside observer. And, at
the very base of the iceberg lies the vision, the ambition, the
dream.

For Indian managers, the framework presents a starting
point for thinking about their own strategic priorities. Figure
4.3 suggests a simple format for structuring such thinking and
discussion within the management group of a company.

Start by looking at your strategic architecture (area 1 in
figure 4.3): make an honest assessment of your key resources
(such as brands, facilities, distribution infrastructure, etc.) and
competencies (e.g., brand building, project management, new
product development, etc.). How good are they, in comparison
to those of your key competitors? Which are the ones that
genuinely offer an edge, and on which you can build the
foundations of your competitive advantage?

Core competency is an evocative and powerful concept, but
it is devilishly hard to identify such competencies for your own
company with any degree of reliability. Most managers believe

that whatever they do—whichever activity they are personally responsible for—is a core competency for the company. As a result, in a first analysis, you may come up with a whole slew of things that people would claim to be core competencies. Force the group to confront reality: are these really your core competencies? For all the items on the list, are you as good as or better than your key rivals? Where is the evidence?

Figure 4.3: From Framework to Action Plans

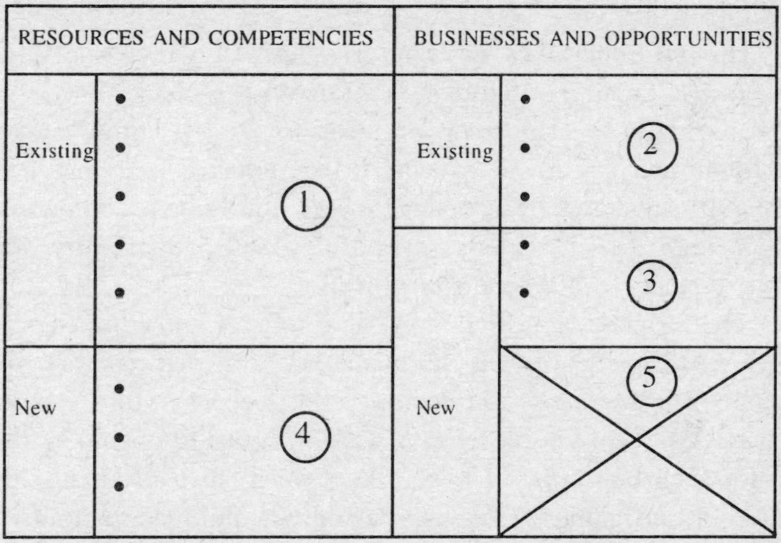

RESOURCES AND COMPETENCIES	BUSINESSES AND OPPORTUNITIES
Existing	Existing

Such a challenge, in all likelihood, will swing the pendulum to the opposite end. As you reflect on all the items on the list and compare yourselves to others, it may appear that you have no real competencies at all: 'There is nothing that we are really good at.' For a few Indian companies, this may well be true. Having grown and made money primarily through their ability to 'manage the environment', they may actually have no real competitive capability for surviving in a deregulated era. But, for most companies, this conclusion may be just as incorrect as the earlier long list: it is most likely that, over time, they have built distinct strengths in some areas even if—like fish in water—they may not be consciously aware of those strengths simply because they take them for granted. The challenge would lie in being insightful, creative and yet logical and disciplined enough to identify these key resources and strengths. One can never be sure if the final list is 'right'—indeed, being right may be less important than being together, to arrive at a collective agreement on the list. At the end, the list must represent the things that the management group is jointly willing to bet on.

Having undertaken this exercise, shift to a review of your businesses (area 2 in figure 4.3). Start with a quick analysis of the market(s) to evaluate your position vis-à-vis those of key competitors. Try to assess where the industry is going, how different segments are evolving, where you have a competitive advantage (as revealed, ultimately, by profitability and performance) and where you don't.

Then, relate your discussions on resources and competencies with your discussions on the businesses and markets: are you using your strategic architecture effectively in your existing businesses? Can you develop a way of doing the business that is not a carbon copy of how others do it; instead change the rules of the game by cleverly using the unique portfolio of resources and competencies you have?

This is perhaps the most important step in the process—the discussion that is most likely to lead to a genuine breakthrough. All businesses, over time, develop 'industry recipes'—taken-for-granted ways of managing the business emerging from its history.[5] Following industry recipes leads to 'me-too' strategies that are really not strategies at all. Strategy, by definition, requires distinctiveness. It is about being different. The real upheavals in a business typically come when one competitor

---

[5]See J.C. Spender, *Industry Recipes: An Enquiry into the Nature and Sources of Managerial Judgement.*

challenges the industry recipe by creating a strategic innovation—
a new way of conducting the business, with or without any
product or technological change.

Typically, strategic innovations come about when a
company—often lacking the resources and capability that are
demanded by the industry recipe—finds a way to create a new
business system by using what it has. In chapter 1, we told the
story of puny Canon taking on the dominant Xerox in the
photocopier business. Canon succeeded, not by copying Xerox—
it simply did not have the brand, distribution, servicing and
financial resources that would be necessary to take on Xerox
head-to-head—but by playing a very different game than Xerox.
Xerox thought that only big organizations needed photocopiers;
Canon imagined that individuals and small businesses could
find the product useful, if only they could afford it. These
potential customers did not require high-volume output—Xerox's
product development focus—and could be reached with dealers
rather than through a company sales force. The appropriate
technology for a small, value-for-money machine for such
customers would also be different from Xerox's patent-protected
technologies. Canon pieced together all these elements to build
a completely different business system for its personal copiers.

In essence, Canon used the resources and capabilities it
had—optical technology, an established dealer network, a
consumer franchise in the Canon brand name—to create a
strategic innovation. It is this kind of a conceptual breakthrough
that can arise when a company can creatively link its core
competencies with the needs of its customers.[6]

But, beyond the breakthrough of doing the business
differently, thinking about the competency-business linkages

---

[6]In *Competing for the Future*, Hamel and Prahalad have labelled this process
as 'competitive innovation'. We have called it strategic innovation, following
Constantinos Markides, whose book *All the Right Moves*, Boston: HBS Press,
1999 provides a detailed description of how companies can proactively create
such winning new strategies.

can also yield ideas about doing the business better. Where are you not fully using your resources to support a business? Where are the barriers? Is there any aspect of your organizational structures and processes that is preventing you from fully exploring your competencies in your existing businesses? How can you overcome those barriers?

After thinking about how you can better use your competencies in existing businesses, you can also review what new businesses and opportunities can you exploit on the strength of your existing competencies (area 3 in figure 4.3). This is the essence of successful diversification—just what Canon did to move from cameras to copiers, or Hindustan Lever is trying to do to move from branded detergents, cosmetics and tea to branded salt, atta and other basic staples. Ability to build brands, large-scale distribution, and high-quality processing of large volumes—Hindustan Lever's undeniable core competencies—are clearly great strengths for these new business areas.

Finally, review the needs for improving your strategic architecture (area 4 of figure 4.3). Given the way you anticipate the businesses to be evolving, what new resources and competencies will you need? Over what time-frame? How will you acquire or develop them?

There are two different ways to create new resources and competencies. The first is to make dedicated investments—in acquiring companies, technologies or brands, in building new production, marketing or distribution infrastructure, and so on. And, there will be times when such investments will be necessary. In moving from bicycles to motorcycles, Hero Honda could use its existing resources of a strong nationwide dealer network, a trustworthy group of suppliers, and a well-known brand, but it needed to acquire new product and process technologies— which it did by establishing an alliance with Honda. But, new competencies can also be accumulated as a byproduct of day-to-day operations—through a process of continuous learning.

Such opportunities are available to every company, but most lack effective processes for capturing such knowledge and institutionalizing it as organizational competency. This is the essence of a learning organization—the ability to use day-to-day learning about customers, markets, technologies and so on and codify and integrate that learning to build new knowledge and capabilities.

The crossed-out area in the diagram (area 5) is 'no-no land'—new businesses requiring competencies that you do not have. While there are a few instances of companies making a success of such a high-wire act, in general this is the area of disaster.

Consolidate this entire analysis, and project it into the future—where do all the ideas you have generated, taken together, take you? What would the company be like in two, five or ten years? What would it be doing? How would it be doing those things?

Then turn to the last issue, the battle for dreams. Start with a zero base—not the analytical advances of the process up to now—but afresh, from the question: Do we, individually and collectively as a management team, have a vision about the company and its future? What would make us feel proud? Is there a possible future of the company that, if achieved, would be exciting and enormously fulfilling?

In chapter 1, we suggested that you form multiple stories about the company's future to come to a collective vision. Ask each individual member of the management team to write his or her own story. Ask them, for instance, to write an imaginary piece that would appear in a famous business journal in five years time, describing and celebrating the company's grand success. What would that piece say?

As you review all these different dreams in the minds and hearts of different individuals, gradually a coherent, integrated and shared picture will emerge—about what the company could and might become.

Now, test this vision, arrived at through a creative and right-brained process, with the consolidated picture arising from the earlier analytical and left-brained process. Is there a match between the two? In other words, if you executed all the ideas that emerged from an analysis of your strategic architecture and competitive strategy, will you get to your dream? If not, where are the gaps? What can you do to meet those gaps?

Iterate through each of these analyses. Try to find a coherent pattern that would link your vision and strategy through each of the three stages of competition. The competition for dreams is very long term, often stretching into five, ten or more years. The competition for markets is very short term, reflecting in quarterly profits and market shares. If you do not win in the short term, there will be no long term to worry about. Yet, short-term gains lead nowhere unless they are related to where you want to get to. Ensure that you, and all members of your team, understand the linkages in your strategy, across all the three stages of competition. And then, practise regularly. Soon, you will be surprised by how much you have improved in the strategy game.

5

ALIGNING FOR GROWTH

Just an overall vision and a coherent plan are not good enough for creating a sustainable growth process, to shape and manage the future a company also needs the ability to effectively act on the vision and implement the plan. For managing growth, attention must be paid to both the content and the process. In the preceding chapter we presented a framework on how managers can think through the content of their vision and plan for growth. In this chapter, we will focus on implementation; on what they need to do internally to facilitate the growth process.

To manage sustainable growth, a company needs to create an effective alignment among three key elements: its value-creation logic, its organizing principles and its people processes (see figure 5.1). Much as an attractive and durable building must be built on a harmonious and stable structure, similarly in thinking about growth, attention must be paid to each of these three attributes that collectively lead to a self-reinforcing growth model. In a building, if any part of the structure is weak, or inadequately supports the other parts, the whole edifice is undermined. Design of any part must take into careful consideration the effect on the whole. Failure to understand the interdependent nature of these different elements in a company will jeopardize its efforts to grow, as piecemeal alterations are made without taking into account the effect on the total structure.

Figure 5.1: Aligning for Value Creation

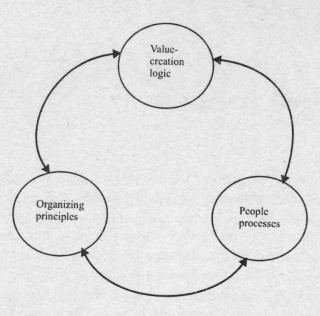

Value-creation Logic

To create a coherent growth path, a company needs a clear value-creation logic[7]—a rigorous answer to the question, 'What is unique or distinct about the way in which we create value?' The word 'value' here does not imply shareholder value, which relates not to value creation but to value distribution. Value creation is all about utility and functionality and refers, therefore, to those the company serves, rather than to those who own it.

---

[7]The term 'value-creation logic' was, to our knowledge, first used by C.K. Prahalad and Yves Doz in their unpublished article 'Value-added of top management'.

Profits and growth are the outcomes of an effective value-creation logic, but they are never the basis for it.

Successful companies can create value in many different ways. Some, like 3M, create value through continuous innovation, maintaining profitability and growth by developing and introducing new products. Others, like Lincoln Electric, create value through operational excellence—with highly disciplined operational processes, typically backed by high-quality and high-efficiency plants and infrastructures—which leads to significant cost and quality advantages. Still others, such as McKinsey, create value by building close relationships with customers, providing tailormade solutions that uniquely meet individual customer needs.[8] And some build layers of advantage, combing two or more distinct sources of value creation.

For more than twenty years, Hanson Trust—the acquisitive UK-based conglomerate—prospered because of its unique and distinct value-creation logic. Lord Hanson, the creator and leader of the company, had perfected a system of arm's length management of businesses through a combination of sharp personal incentives, a tight budgeting and control process and strict organizational discipline. He would buy underperforming companies in relatively mature businesses that were not overly dependent on technological or marketing innovations, and squeeze improved productivity out of them through the 'Hanson way'.

The value-creation logic of 3M—a perennial winner in *Fortune*'s annual list of the ten most admired companies in the United States—has been very different from that of Hanson. Located in the Midwest, the agricultural heartland of America, 3M has grown from its humble roots in the sandpaper business by consistently following a principle that frugal farmers and

---

[8]For a more elaborate discussion of these three value-creation logics and their supporting requirements, readers are encouraged to look at Michael Treacy and Frederik D. Wiersema's book *The Discipline of Market Leaders*, Perseus Press, 1997.

housewives follow around the world—to stretch all resources
to their maximum possible use. 'The last squeak from the pig'
is the Midwest expression for this principle. Following this
philosophy, 3M has continuously used its technologies in as
many different applications as possible, thus growing organically
into new areas and creating opportunities for building new
technological competencies.

In India, under the leadership of Rohinton Aga, Thermax
developed a value-creation logic very similar to 3M's. Just as
3M expanded from its roots in sandpaper to move into masking
tape, then, as cellophane was invented, into cellotapes, and
then into insulating tape, and so on, Thermax has used its
origin in small boilers to expand around both the inlet and the
outlet sides of that product (see figure 5.2).

Figure 5.2: Value Creation through Innovation

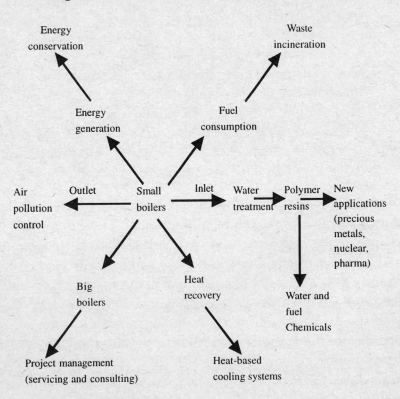

On the inlet side, boilers need water, and poor water quality affected the performance of Thermax boilers. So, the company expanded into water treatment and, as it developed a better understanding of water chemistry, into polymer resins. Then it found new applications for its knowledge of resins, for recovery of precious metals, and in the nuclear and pharmaceuticals businesses, for instance, developing small niche businesses at each step.

On the outlet side, boilers produce energy. As Thermax built up its technological strengths in the heat transfer area, it expanded into heat utilization, thereby spawning new businesses in both energy generation and energy conservation. Boilers also produce pollution, and to help customers solve this problem, Thermax got into pollution control and waste incineration.

Competencies in heat recovery led to heat-based cooling systems. Entry into big boilers took Thermax deeper into the customer's world, and from there into project management and a slew of service businesses. Its expanding skills in combustion systems similarly led to a range of new applications, from tea drying to paint stripping. While most other Indian companies grew and diversified into completely unrelated fields, based on the availability of licences and government patronage, Thermax grew and diversified by using its technology in new areas, and finding new ways to solve its customers' problems.

Located twenty miles away from Thermax's Pune head office, Bajaj Auto has historically prospered by following a dramatically different value-creation logic. As we described in chapter 2, in an environment that restricted both competition and its own capacity to grow, Rahul Bajaj basically focused the company on one core product—first the Vespa and then, after the termination of its partnership with Piaggio, the Chetak— and standardized and refined the operational processes to become the lowest cost two-wheeler producer in the world. Innovation was not central to Bajaj's value-creation logic; instead he focused on giving customers 'the best value for money' with tight control over all costs and by building a high-scale infrastructure for both production and distribution.

What these illustrations demonstrate is the diverse range of effective value-creation logics that are possible. The challenge, therefore, is less of finding the one right formula than of making a clear choice. A lot of companies in India do not have a value-creation logic at all—their managers have never had to confront that question. In a licence raj period, what they produced sold and nothing more was really necessary. In a context of deregulation and intensifying competition, they will now require to identify and commit to a clear value-creation logic. The reason that commitment is necessary is because the value-creation logic, in turn, will influence their choices and actions for the other two elements shown in figure 5.1.

Organizing Principles

Looked at in fine-grained detail, each company's internal organization is unique but, at a more general level, each organization represents a set of choices around a few key parameters. A company's organizing principles provide the basis for these choices.[9]

Autonomy versus synergy: The first choice lies in the levels of autonomy for different businesses and activities vis-à-vis exploiting potential similarities and synergies across them. How tightly coupled should the different businesses, product lines or functions be to each other? Should they be thought of as a 'portfolio' of relatively independent activities, or do they together form an integrated enterprise? Loose or no coupling allows freedom of movement for each business, but renders the enterprise merely a collection of parts. At the extreme, with no synergy at all, there is really no reason to keep together. At the

---

[9]These parts of our discussions are drawn from Sumantra Ghoshal and Henry Mintzberg, 'Diversifiction and diversifact', *California Management Review*, Fall, 1994.

same time, an excessive focus on synergy may amount to a sack race—with their feet tied together, all the businesses may fall down. At the extreme, the search for synergy may destroy all the benefits of diversity and, by seeking a grand compromise, may end up meeting the needs of none. Thus a key organizing principle for a company lies in nuancing the trade-off between autonomy and synergy.

This trade-off operates at many different levels. At the broadest level of overall leadership and direction, there is a choice between the loose coupling of opportunistic decisions to respond to emerging situations and the tight coupling of adherence to a clear and shared vision. In terms of the company's planning processes, the choice becomes one between the loose coupling of performance planning, with a view to managing only financial transfers across businesses or activities, to the tight coupling of developing an integrated strategic, operational and logistics plan, to build and manage a thick web of beneficial interdependencies across all the activities at functional and operative levels. With regard to entrepreneurial activities, the trade-off appears between the weak coupling of autonomous venturing by each unit and the tighter linkages of competency leveraging and cooperative team-working across the units.

Control versus initiative: Whatever the balance between synergy and autonomy, both can be managed by formal central controls or they can be left to decentralized informal initiatives. The trade-off then becomes the extent to which there are efforts to rationalize from the centre as opposed to allowing for revitalization within the businesses or activities.

The choice between autonomy and synergy is a horizontal trade-off across the businesses; the choice between control and initiative is a vertical trade-off because it pertains to the degree of decentralization to the individual businesses (as well as within them) and to the relative primacy of formal planning imposed from the top as the basis for coordination versus mutual adjustments and adapting among the businesses on a cooperative basis. Should the company, for example, favour performance controls to drive behaviour or should it encourage autonomous venturing?

Some key differences between the two ends of the choice spectrum need to be kept in mind. Planning is essentially an exercise in disaggregation; it decomposes the organization into component parts so as to aggregate up to the whole. It is deductive, treating strategy making as a deliberate process and concentrating attention on tangible contents, such as identifiable resources like cash, jobs and machines. Adapting, on the other hand, is less amenable to such disaggregation; it deals in ideas and perspectives. Because these can be known only after the fact, the attention is not on content so much as on process, which tends to be inductive in nature, therefore rendering the strategy-making process more emergent than deliberate. Thus, top-down planning and mutual adaptation relate to each other much as do yang and yin of Chinese philosophy, one hard, the other soft, one rooted in categories, the other in images.

And much like yang and yin, while the substitutability is evident, the complementarities are no less important. In the horizontal trade-off between autonomy and synergy, there is the complementarity of what Peters and Waterman described as the 'simultaneous loose-tight properties' of excellent companies;[10] similarly between planning and adaptation there is the complementarity of 'hard and soft'. No company can do without the revitalizing efforts of adaptation, which bring in new ideas, nor the rationalizing efforts of planning, which help to order these.

Leadership versus culture: The vitality of a company comes, to a large extent, from the energy of its leadership. But an energetic leadership also sets up centrifugal forces that can be damaging. Unless held together, the parts can fly apart. For example, as a new leadership comes in and initiates a change

---

[10]See Tom Peters and Bob Waterman, *In Search of Excellence*, Warner Books, 1988.

process, established procedures break down, and despite a new vision, the net result can be less coordination and a loss of synergy. In other words, organizations can have too much energy—at least at certain times. A necessary compliment to the thrust of leadership must, therefore, be the glue of culture. And, the greater the energy pumped in by top management, the stronger must be the bond of culture to keep the enterprise in coherent, coordinated motion.

Once again, the substitutability of leadership and culture must be recognized alongside the complementarity. Companies can, for example, integrate through the conceptual vision of current leadership or the norms of its historically entrenched culture—i.e., through an image of the future or a sense of the past. Strong leadership can partially make up for a weak culture, holding the enterprise together by the sheer force of its ideas and will. Likewise, a strong culture—established beliefs, deeply rooted traditions—can sometimes sustain a company through periods of weak leadership.

But these forces act on each other too. The stronger the bonds of culture, the more difficult it becomes for leaders to create new energy and thrust. Turnaround is most difficult in companies that stagnate with strong cultures. At the same time, while it may be relatively easier to create energy and thrust in organizations with little or no cultural integrity, the risk is that it can slip off in almost any direction. Put differently, without culture to hold an enterprise in one place, management can all too easily become opportunistic. Leadership and culture must complement each other—a point that was once vividly made by a manager of Royal Dutch Shell: 'It is a bit like flying model aeroplanes,' he said. 'I see my son assembling these planes and they never fly. Sometimes, he puts too little glue, and the plane disintegrates when he hurls it; and sometimes he puts too much glue, and the soggy mass drops like a stone.'

As our discussions of the various trade-offs suggest, the organizing principles of a company must seek a balance among the different elements—and a few companies do manage to achieve such a balance. They tend to be relatively stable, with little need for sudden or dramatic changes, and they are rarely written up in the popular press except in brief reports about their steady growth in sales and profits. Among Indian companies, HDFC—the Housing Development Finance Corporation—appears to have found such a balance.

HDFC has historically developed a wonderful symbiosis between strong leadership, provided by the legendary H.T. Parekh in the early years and by Deepak Parekh, his nephew, more recently, and a powerful culture based on a well-entrenched set of core values. The growth of HDFC has been driven by the initiative and entrepreneurship of its front-line employees, and yet, since inception the company has had to charge off a mere Rs 0.8 crore as bad debt against a total loan disbursement of Rs 11,200 crore—a result of its strong internal discipline and risk control. HDFC employees have historically been granted exceptional levels of autonomy and large responsibilities much earlier in their careers, compared to other Indian financial institutions, and yet established norms such as 'no stars', 'no politics' and 'free sharing of information' have allowed the company to exploit all the synergies available within its diverse portfolio of customers.

At the same time, the nuances of a company's organizing principles must also reflect the demands of its value-creation logic. The logic of expansion through constant innovation into new application areas that Rohinton Aga embedded in Thermax needed the support of exceptional front-line entrepreneurship. The organizing principles of Thermax reflected that demand by tilting towards autonomy, at the cost of synergy; towards initiatives with some resulting loss of control; and, ultimately, a stronger reliance on culture than on individual leadership. This alignment between its value-creation logic and its organizing principles provided the historical strengths of Thermax, undergirding its growth under Rohinton Aga's leadership, but it has also led to limitations that Abhay Nalwade, the current managing director, will need to find ways to overcome.

Reliance's value-creation logic of competing on scale efficiency and low cost, on the other hand, required close control over project management, production and finances. As a result, in these functional areas, the company has tended to be very centralized, with top-down planning, decision making and control. But, in the downstream side, the large outputs of its high-scale plants have required a strategy of entrepreneurial demand creation and this has led to a primacy of decentralization and front-line initiative in its marketing organization. Once again, like Thermax, Reliance has benefited through these alignments between its value-creation logic and its organizing principles, but, in the context of a changing business environment, may now need to rethink and refine its historically effective choices.

People Processes

In his very first week at Enron, CEO Kenneth Lay asked his head of human resources, 'What's our graduate recruitment policy?'

The answer he received was both pragmatic and reasonable. As a utility company in the unexciting business of producing and trading natural gas, Enron could not really attract graduates from the Ivy League schools in the United States. So it focused on the next tier of schools. There too, past efforts at attracting the top quartile students had proven futile. Even those who could initially be persuaded to join the company soon left for greener pastures in more exciting businesses like financial services, consulting or software, wasting Enron's investments on their recruitment and training. Enron had therefore settled on recruiting from the next cut of students who had proved to be less footloose and more willing to live with the gruntwork of a utility.

Lay's reaction to this analysis was far less measured and

patient. He got a new HR head. 'How can we become a world-class company unless we have world-class people?' he asked. Over nearly a decade since, he has transformed Enron into one of the most exciting companies in the world, driven largely on the strength of a very different breed of Enroners. And how the rules have changed! Enron now competes successfully for Harvard MBAs against McKinsey—the world's most attractive MBA employer.

In a changing world in which human and intellectual capital are increasingly replacing financial and physical capital as the key scarce resource, many Indian companies have recognized the need to fundamentally rethink their policies for attracting, developing and retaining the best talent. In most cases, however, all that has really happened is that the rhetoric has become sharper and the HR presentations have become fancier. Nothing has fundamentally changed in terms of the quality of people the company is able to attract. The reason is that, in most cases, while top managements have articulated the need for upgrading the quality of people, in few cases have they been as demanding and as relentless as Ken Lay, or as unreasonable.

As the CEO of a 'boring' utilities company, it was unreasonable for Kenneth Lay to expect that Enron could attract the world's most sought after talent—his ex-HR head certainly thought so. Yet, this is what is common among all managers who really believe in competing on human capital. They cannot be merely reasonable when it comes to people. They cannot accept taking what they can find. They are passionate about getting the very best talent there is, and no compromise is acceptable.

To compete on human capital, managers have to become equally unreasonable on all aspects of their human resource management systems—not only for recruitment but also for development, compensation, career planning and performance management. This is what Jack Welch has done in GE, committing huge resources—above all, his personal time—to create the world's best training and development facility. 'I cannot dream of working for a company that does not have a Crottonville,' said Welch, referring to GE's in-house management school. This is precisely what John Browne is doing, to transform British Petroleum, and what Andersen Consulting has built its rapid global success on.

In India, while most companies continue to fill vacancies, 'selecting' among those who wish to join the club, there are a few companies that demonstrate the same passion and commitment that Enron and GE have for 'seducing' the best people there are, and then helping them become the very best they can be. They go to similar extreme lengths, and their top managements possess the same fervour about people. Reliance and Hindustan Lever are both good examples. This does not mean, however, that they look for the same kind of people, or go about it the same way. Each collects and develops talent in ways that are attuned to its own value-creation logic and are unique to its organizing principles and management philosophy.

What is striking about Reliance's approach to people is the diversity and variety they seek. A Stanford MBA with venture capital experience in the US is pursued with the same relentlessness for a senior management position as a young entrepreneur with a B.Com. degree who has built a successful small business in India, or a high-energy public sector executive hemmed in by the bureaucracy. What Reliance values and looks for are the capacities for entrepreneurship, risk taking and the will to win—hallmarks of the Reliance culture etched indelibly by Dhirubhai Ambani into the psyche of the company. To all of them, Reliance's pitch is the same: 'You are too talented to work in the small pond; come and build India's first great company.' Both Mukesh and Anil Ambani maintain large networks of friends and associates around the world to tip them off when they find attractive talent. 'Once you are on their list, they have endless time to meet you. They will not give up till you say yes,' said a recent convert to Reliance.

Hindustan Lever, in contrast, hires very few people directly in middle and senior management positions. It recruits either fresh graduates or young professionals with a few years in another company, and then develops all of them through a uniform, highly structured and very high quality process into a common mould of professionally competent, highly competitive, yet loyal and decent executives who have high ethical standards and are the envy of all its competitors. Unlike Reliance, Hindustan Lever values professionalism more than entrepreneurship and both seeks and creates uniformity more than diversity; but, like Reliance, it goes to extreme lengths to attract the very best talent at the input stage. Generations of Hindustan Lever top managers have shared a common paranoia: are we still attracting the best graduates? We used to be the employer of first choice, but do we still hold that position? They spend endless hours agonizing over these questions. It is this paranoia that has so far allowed the company to remain one of the most attractive employers in the country, in spite of competition from prestigious global consulting companies and financial institutions as well as the new domestic technology companies and entrepreneurial start-ups.

The Failure of Success

Let us recapitulate the argument we have made so far in this chapter: to create an effective growth path, a company needs to align a clear value-creation logic with its organizing principles and people processes. It is precisely such an alignment that has underpinned the historical successes of companies as diverse as Reliance, Hindustan Lever, Thermax and Bajaj Auto.

But, such an alignment also creates a great source of danger. Effective alignment leads to success, resulting in both internal and external satisfaction, and that satisfaction further reinforces the alignment. Over time, this self-reinforcing process acquires greater and greater momentum, with the alignment becoming tighter and tighter. As long as the environment remains largely the same and, therefore, the fundamental value-creation logic remains valid, this tighter alignment only improves the company's performance. The danger, however, arises when the environment changes, and the historical value-creation logic becomes invalid. Then the once effective alignment becomes a rigidity that, because of the historical reinforcement, becomes almost impossible to overcome. Over time, the company becomes a victim of its past success. In fact, if nothing fails like success, nothing fails as spectacularly as spectacular success. So, the greater the past success, the tighter the links between a company's value-creation logic, organizing principles and people processes, and the more difficult it becomes to reignite the growth process when environmental changes make obsolete the old growth formula.

TI Cycles provides a vivid example of such ossification of a success formula.

Twenty-five years ago, TI Cycles dominated the bicycles market in India. BSA and Hercules, its flagship brands, were widely known throughout the country and had immaculate reputations for quality and durability. For over three decades, TI maintained its market leadership based on a successful alignment of its value-creation strategy, its organizational processes and its values and people.

Originally a joint venture with TI of UK, the company was managed in its early days by British expatriates. They viewed a bicycle as they did in the UK, and formed the company's strategy based on that view. They built high-quality, elegant bikes based on drawings and designs from England.

To implement this strategy of producing high-quality, beautifully designed cycles, and confronting a poor infrastructure and paucity of quality component suppliers, TI adopted a policy of vertical integration. It produced most components in-house, all the way down to the steel tubes needed for constructing the basic frame of a cycle.

This strategy, based on producing high-quality bicycles on the strength of vertical integration, was implemented through a set of organizational values and people processes that were also shaped by the British expatriates. Their colonial mindset created a relatively formal and hierarchical organization dominated by a manufacturing rather than customer orientation. Bureaucratic values, reflected in an organization with over 1000 managers in a company with Rs 620 crore in turnover and Rs 28 crore in profits, shaped its people's behaviour toward disciplined but rule-bound implementation.

Then the environment changed, with the arrival of new competition. Over the 1970s and '80s, Hero Cycles grew from its origin as a small producer of bicycles in Ludhiana to the largest manufacturer of bicycles in the world, right under the nose of TI. For much of this period, TI scarcely paid any attention to this competitive threat, far less try to respond to it.

At the heart of Hero Cycles' success lay a fundamentally different value-creation logic. While TI continued to build its bicycles based on the drawings and designs from England, Hero Cycles developed its products to meet specific Indian needs. It designed a cycle that could carry two people plus a heavy load, and that could be manufactured at the lowest possible cost. Not quite as elegant as the BSA or Hercules models of TI and, therefore, not perhaps as appropriate for leisure cycling in the meadows of Sussex, its bicycles, nevertheless, helped the farmers of Punjab carry a heavy load of vegetables to the village market.

In contrast to TI's strategy of vertical integration, Hero Cycles outsourced most of the components and focused on creating a highly efficient assembly operation in-house. Indeed, to a significant extent, the Munjal family—owners of Hero Cycles—created the local component supplier infrastructure by inducing friends and family to set up ancillary units, often supporting them with both funds and technical assistance. Much before the concept of just-in-time production became famous, the Hero group adopted the system, leading to extremely low costs which allowed them to undercut TI's prices by over Rs 150 even for the cheapest models.

Figure 5.3: The Ossification of Success

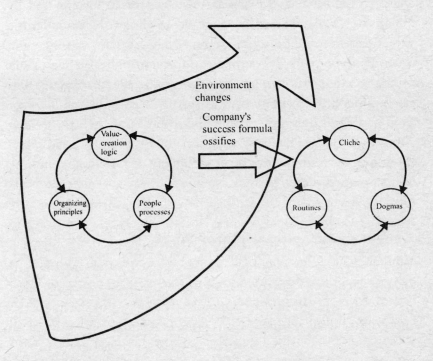

The reason TI practically ignored the rapid ascendance of Hero Cycles for over two decades was because of the enormous inertia created by its formerly successful alignment of strategy, organization and people. Its value-creation logic had become a set of clichés about markets, customers and competitors, with the supporting resources such as the component-producing units having become millstones around the company's neck—organizations, facilities and costs that had to be carried along, thereby preventing the adoption of any new strategic approach that would have no need for those resources. Its organizational principles had hardened into routines—the 'company way' of doing things—that had become ends in themselves. And its beliefs about people and management had degenerated into dogmas—assumptions that were too venerated to be even discussable (see figure 5.3). The tight coupling of value-creation logic, organizing principles and people processes had made TI blind to the competitive threat posed by Hero Cycles.

In the 1990s, TI finally woke up to the problem but it has faced enormous difficulties in responding to it. It was stuck with the component production infrastructure. It has been trying to overcome this constraint—hiving off Diamond Chain as an independent company and separating the bicycle division (still called TI Cycles) from the tubes and strips division (known as Tube Products of India). But the old infrastructure continues even now to be an impediment for TI in changing its value-creation logic and in bringing down its costs to Hero Cycles' level.

Combining Alignment with Evolution

The need, then, is for both alignment and evolution; for both fit and flexibility. To successfully grow, a company must align its strategy, organization and people processes. But the alignment must not be so strong as to prevent change. In a dynamic environment, no success formula can last for ever. A key challenge for top management in creating growth opportunities in turbulent and highly competitive environments is to continuously remain alert to the problem of ossification, and to challenge the organization into changing the strategy–organization–people configuration with changes in the external environmental demands.

This is precisely the challenge Bajaj Auto faced, when it missed a step or two in the second half of the 1990s.

Historically, Bajaj Auto had shaped a value-creation strategy that had represented a perfect fit with the Indian market context (see figure 5.4). In a regulated economy, there were few competitors and, because of rigid licensing requirements, the market was supply constrained. Consumers had limited choice and, therefore, there was little need for innovation, and the prices were reasonably high.

Figure 5.4: The Bajaj Juggernaut

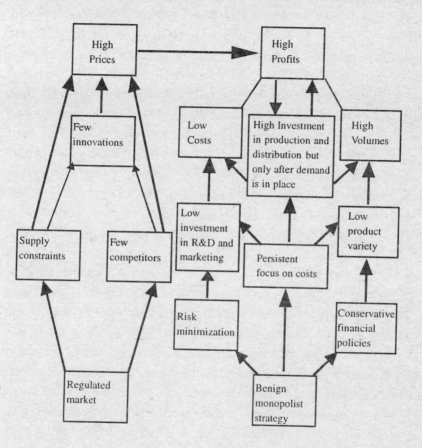

INDIA'S MARKET CONDITION   BAJAJ AUTO'S STRATEGY

In this environment, Bajaj adopted the value-creation logic of the benign monopolist. It minimized the risks, developed a conservative financial policy and focused on bringing its costs to the lowest levels. Given the limited need for innovation, R&D was minimized, and given limited competition, low product variety and minimal marketing expenses helped to keep

Bajaj's overall costs at very low levels. High investments in production and distribution capacities yielded high volumes together with economies of scale, mirroring the value-creation logic Reliance adopted in the petrochemical business. Overall low costs, high volumes and high market prices maintained Bajaj's high profit levels, which it could reinvest to augment production, thus creating a close equivalent to a perpetual profit machine. To keep this machine humming, Bajaj needed a disciplined, functionally focused organization, with a firm central control on costs. Decentralized entrepreneurship was not necessary, nor did the company need outstanding technical or marketing talent. It essentially needed ordinary skills but total loyalty and commitment, and Bajaj's people processes were aligned to attract and retain such individuals. The result of this alignment, as we described in chapter 2, was outstanding success all through the 1980s, with a growth rate that exceeded even Reliance's.

Then, in the 1990s, the market conditions changed. With deregulation, new competitors entered the business, relaxing the supply constraints and creating customer choice. Innovation became key, and prices started coming down. Bajaj took a few years to recognize this shift, leading to the erosion of its market position and share, but then launched a transformation strategy that we have described in chapter 2.

Bajaj Auto confronted environmental change, faltered, and then initiated a radical response. In some ways, Infosys represents a more interesting example because, while building its success on successful alignment, it has continuously adapted to change, instead of a freeze alignment–unfreeze–change–freeze again kind of stop-go transformation process. It has seamlessly combined alignment and evolution in a more organic way.

For over ten years since its founding in 1981, Infosys looked like a very ordinary company, with modest to disappointing growth in revenues and profits. To a large extent, it looked like any other software services company in India, earning its revenues primarily though body shopping. The employees of Infosys would go to the customer sites abroad and plan, prepare, develop and implement the systems and train customers' employees on-site. The profits of the organization came from the price differential between the cost of software developers in the US versus the cost of employing, training and deploying equally qualified software engineers from India. Indeed, over these ten years the only reason Infosys performed any better than other Indian software houses was because the original seven founders lived very frugally abroad, on less than $500 a month, saving the rest for the company.

The basis for Infosys' outstanding performance since 1991 lay in the new value-creation logic it pioneered around the concept of Offshore Software Development Centres (OSDCs). As opposed to relying purely on body shopping, as most Indian software companies continued to do, Infosys created the OSDCs in Bangalore, where most of the actual software development work could be done. In essence, an OSDC functioned as an extension of the customer's own Information Systems (IS) department. Bringing work back from the client site enabled economies of both scale and skill, maximizing internal learning of individual software engineers while at the same time continuing to derive maximum benefits from the wage differential between the US and India.

Infosys' organization and people processes were fully aligned to this value-creation logic of offshore software development. For example, with regard to people, Infosys demonstrated the same commitment to recruiting the best talent that we described earlier in this chapter as the hallmarks of Reliance and Hindustan Lever. But, while Reliance sought out entrepreneurial go-getters to match its strategic approach and Hindustan Lever valued professionalism more than entrepreneurial flair, Infosys built its organization on the strength of a very different kind of people.

As a leftover of India's colonial legacy, public school English, sharp dressing, good debating skills and clubbability continue to be highly valued in corporate India. These are also the kinds of people that foreign companies find very attractive. As a result, middle-class Indian men and women, brought up in traditional, conservative homes, tend to find it difficult to join the elite league, despite their often superior academic records, technical skills and ingrained capacity for hard work. These were precisely the people that Infosys targeted.

Given the need for intense collaborative teamwork to deliver software projects on time and on budget, Infosys deliberately avoided recruiting the 'stars' from prestige business schools who tended to be both very bright and very competitive and who required prima donna treatment. Instead, Infosys finely honed a recruitment process to select individuals with high 'learnability'—an often used term within the company to describe people's willingness and ability to quickly learn new skills and grasp new materials. Often these were modest young men and women, not always from the IITs and IIMs, who had a great deal of respect and hunger for knowledge which they viewed as key to both personal and professional success.

Infosys' organizational processes and values were perfectly matched to the needs of its young workforce. 'We are a group of middle-class people with middle-class values who started this organization to reflect these values,' said N.R. Narayana Murthy, Infosys' founder and chairman. 'These are the values of honesty, transparency, modesty and the highest ethical standards.' Cultural norms at Infosys encouraged debate and challenge but not impoliteness or unpleasantness. The core value of modesty was constantly reinforced through the behaviour of the senior management team: while being worth a billion dollars personally, Narayana Murthy often travelled economy in domestic flights, lived in the same modest house he had moved into in the early days of the company, and drove a very ordinary car. A deep respect for knowledge was institutionalized throughout the company, reflected in its commitment to employee training and symbolized in actions such as Narayana Murthy himself teaching a technical course to young recruits.

This marvellous alignment between its value-creation logic, its organizational values and its people processes powered Infosys' success for over a decade. By the late 1990s, however, the environment had changed, demanding another round of evolution in Infosys' growth formula. Three forces had contributed to this need for change in India's most successful corporation.

The first was the force of commoditization. As described by Nandan Nilekani, Infosys' managing director, 'There is the legendary tendency in the software industry within India to commoditize all its businesses. The only discriminant in a commodity business is price.' In the software business, people were the ultimate commodity. As little garages and back rooms all over India were converted into outfits for recruiting, training and exporting young software professionals cheaply, the market was taking more and more a commodity-like look, resulting in ever-growing pressure on price and margin.

The second force for change lay in sharply rising costs. Salaries accounted for over 30 per cent of revenues for software companies, and wages of software professionals were rising by about 25 per cent per year. Travel and other direct expenses were also rising by about 10 per cent annually. What this meant was that a company's margins would inevitably decline sharply unless per capita revenues went up significantly to offset the cost increase. Besides, just offsetting the cost increase would not be good enough—to invest in the physical and technological infrastructures necessary to keep up with the rapidly changing business, a company had to constantly improve its margins simply to retain its position.

Finally, intensifying competition was perhaps the most critical of the three forces of change. 'The industry as a whole is teaching the customers how to negotiate,' said Nilekani, referring to the growing tendency of even major players to snatch others' customers by offering price discounts. 'It is extraordinary; the industry is killing itself.'

To respond to these three forces of commoditization, cost and competition, in the closing years of the '90s Infosys had embarked on a process of transitioning to a new value-creation logic of 'value-based selling'. Nilekani described this new approach as follows:

> Because of the value that a customer perceives in the product, they are willing to pay on that basis. There is negligible negotiation based on the actual specifics of inputs from Infosys in terms of hours of manpower. Infosys has articulated that it must have a 20 per cent margin of profitability after tax for the next five years. To meet this, the model of selling must move from cost-based to value-based.

This new value-creation logic needed similar evolutions in Infosys' organizational principles and people processes. It is precisely this evolution that the company was in the midst of as the 1990s came to a close.

A cost-based model of software development was best supported by a technologically adequate, culturally homogeneous and highly disciplined professional workforce. A value-based model would continue to need that strength, but would also require intellectual leadership and individual entrepreneurship at least at the front end. This would require Infosys to broaden its people processes, and that is precisely what Infosys has been in the process of doing.

A company that primarily recruited engineers and was only a marginal recruiter of MBAs has, by 1999, become the largest recruiter of MBAs in the country. A company that avoided 'stars' and was historically not too keen on being a 'day 1' recruiter at IIT and IIM campuses has now become a day 1 company in most institutions. The new breed of Infoscians must still pass the 'learnability' test and overtly aggressive behaviour is still a strong negative, but increasingly they have to have greater entrepreneurial flair, and are selected for stronger social skills as well as business knowledge to support partnership relationships with clients that are central to value-based selling.

The new value-creation logic similarly demands a realignment of Infosys' organizing principles. Value-based selling will require Infosys to become a truly global company—'one that produces wherever in the world it can achieve the lowest costs and sells wherever in the world it can obtain the highest value,' according to Narayana Murthy—and not an Indian multinational. This would require fundamental changes in the company's organizational structure, management processes and people's mindsets.

In structural terms, the company has already embarked on a journey of creating Proximity Development Centres (PDCs) around the world, to build and support close relationships with local customers. We will describe these structural changes in chapter 8. But, by far the most important and most difficult changes lie in the domains of management processes and people's mindsets. The company's commitment to making these changes happen is reflected in Narayana Murthy's dramatic decision to step down from the managing director's position in favour of Nandan Nilekani, so as to be able to dedicate himself fully to driving the company towards globalization. Immersion in the day-to-day pressures of targets, productivity measures and financial details makes a company's top management a prisoner of its existing configuration of strategy, organization and people. To lead the realignment, top management needs to first step aside from the existing alignment, at least intellectually and emotionally if not physically, as Narayana Murthy has done.

6

MANAGING ACQUISITIVE EXPANSION

In the early 1960s, Sweden's Electrolux was a small and marginal player in the major appliances business, dwarfed by far larger global rivals such as GE in the United States, Philips and Siemens in Europe, and Matsushita in Japan. It had a very narrow product range consisting primarily of vacuum cleaners and absorption-type refrigerators, the latter increasingly uncompetitive against the technologically superior compressor-type refrigerators developed by competitors. With no in-house R&D and outdated production facilities, the company was losing money; in fact, was fast approaching bankruptcy.

Over the next two decades, under the ownership of the Wallenbergs, Sweden's most influential business family, and the leadership of a new top management team led by Hans Werthen, since a management legend in Sweden, Electrolux catapulted itself into the worldwide number one position in the business. By the late 1980s, it had a broadly diversified portfolio of thirty product lines in five business areas and it was the world's largest manufacturer of household appliances. In most of its businesses, Electrolux had a dominant position in Europe and significant market shares in a variety of other national markets including the United States, it had achieved leadership in many areas of relevant technologies and parity with key competitors in most others.

At the heart of Electrolux's dramatic transformation was an aggressive strategy of acquisitive expansion. Between 1962 and 1988, it made over 200 acquisitions in 40 countries that included such celebrated names as Electro Helios in Sweden, Arthur Martin in France, White Consolidated in the US and Zanussi in Italy.

Electrolux is by no means unique in achieving radical improvement in performance and position through such a strategy of acquisitive growth. Over the last two decades, several companies—ABB in electrical equipments, Rhone-Poulenc in agricultural chemicals, WPP in marketing services, GE in medical systems, and many others—have catapulted themselves into global leadership positions through such strategic acquisitions.

In India, Ajay Piramal has built up a strong and highly profitable position in the pharmaceutical industry through a very similar strategy. Starting with the acquisition of Nicholas Laboratories in 1988, he has built up Nicholas Piramal into one of the fastest growing companies in India—increasing sales twenty-sixfold in ten years, from Rs 19 crore in 1988 to Rs 543 crore in 1998, and growing profits a staggering seventy-three-fold, from Rs 80 lakh to Rs 57 crore—through a string of acquisitions that have included the Indian operations of Hoffman La Roche of Switzerland, Boehringer Mannheim of Germany, Hoechst's R&D facility, Lacto Calamine's OTC products, and the bulk drugs business of Sumitra Pharmaceuticals and Chemicals.

While not quite an Indian company—it is incorporated in Holland and headquartered in London—Ispat International N.V. is very Indian in both its spirit and management. In less than a decade, Lakshmi Niwas Mittal has spectacularly expanded the company from a wire rod manufacturer in Indonesia to the fourth largest steel producer in the world, largely through a similar acquisitive strategy.

Acquisitions, organic growth and strategic alliances provide the three major means for business expansion. They are not mutually exclusive—Nicholas Piramal, for example, has also grown organically through expansion of its manufacturing and marketing capabilities, and has entered into several strategic alliances with a variety of Indian and foreign companies such as Sarabhai, Reckitt and Colman, Boots and US Surgicals. Yet, most companies, at least for a time, come to rely on one or the other of these instruments as the central element of their growth strategy. In India, for example, under the leadership of the late Aditya Birla, the A.V. Birla group largely expanded organically through greenfield ventures; R.P. Goenka drove the growth of the RPG Enterprises group primarily through acquisitions; while B.K. Modi tried to develop Modicorp through a string of strategic alliances.

Why choose acquisition as a growth strategy? When is this strategy relatively the more appropriate? And, if you have chosen this strategy, what are the main dos and don'ts for managing it well? These are the topics for this chapter.

The Strategic Logic of Acquisitive Growth

Leif Johansson, then the head of Electrolux's appliances business and, in 1999, the CEO of Volvo, used the chart shown in figure 6.1 to explain Eloctrolux's strategy of growing through multiple acquisitions. He made two main arguments with this chart.

First, he claimed that in many businesses, including the domestic appliances business, the relationship between profitability and market share was not linear, but followed the more complex pattern shown in the figure. There tended to be a viable and profitable position for small, niche players, focusing on a narrow product or geographic segment (Zone 'A'). Typically, there would be another viable and profitable position for the really large players, who operated in multiple segments and markets (Zone 'C'). In between these two positions lay what Johansson described as the 'no-profit land' (Zone 'B') populated by relatively medium-sized companies who were too large to play the niche game, and yet too small to compete effectively with the leading competitors.

Figure 6.1: Relationship between Profitability and Market Share

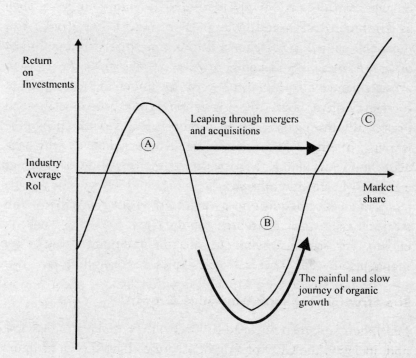

According to Johansson, the cut-off market shares dividing these strategic positions varied both with industry and, for the same industry, over time. The appropriate definition of the market, for calculation of market shares, was also critical. In the domestic appliances business, for example, given the relative costs and economics of development, component production and assembly, on the one hand, and brand promotion, logistics, and service, on the other hand, he believed that geographic continents (i.e., North America, Europe, South East Asia, etc.) were the right strategic units for calculation of market share. Within Europe, for example, in the early 1980s, Britain's Hotpoint occupied a highly profitable position in the 'A' zone, Philips-Bauktnecht consistently lost money in the 'B' zone, and Electrolux was the sole player in the 'C' zone. In other businesses, the strategic unit for defining market shares could be the world (e.g., semiconductors), country (e.g., power generation) or even regions within a country (e.g., retailing). Also, the cut-off zones changed over time, based on evolution of cost structures and competition.

Second, he claimed that companies in the 'A' zone, having reached the upper limits of size that could be supported with the niche approach, faced a choice between two alternative strategic paths. First, they might remain content with the existing size and focus on defending the niche, or even contract marginally to further improve profitability (note that in the upper end of this region, profitability would improve with reduction in market share). In the domestic appliance business in Europe, some companies such as Hotpoint (before its acquisition by GE) and TI-Creda had successfully followed this approach. It was a risky strategy, however, since—according to Johansson—technological and market developments tended, on average, to squeeze the 'A' zone, lowering the market share level at which the no-profit land started. Besides, in an open economy, this strategy was increasingly vulnerable to acquisition by bigger players.

Alternatively, these companies could attempt to grow out of the 'A' zone to the 'C' zone. They could do so in one of two ways. First, as many Japanese companies had tried to do, they might grow organically, through internal development. Such growth, however, took a long period of time—typically between five and seven years—before the investments started generating positive returns. Over this period, the company would have to travel through the unprofitable 'B' zone and would face a prolonged period of unsatisfactory financial results. Because of internal administrative processes, management evaluation systems and career paths and also because of external capital market pressures, most companies and managers preferred to avoid this long hard journey of organic growth. They opted instead for a transition from the 'A' zone to the 'C' zone by leaping across the 'B' zone through mergers and acquisitions. In essence, they preferred to take a one-time hit in the balance sheet instead of a year-upon-year attrition in the P&L. Further, in an era of widespread industry overcapacity, creating new capacity through internal development could often be disastrous for all. In the face of rapid industry restructuring, the opportunity window might also be too short for the slower process of organic growth. According to Johansson, the combination of these external strategic considerations together with the internal administrative constraints led his company, and many others, to prefer the process of acquisitive growth.

Leif Johansson's premise about such a Carvellinear relationship between market share and profitability is not uncontroversial. Many academics and consultants will challenge both its theoretical merit and its empirical generality across different businesses. Johansson's justification for this pattern was based on the argument that presence in each product or geographic market required some minimal levels of advertising, service, logistics and administrative expenses which, even though typically accounted by companies as variable costs, were, for all practical purposes, fixed. Operating in one or a few such markets in each of which they enjoyed relatively high shares, companies in the 'A' zone could appropriate these costs over larger volumes. Companies in the 'B' zone typically found themselves operating in a number of such product and market segments in most of which they had relatively low volumes. Consequently, these fixed costs of segment presence weighed heavier on them and led to a decline in financial returns. The larger overall market share of companies in the 'C' zone translated into relatively larger volumes in each segment and hence, to a decline once again in the allocation burden. This, coupled with larger potential scale and scope economies, provided them with a higher profit opportunity compared to companies in both the other categories.

Value creation versus Value Capture

A strategy of acquisitive growth is by no means a novelty in India. It has been widely practised well before the onset of market liberalization, and was in fact one of the few routes to growth available to 'monopoly houses' in the 1980s.

Among those who preferred this route to any other was R.P. Goenka, a blue-blooded member of Calcutta's Marwari aristocracy, and he used it to carve out a sultanate which touched the lives of ordinary people in countless ways. Switch on a light, sip a cup of tea, have a shave, listen to music, drive to work—and you could be using products and services offered by CESC, Harrisons Malayalam, Wiltech, HMV and Ceat. Companies making tyres, pharmaceuticals, textiles, computer hardware, cables, transmission towers and running plantations and hotels: Goenka bought them all, and a few more.

Even further back, J.R.D. Tata built a number of companies from scratch, foremost among them Tisco, but he also acquired many others. Starting with the acquisition of ACC in 1936, JRD bought tea plantations, companies making locomotives, air-conditioners, textiles, chemicals and everything in-between during his long career as head of India's biggest business dynasty.

But, there is a fundamental difference between these empire-building acquisitions of the past, and the wave of mergers and acquisitions that have now begun to reshape the structures of several Indian industries. Hindustan Lever's acquisition of Tomco—to support and strengthen its core detergent business— was very different in character from the RPG group's acquisition of CESC or HMV, and even more so from Manu Chhabria's acquisitions of Dunlop and Shaw Wallace. For Chhabria, the key attraction for the acquisition, as well as the key management challenge, was value capture—from earlier owners by buying cheap, or from the government by using tax credits and incentives or through the sale of assets, and so on. While the deal-making part was still important for Hindustan Lever when it acquired Tomco, by far the greater challenge lay in integrating the acquired operation with its own existing business. This was an acquisition more for value creation than for value capture, and all value creation occurs through the integration process.[11]

Increasingly, it is these kinds of acquisitions, aimed at industry restructuring and value creation, that will become common in India. It is precisely such acquisitions that have supported the growth strategies of Electrolux, Ispat and Nicholas Piramal. And, from their practices and experiences, it is possible to distil some simple lessons about how to manage such a process of acquisitive growth. There are, of course, some variations depending on the nature of the industry, the history of the acquiring company, and the specific circumstances of each acquisition. But, overall, there is a certain commonality in the approaches that each of these companies seem to have adopted in both the pre- and the post-acquisition phases. Before presenting these commonalities in the form of a general framework for acquisition management, let us describe one case in some detail that illustrates most of the elements in the framework.

The Story of Ispat Mexicana (Imexsa)[12]

Lakshmi Niwas Mittal's (widely referred to as LN both inside and outside the company) faith in DRI (direct reduced iron)

---

[11]This distinction between acquisitions for value creation and value capture has been made by Philippe Haspeslagh and David Jamison in their book *Managing Acquisitive Growth*, New York: The Free Press, 1988.

[12]Largely based on the case 'Ispat International N.V.', written under the supervision of Professor Don Sull at the London Business School.

technology governed his choice of acquisitions. He believed in its future long before others. 'This has spelt success for so many of my plants,' he says. Starting in Indonesia in 1976, he bought mini-steel mills using the DRI route in various countries and turned them around. Eventually, in January 1995, Mittal acquired Hamburg Stahlwerke, the originator of DRI technology on which almost all LN's plants depend.

According to Peter F. Marcus, director of Paine Webber, 'Lakshmi Mittal championed the practice of mini-mills becoming integrated producers through the use of scrap alternatives.' This faith created 'the only true global steel company', according to the *Financial Times*, and Mittal's reputation as a doctor of sick steel mills. In 1991, this reputation brought the Mexican government knocking on his door.

In the early 1980s, the Mexican government decided to build a new steel mill—Sicartsa II—adjacent to its existing Sicartsa facility located in Lazaro Cardenas. It invested $2.2 billion in a state-of-the-art facility, which included a pelletizer plant to produce iron pellets from ore, the first DRI plant in the world using the HyL III technology, electric arc furnaces, casters to roll molten steel into flat slabs and a mill to convert these slabs into plates to produce pipes for the then booming oil industry. Before the factory was completed, however, the end of the oil boom coincided with a faltering economy which forced Mexico to devalue the peso. The government curtailed investment in the planned pelletizer plant, which forced the Sicartsa management to source high-cost iron pellets on the open market. The government also abandoned the planned plate mill, forcing the plant to sell steel slabs—an intermediate product—rather than finished steel plates. Three years after opening, the plant operated well below its capacity of two million tons per year and incurred significant operating losses. Mexican government officials publicly blamed the management and employees of the factory for the losses, and decided to privatize both Sicartsa factories in 1991. Based on Ispat's reputation for turning around Iscoot, a steel mill in Trinidad, the Mexican government invited Ispat to join two other steel companies in bidding for Sicartsa.

The Pre-Acquisition Negotiation Process

The team: Mittal sent a due diligence team consisting of twenty managers representing all line and staff functions chosen from Ispat's Trinidad and Indonesian plants and instructed them to develop plans to turn around the plant. Mittal also explained that some members of the due diligence team would have an opportunity to remain in Mexico if Ispat acquired the facility. There were no merchant bankers.

The team was divided into sub-units to look at specific areas such as finance, marketing, management and costs. Each team had to make specific recommendations. 'These had to be solid and doable as the person making the recommendation could easily be called upon to implement it,' said one manager. 'This eliminates consultants and their ivory tower analyses. After this process, targets are fixed and LN largely steps out of the picture.' Each team's report provided a valuable check on the other's to eliminate biases and oversight.

The team's due diligence revealed a factory plagued by technical problems, running at 20 per cent of capacity, producing low-quality slabs and manned by a dispirited workforce. The Ispat team was impressed, however, by the recent vintage of the assets, a young workforce with an average age of 27 years, and the supporting infrastructure. The team recommended bidding for the plant, and developed a turnaround plan.

The bid: Ispat proposed acquiring all the Sicartsa II factory's assets and liabilities, excluding contingent environmental liabilities. Ispat also bid for 50 per cent equity stakes in several of the businesses that supported the Sicartsa II plant, including PMT, a producer of welded pipes, Peña Colorada, which provided the factory with iron pellets and Sersiin, which managed the deep-water port facilities and distributed electricity. It took eight months to sew up the contract.

Ispat proposed a total consideration of $220 million, consisting of $25 million in cash and $195 million in ten-year bonds (at 15 per cent interest) issued by the Mexican government and secured by a warrant for 49 per cent of Imexsa (not Ispat) equity. Of the cash component, $5 million was a loan from Trinidad and $20 million came from LN's personal resources. Ispat's bid outlined the company's five-year plan for improving Sicartsa's operations, and included a commitment to invest an additional $350 million, with a $50-million penalty if the company failed to follow through on its promised capital spending.

Ispat's proposal also included a clause capping the number of employees it would lay off at 100 of the 1050 workers. Impressed by the business plan, the Mexican government selected Ispat's bid. Ten members of the due diligence team remained in Mexico to run various departments, including Dr Johannes Sittard, the former head of Iscoot, who served as the managing director of Imexsa from 1991 to 1993.

The Post-Acquisition Integration Process

Stopping the bleeding: Ispat took control of Imexsa on 1 January 1992 in the midst of a global recession in the steel industry, and had to briefly shut down the furnaces because there were no orders for the steel and no place to store the finished slabs. Despite the shutdown, Imexsa laid off only seventy people—thirty fewer than the agreed upon limit—and ultimately hired an additional 270 employees.

The $220-million consideration which Ispat had committed to more than halved almost instantly. The plate mill which had been lying abandoned, still packed in crates, was shipped to a Korean company. 'Our focus is slabs and we didn't need the plate mill,' R.R. Mehta, Imexsa's executive director, told

Business India.[13] The deal brought in $135 million—much of this went towards upgrading facilities.

Mittal recalled his first steps at Imexsa:

> In Mexico we did what we do with every business . . . we sat down with management of the acquired company to discuss various options for improvement and we developed the business plan. We sat down with each of the departments to understand their problems and viewpoints and gave our input based on international experience and our due diligence. Together we set very aggressive targets because we don't benchmark companies based on local standards, but on international standards. If the management of the acquired company is willing to commit to these targets, they stay. If they have any problems following our business plan and vision, they go. The Imexsa managers stayed.

Production Planning Manager Oscar Vasquez recalled his first meeting with Mittal:

> In our first meeting, we presented two alternative production plans, one for 600,000 tons—it was conservative and based on our past experience—and another plan for 1.2 million tons. Mr Mittal saw both and said 'Forget the small plan, just let me know what you need to implement the second plan.' We expressed concern that we might not find a market for the additional slabs, but Mr Mittal said, 'You will have the volume because I'm going to take care of that for you.'

Mittal used Ispat Indo's sales network to identify Asian customers for Imexsa's slabs, including a contract for 400,000 tons per year with a Taiwanese steel manufacturer. Although these orders provided low margins, they allowed Imexsa to increase capacity utilization while improving quality to win more profitable business. Imexsa also reduced costs by switching to suppliers willing to match the lowest costs provided at Ispat's Trinidad and Indonesia plants.

---

[13]*Business India*, 27 July 1998, p.50.

The next step was to quickly develop cost consciousness and discipline among the Imexsa management team. Jai K. Saraf, Ispat International's finance director, and Sittard instituted a daily meeting of the heads of each department in the plant, which began after the day shift ended at 5:00 p.m. and generally ran until 9:00 or 10:00 at night. The team evaluated the previous day's cost, volume, productivity and quality performance, discussed the current day's results, and agreed on detailed targets by department for the following day.

Om Mandhana, purchase director, described the purpose of the daily meeting:

> The idea of the daily meeting was to cut red tape. You got together all of the people involved to talk through any issues, and as a means of coordinating and resolving day-to-day problems. The idea was to take a decision then and there rather than refer to committees.

Raul Torres, melt shop director, recalled his first impressions of the daily meetings:

> Before Ispat bought the plant, the boss just told us how we should do things, but the daily meetings were nothing like that. Dr Sittard asked a lot of detailed technical questions to force us to think through problems to their root causes. If we were consuming too much steel in the electric arc furnaces, for instance, Dr Sittard would ask: 'Why are you consuming this amount of steel? Is there leakage? Why do you have this amount of leakage? Are you losing steel in the slag? How do you plan to improve this? Is that the cheapest way in the world? Who does this best in the world? Can we adopt their technology?
>
> We had open and sometimes heated discussions, but once we agreed on the right thing to do, it was easy to get Dr Sittard's approval and any resources you needed to make it happen. But you had to commit to improvements—how much you were going to achieve and by when, and the entire team monitored how you did against the promised target. And Dr

Sittard was always asking for higher targets—he always kept the pressure on us to increase volume and quality and cut costs.

Imexsa's existing cost accounting system reported only aggregate production costs on a monthly basis, and was first available three weeks after the previous month ended. One of the first things the new management team did was to implement Ispat's daily reporting system, which provided overall figures for each day's operations by the next morning. Led by Saraf, Imexsa's accounting department began collecting detailed volume, cost, quality and productivity data for each step in the production process on a daily basis. Initially, Imexsa's accountants collected these data themselves every day, and analysed them by hand. To monitor raw material usage, for example, the accountants asked warehouse workers to track the volume of materials leaving the storeroom each day.

As the discipline steeped in, kudos flowed back. A J.P. Morgan report hailed Imexsa as the lowest cost slab producer in the world, while Credit Suisse First Boston reported, 'At Imexsa, Ispat makes Nucor's cost position look almost amateurish.' Imexsa could land a slab in the middle of America at $35 a ton below Nucor's cash cost of production of $210 a ton. And Nucor founder Kenneth Iverson acknowledged, 'Ispat comes in and runs the operations very well. They control costs very very closely.'

In 1992—the first year under Ispat ownership—Imexsa increased shipments from 528,000 tons to 929,000 tons, decreased the cash cost per ton produced from $253 to $178, and earned a small profit. From 1992 to 1998 Imexsa increased annual steel shipments from 929,000 tons to over 3 million tons, and improved productivity from 2.62 to 0.97 man-hours per ton. Antonio Gonzales, the pelletizing plant supervisor, observed, 'There is no feeling of having finished the turnaround . . . we keep resetting the targets, and now we are aiming for 4 million tons per year—that's double our rated capacity.'

In 1997, M.R.R. Nair joined Imexsa as managing director from the Steel Authority of India, the seventh largest steel company in the world, where he had served as chairman and CEO and had been awarded the Best CEO in India award. Nair cited four mechanisms for maintaining constant improvement at Imexsa: daily meetings and reports, quality programmes, global integration and stretch goals.

Daily meeting and daily report: The daily meeting, now held each morning for one or two hours, continued to play a pivotal role at Imexsa. A typical meeting (in March 1998) was attended by representatives from each of the departments, most of whom wore the khaki Imexsa uniform. A few of the managers, however, wore red Imexsa jackets awarded to recognize achievement of ambitious goals, such as increasing one of the DRI facility's production nearly 50 per cent above its rated capacity. On several occasions during the meeting, participants jokingly asked whether their targets were ambitious enough to earn a jacket. Nair guided the meeting with a series of questions, inquiring about the results of previous experiments to improve performance, asking what level of performance was budgeted for the following month, and probing why targets were not higher. Nair left the room for extended periods on two occasions during the meeting, but the discussion continued with the members of the different departments discussing targets and experiments among themselves. The participants frequently referred to the daily report which provided detailed data on cost, productivity, volume and quality for each of the departments.

Quality programmes: In 1998, Imexsa used standard quality tools, such as ISO methods, to describe existing processes. Imexsa's quality efforts won numerous international awards and earned it the British Standards Institute's prestigious Company-Wide Recognition, one of only two steel companies in the world so honoured (Iscoot was the other). Imexsa's quality initiatives helped the company upgrade its products to serve more demanding customers. Imexsa enhanced its product mix from 97 per cent low-grade steel sold into construction applications in 1992 to 47 per cent of slabs sold for demanding automotive and coated plate applications in 1997. Despite Imexsa's success, the quality director, Rafael Mendoza, wanted more: 'Traditional quality programmes such as ISO 9000 provide excellent statistical tools for documenting your current processes, but they are not as useful in accelerating continuous improvement. For this we introduced benchmarking, Top 10s and internal agreements.'

In benchmarking operating processes, quality team members looked at best practices within the Ispat network, the steel industry as a whole and also identified and studied related processes at global leaders such as Ericsson and General Electric. When Imexsa management wanted to improve cafeteria service during the busy lunch hour, for example, a quality team studied the restaurant in a busy soccer stadium renowned for serving large quantities of excellent food quickly during half-time. Imexsa would only work with customers and technology suppliers who agreed to openly share information on new technological developments and applications, and in turn agreed to open their plants for benchmarking. Mendoza was not worried that Imexsa would surrender competitive advantage by allowing other companies to benchmark the plant: 'In the steel industry these days, all companies have access to good ideas through customers, suppliers and consultants. The difference is who can implement them successfully.'

In the Top 10 programme, each department identified projects to either cut costs or improve quality, quantified each project's financial impact (in US dollars per year), and rank ordered the projects from one to ten based on their bottom-line impact. Each project was assigned to a project owner charged with selecting a multidisciplinary team to quantify the benefits of the project, develop an action plan and monitor progress against agreed process milestones. In Mendoza's view, the Top 10 programme introduced a consistent discipline in translating proposed projects into financial results and allowed each department to prioritize its own projects for improvement.

In 1996 Imexsa initiated a systematic programme for making internal service agreements between Imexsa's departments and monitoring service delivery levels against these agreements. The head of the department receiving a service would meet once a year with each internal supplier to articulate their key requirements and agree on targets and concrete measures of service delivery. Before agreeing to target service levels, a service provider could request any prerequisites necessary to guarantee delivery. The maintenance department might agree to provide preventive maintenance on time, for instance, provided that they were notified at least one week in advance of the scheduled downtime. The head of the department providing the service was responsible for monitoring performance on a daily basis and reporting to the head of the internal customer on a monthly basis, who would sign off on the performance evaluation. If a service provider repeatedly failed to meet goals, the failure would be elevated for discussion in the daily meeting, but this had occurred only once in the programme's first two years.

In 1998 Imexsa had 140 internal service agreements across twenty-eight production and service departments and sub-departments in the plant. Seventy per cent of the agreements fulfilled 100 per cent of the requirements, 11 per cent of the agreements met between 95 per cent and 99 per cent, with the remainder fulfilling less than 95 per cent. These internal agreements yielded significant improvements in operations.

Knowledge Integration Programme: The Knowledge Integration Programme (KIP) was an Ispat corporate initiative designed by Mittal to 'keep stirring the whole organization'. A few representatives from each operating and staff function (twelve in all) at each Ispat plant would meet twice each year. These

KIP meetings lasted two to four days, and rotated among the plants in the Ispat network. Prior to the meeting, the department heads would send their suggestions for discussion topics to Ispat group headquarters in London, where the agenda would be set and then distributed to each of the participants in advance. During the meeting, the participants would review their performance against targets, including major accomplishments and disappointments, discuss common technical problems, update each other on developments in their plant and commit to future targets. The participants also communicated between KIP meetings, as Torres described: 'If I have a question, I don't have to wait until the next KIP meeting. I can make a phone call or send an e-mail to Canada or Trinidad. I probably exchange at least one e-mail every week with them.'

Stretch goals: Each department in Imexsa committed to annual targets for production volume, productivity and costs, and presented their plan for achieving these goals. The process was based on a firm philosophy of Ispat. As described by Nair, 'Senior managers should ask the departments what they plan to do, rather than telling them what to do.' At the same time, however, it was not a laissez-faire. Nair and his team asked a lot of questions on the plans that were presented. 'You achieved this level last year, why can't you do it again? They can achieve the level at another factory, what prevents you from doing the same? What can we do to help you achieve more?' At the end of such discussions, while the targets were very demanding, they were owned by the departments instead of being perceived as coerced from above. As Raul Torres described:

> I feel the need to constantly improve performance every day, but it's not forced on me by management. I'm not fighting against somebody else's budgets—I agreed to the goal, and the best way to reach a goal is not with a big gun to your head. I set stretch goals because I want Imexsa to win. At first, I wanted Imexsa to be the best steel plant in Lazaro Cardenas, then the best steel plant in Mexico, but now I ask why can't

we be the best steel plant in the world? We always wanted to be the best, but we couldn't because the old management put up too many limitations.

A Blueprint for Managing Acquisitions

We have described the story of Imexsa in such detail only because it is almost a textbook example of some of the key lessons that emerge from the experiences of a diverse range of companies on how to manage the pre- and post-acquisition processes. Table 6.1 summarizes these lessons.

THE PRE-ACQUISITION NEGOTIATION PROCESS

Moving Rapidly

The first success factor in the pre-acquisition process is to develop the ability to move very rapidly. The moment an acquisition candidate surfaces in the market, a frenzy of activity follows. Multiple buyers jump into the fray with competitive bids. In this situation, speed is often the vital difference between the winners and the losers.

One way to achieve speed is to be prepared in advance. In the 1980s, when Electrolux was still building its global infrastructure through a string of strategic acquisitions, there was a shelf in the room of Leif Johansson, crammed with a set of folders. Each folder was a complete analysis of a domestic appliances company, with details of what Electrolux should do if an opportunity arose for acquiring the company—not just how much it should pay, but what actions it should take should the deal go through. Johansson had one such folder for each and every significant domestic appliances company in the world, and had instituted a process for keeping the folders updated on a regular basis. Because of this head start, he could move very rapidly whenever any of these companies actually came to the market.

Nicholas Piramal did not have the same systematic approach

Table 6.1: A Blueprint for Integrating Acquisitions

Pre-acquisition Negotiation Process	Post-acquisition Integration Process		
	Phase I	Phase II	Phase III
	Cleaning up and building foundation	*Strategic and Organizational Revitalization*	*Integration of People and Operations*
• Prepare so as to be able to move very rapidly	• Align top management	• Establishing a vision and stretch goals	• Broadening the interface between acquired and acquiring units
• Careful structuring of evaluation/negotiation teams	• Instil discipline through reporting and control systems	• Investment for enhancing basic functional competencies and employee skills	• Joint rationalization of production, marketing, IT, etc.
• Involve operating managers and protect against escalating commitments	• Pick up the pennies lying on the floor	• Structural reorganization if necessary	• Two-way flow of people at different levels
• Understand seller's motivation to secure the best deal	• Few quick hits to improve performance and morale	• Continuing commitment of corporate top management	

that Electrolux had perfected, but it still achieved the same benefit of rapid response through the personal involvement and push of Ajay Piramal. In each of his key acquisitions—that of Nicholas Laboratories, Roche and Boehringer Mannheim, in particular—Piramal was the underdog in the bidding process. Nicholas Laboratories wanted to sell the business to Reckitt and Colman, who took their time thinking about it. Roche had first approached the Tata group, which already held a 12 per cent stake in the Indian subsidiary. In each case, Piramal snatched the prize simply by moving very quickly. For example, the managing director of Boehringer Mannheim's Indian subsidiary called him at 10.30 p.m. one night in August 1966, in the course of which he suggested that Piramal should meet the company's corporate managers in Frankfurt. Piramal caught the flight to Germany that same night and ultimately finalized the deal by October. In his earlier acquisitions Mittal played an exactly similar role to ensure quick decisions and actions on every acquisition proposal.

Structuring the Teams

The second requirement is to pay careful attention to the structure of the pre-acquisition teams. Ideally, the task should be divided among two different teams. The first team should focus on strategic, organizational and operational assessment of the target, and it must include the operating managers who would actually have to run the business should the deal go through. The second team, consisting of financial and legal representatives, should carry out the actual negotiations. This team should have one or two operating managers, largely in a silent observer role, and it must have the autonomy to arrive at the best possible terms, unconstrained by anything that the operating team might have implied.

The acquisition negotiation process is notoriously susceptible to the problem of escalating commitments. Outsiders involved in the deal, such as investment bankers and consultants, make money only when the deal goes through. Even for internal managers, the thrill of the chase leads to an emotional need for closure. That is why it is important for the first team to include those managers who have to actually deliver on any improvements that are anticipated and for the second team to be totally different so as to retain its capacity to walk away from the deal unless the legal and financial terms are satisfactory. For example, in 1997 the due diligence team recommended that Ispat should acquire the 3.7-million-ton Sidor plant in Venezuela. But Mittal walked away from the deal because the financial negotiation team thought that the price was too high.

Understanding the Seller's motivations

The trick for getting the right price is to fully understand the motivations and priorities of the seller, and to have better information on all possible aspects of the deal than the rival bidders. Mittal recognized that protecting employment and assured revitalization of Imexsa was of vital importance to the Mexican government, and he got an outstanding deal by meeting these two needs of the seller. Similarly, in the negotiations with Roche, Piramal won because of his accurate analysis of what the Swiss company was looking for:

> They were actually looking for a company who would be more like a partner than just a simple acquirer. They did not want to lose the brand image that they had built in India because they felt that it might be useful to them in the future. They wanted to continue supplying chemicals into India. So, the partner had to be able to implement a successful turnaround of the company. Besides, they did not want the acquirer to compete against Roche in the international arena via export of generic products. They also wanted a company with a strong sales and distribution network in India that would give a boost to new product launches—and royalty revenues.

In his presentation to Roche, Piramal clinched the deal by using a very Indian concept—that of matching the horoscopes of a prospective couple—to show why he was the ideal partner. Using·this analogy, he showed how his company ideally met all Roche's needs, and why his rivals did not.

Beyond getting the seller to be favourably disposed towards him, this focus on understanding their motivations and priorities also helped Piramal in reducing the price:

> They asked for a price of Rs 150 per share which they subsequently brought down to Rs 115; but we were not willing to pay more than Rs 85. Here again, it was essential to get into their minds—when we asked them for the logic behind the value that they arrived at, they said that they needed to pay tax in India on the transaction. They explained that they wanted a net realization of Rs 57. However, we knew from our homework that there would be no taxes payable on this transaction. So, I told them that they would receive a consideration of Rs 57 from us, and any taxes would be my responsibility.

An important rule while negotiating the price is to stay focused on the hard structural realities of the acquisition candidate and to ban all discussions on potential synergy benefits that the acquiring company might obtain through the acquisition. Synergy with its existing operations is something that the acquirer possesses, and you never pay for what you bring to the party.

The Post-acquisition Integration Process

In integrating strategic acquisitions, the key issue is to avoid the temptation of trying to do everything immediately. Typically, the acquired company would be in a bad state; otherwise, it would not have been sold. The first task is to clean up the mess, and to pick up the money on the floor—if this is not done immediately, it becomes much harder to do later on. Then, when the basic foundation has been built, the focus must shift to strategic and organizational revitalization of the acquired unit. Finally, only in the third phase should the actual integration of operations and people be carried out across the acquiring and acquired organizations.

Cleaning Up

More often than not, an acquired unit would have been poorly managed for a while, with poor productivity, poor capacity utilization, poor discipline and poor morale. The first task is to deal quickly and effectively with these problems, and to achieve some quick successes.

Perhaps the most critical task in this phase is to immediately establish a fully aligned top management within the acquired company. Sometimes, as in the Imexsa case, the existing senior management may jump on board; more often, however, it may be necessary to remove the old top management, and put a strong new team in place. This was a cardinal rule for Electrolux: protect the managers below the top, but remove the top. The temptation to give the old team another chance is often strong, not the least because of the relationships that are developed in the course of the pre-acquisition negotiations. But, not putting in a fully aligned team at the helm inevitably delays the post-acquisition changes and it is better to bite the bullet at the beginning than later, after a lot of conflict has been generated and costs incurred.

It is also important to install the acquiring company's financial reporting systems into the acquired company as soon as possible. This is exactly what Ispat did in Mexico—installing its very traditionally Indian 'parta' system of daily reporting as almost the first post-acquisition action. Similarly, one of the first things ABB does after an acquisition is to link it to its worldwide ABACUS system.

Often, because of a history of poor management, an acquired operation can provide significant opportunities for immediate cost savings and productivity improvement. Disposal of unwanted assets is one key avenue and, at times—like in the still-crated plate mill at Imexsa and the outstanding real estate in Piramal's acquisition of Glaxo India's R&D facility—the resources so released can be very large. But, beyond one-time sale of assets, there may be significant opportunities for picking up pennies lying on the floor. For example, the acquired company would have faced financial uncertainties for a while, and suppliers would have incorporated the resulting risks into their pricing structures. The financial strengths of the acquiring company, together with its own purchasing power, should lead to an immediate and substantial reduction of these prices. These actions must be taken immediately because, over time, they become more difficult to both see and implement.

While the financial discipline starts the clean-up process on the cost side, it is also important in this phase to earn some quick hits on the revenue side. One of the most important sources for revenue enhancement lies in improving capacity utilization. Small investments in debottlenecking the production process and some marketing support from the acquiring company are usually enough to significantly enhance outputs. In some instances, it may also be possible to transfer some manufacturing volumes from other plants to the acquired operation. Perhaps the greatest benefit of this increased output comes from improved morale within the acquired company, and from its improved credibility externally, with suppliers and customers.

Strategic and Organizational Revitalization

Even after the first phase of operational turnaround, full integration of the acquired company within the existing operations of the acquiring company must await a second phase of strategic and organizational revitalization. This is the recuperation time, after the surgery, and before the patient can re-enter normal life.

Undisciplined employees, poor skill levels, demotivated middle and junior managers and an intransient labour union are typically the consequences of a spell of bad management. The acquired company is likely to suffer from each of these maladies. The time to deal with them is not at the very beginning, but after the first phase of improving performance and earning some initial legitimacy within the acquired organization.

Perhaps the most vital instrument for fighting these diseases is a sense of purpose—a clear vision, supported by stretch goals, and a meaningful set of values—that can create an environment of optimism, anticipation and pride within which the changes in strategy and organization can be brought about. Some of the changes will be painful: it may be necessary to rationalize the workforce and the wage structure, some junior and middle managers may not have the needed energy or skills, and some parts of the business may have to be restructured. Without a clear articulation of the vision—of the future possibilities—the pain becomes much harder to take.

When Electrolux acquired Zanussi, a proud Italian company that had fallen on bad times, the new management took about eight months for the clean-up operation, and then initiated a team-building process, one of the key outcomes of which was a statement of mission, values and guiding principles. That statement then served as the anchor for an extensive management development programme, and also as the platform for building a very different relationship with the employee union.

Another key task in this phase is to enhance the basic competencies of the acquired company: upgrading of technology, improvement of quality, enhancement of R&D, and updating the skills of the workforce. This is what the quality management and benchmaking processes achieved at Imexsa.

In many cases, top management of the acquiring company loses all interest in the acquired company after the deal is announced. In contrast, both the Electrolux and Ispat top managements remain highly visible in the acquired company throughout this phase of strategic and organizational revitalization. Their frequent visits and manifest personal commitment serve as a continuous source of energy to keep up the momentum through this often difficult and painful phase.

Integration of People and Operations

Finally, only after the acquired unit has become stronger and more confident, does the actual integration of people and operations between the acquired and the acquiring company take place. Up to this time, the interface between the two companies is kept under careful control, with a few individuals on both sides acting as the bridge. In this final phase, that interface is broadened, with more two-way flows of people to ultimately forge the existing and the acquired operations into one integrated organization.

This is the time to rationalize production and the sales force, to implement integrated IT systems (ERP), to completely combine the top managements—in essence to absorb the acquisition. For Ispat, the Knowledge Integration Programme (KIP) served as one of the key levers for managing this final phase of integration. But, by this time, it is no longer an issue of integrating acquisitions. The acquired unit has now become a fully paid-up member of the corporate network and the actions become those of day-to-day good management in a large, multi-unit operation.

7

DIVERSIFICTION AND DIVERSIFACT

What a difference an 'a' makes! Drop the letter from the word *diversification*, as a secretary of a friend once did, and it comes out as *diversifiction*. There is much fiction about the management of multi-business enterprises, and there are some facts. In the current context of change, not only in the economic and competitive landscapes but also in the fads and fashions of management thinking, sorting out of the facts from the fiction is a major challenge for many diversified Indian business groups.

Let's begin with the management fads and fashions. In the 1970s, diversification was the essence of strategy. Driven by the seductive portfolio models, companies worldwide were urged to exchange dogs for stars in order to maintain perpetual corporate youth on the strength of their internal capital markets. Problems in the many companies that adopted this consulting formula then led, in the early 1980s, to the dogma of 'stick to your knitting'. Once again, companies that adhered to this dogma missed the enormous opportunities that were opening up around the globe as markets and technologies converged to create huge new businesses.

By the mid 1980s, strategic business units become the darling of academics and consultants who, like Johnny Appleseed, spread the message of the multidivisional enterprise from company to company and from continent to continent. Creating independent SBUs, with full functional control and complete profit responsibility, did indeed improve short-term performance for some companies but, in the long term, internal fragmentation sapped their abilities to create new products and new capabilities. In the 1990s, SBUs became the villains amid the new mantra of core competence which, in effect, called for both refocusing of the portfolio and corporate-level integration of key functions and core processes.

In the late 1990s, the pendulum began to swing the other way. Highly diversified companies like General Electric, ABB, Sony, Virgin, Disney, 3M and others made diversity fashionable once again, though perhaps in a somewhat different form.

In each of these periods, both management academics and consultants claimed to have found the truth about diversification. In each period, they were wrong. This is diversifiction—the notion that there is any one general formula for deciding the nature and extent of optimum diversification. In each of these periods, some highly diversified companies did very well while some others performed poorly, just as some highly focused companies chalked up great successes while others failed. That is diversifact—the correct level of diversification depends not only on the nature of the external environment and the potential synergies within the portfolio, but also on the nature of the company itself and on the quality of its management.

Indian companies are right now in the grip of one such wave of diversifiction. Having diversified helter-skelter in the licence raj period, company after company is surrendering itself to consultants for reorganization around its core competencies. In the process, many are recognizing that they really have no core competencies but, since complete liquidation is not an option, they are inventing slogans and pretending that they are competencies in order to justify being in business while simultaneously appearing to have entered the modern age.

The underlying theory of diversification is simple. There is a constant battle between the management capabilities of a company and the discipline of market forces. The market forces try to dismember companies so as to achieve the economist's ideal of a perfect market in which each company is a small, powerless actor in a narrow business niche. Corporate managements, in contrast, try to grow, to diversify, to achieve high profits, and to become powerful enough to control their own destiny. When a company has a high level of management capability, it can buck the market into submission and, thereby, grow, diversify and earn sustained high profits. As the markets become stronger—more efficient capital markets, more competitive product markets, more flexible labour markets— companies need higher levels of management capability to protect their diversity and their profitability. Those that cannot enhance their management capability have no option but to surrender ground.

This is precisely what is happening in India. The markets are becoming stronger in the sense that they are becoming both more efficient and more complete. Companies, therefore, have two options. Either they must match the growing strength of the markets by rapidly enhancing their own management strengths. Then, they can protect themselves and continue to both grow and diversify. This is what Reliance Industries, Zee, HDFC and Hindustan Lever are doing with such aplomb. Alternatively, if they cannot enhance their management capability, they must indeed shrink, refocus—perhaps even go out of business. That appears to be the way many of India's traditional family businesses are headed.

Managing Integrated Diversity

What does the word 'management capability' mean? What capabilities do companies like GE, ABB and 3M have that have allowed them to prosper, despite the diversity of their businesses?

In essence, they have the ability to build and manage their organizations in a form that can be described as an integrated network (see figure 7.1). This is an organization that combines three key features: (i) strong, entrepreneurial business units, with their own resources and capabilities, managed with high levels of strategic and operational autonomy; (ii) rich, horizontal flows of knowledge, best practices and other resources across those units, in an environment of strong mutual trust; and (iii) a corporate engine that creates and maintains an exciting sense of purpose—a shared ambition, a set of values and a sense of identity—which acts as the glue to integrate the organizational diversity.

Figure 7.1: The Integrated Network Organization

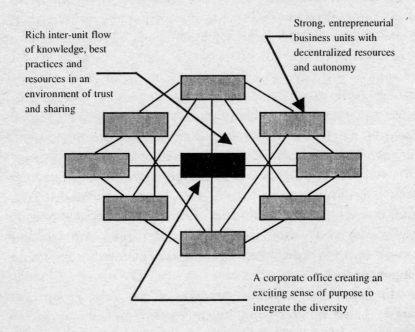

Rich inter-unit flow of knowledge, best practices and resources in an environment of trust and sharing

Strong, entrepreneurial business units with decentralized resources and autonomy

A corporate office creating an exciting sense of purpose to integrate the diversity

Entrepreneurial, empowered businesses: Frustrated by the business-level satraps that were created over decades of operating under laws like the MRTP, which forced companies to minimize group level influences on their diverse holdings, some Indian business houses appear to be on their way to creating a centralized hub organization. In this model, all key resources and authority are centralized to capture the benefits of scale and scope, and to force disciplined implementation at the level of each of the businesses. This is a recipe for eventual failure.

Such centralization, coupled with the new layers of hierarchy and the complex systems that are needed for corporate management to exercise control over the businesses, inevitably chokes the business-level entrepreneurship that is vital for any diversified group. In a centralized hub, managers of the businesses either retreat into a mode of obedient conformity or assume a defiant, subversive posture to 'beat the system'. In either case, the relationship between business and corporate-level managers becomes increasingly pathological and mutually destructive.

In contrast, ABB clearly recognizes that those closest to the customer, or more knowledgeable about the technology—managers at the business level—are far better placed than corporate top management to respond to fast-changing environmental demands and market opportunities. This recognition, coupled with an underlying faith in people, has led to a radical decentralization of resources and authority to the forty-plus Business Areas (BAs in ABB language) of the company and, through them, to the 1100 ABB companies spread around the world. Only with such transfer of people and strategic assets does traditional delegation become legitimate empowerment.

In India, the historical strength of the Tata group was largely based on this commitment to entrepreneurship at the business level. J.R.D. Tata, the charismatic patriarch of the highly diversified group, collected an amazing band of highly talented executives—Russi Mody, S. Moolgaokar, Darbari Seth,

Ajit Kerkar and many others, often referred to as the 'constellation'—and gave them both considerable latitude and complete support. He encouraged each of them to operate autonomously and adopt an organizational approach suited to the needs of his business, with the only requirement that the business practices conform to the overall Tata philosophy. Thus one company, Tata Steel, had a functional organization. Another, Voltas, was structured as a matrix. A third, Tata Consultancy, was organized around project groups. As JRD explained:

> Once I get good people, I am able to get the best from them probably because I am somewhat of a democrat. An outstanding manager is usually strong-willed and of independent character with a distinctive style of management and personal behaviour. I give such a person an allowance for his idiosyncrasies in order to draw the best out of him. Of course, this has made it difficult sometimes to ensure that a reasonably uniform style of management prevailed in the Tata group. The Tatas have nevertheless been surprisingly cohesive and successful because their directors and managers have been professional persons and allowed full freedom to deploy their talents and ideas while keeping within the Tata ethos.

However, to prevent such decentralized autonomy from leading into chaos, it is necessary to build a strong sense of discipline in such diversified companies. Discipline is very different from compliance, as we shall see in chapter 9—it is embedded as internalized norms of behaviour and mutual expectations instead of being imposed through corporate command and control. This is precisely what the Tata organization had in its heyday, established though clear standards of both behaviour and performance that were transparent and shared within a network of common directors across the different companies. At the middle-management level, this discipline was inculcated through the institution of TAS—Tata Administrative Services—composed of bright young people recruited at the group level and carefully socialized into the group's culture, values and business philosophy. Finally, the fiercely autonomous business heads themselves were disciplined through a combination of profound respect and affection for JRD and their participation in a set of institutionalized processes of peer-base review and challenge in open forums.

Cross-unit sharing of resources and knowledge: Just decentralized entrepreneurship, however, is not enough to justify a diversified firm: after all, each of the units could be fully independent to enjoy complete autonomy, without the cost of a corporate office. A diversified company must exploit the benefits of bigness and must use whatever form of synergy that may be available because of its diversity. In the integrated network organization, these benefits are captured not through a top-down process of centralization that destroys business-level entrepreneurship but through a horizontal process of integrating and sharing resources, knowledge and best practices across the different businesses.

The extent of such horizontal sharing depends on the nature of the business portfolio. In companies with highly interdependent businesses, such as HP or Sony, such integration may involve joint organizations and shared work in functional areas such as technology development, production and marketing. In companies where the businesses do not have such high levels of operational interdependence, it may take the form of sharing ideas, best practices and management resources. GE, for example, excels in such sharing, despite the diversity of its business portfolio, through intensive processes of best practice transfers across its divisions and programmes such as '16 pounds of plastic in every refrigerator' which identify and exploit opportunities that lie at the interfaces of the different businesses. As we have described in chapter 6, while the Ispat group allowed each company in the nine countries where it had a presence to operate with strategic autonomy and to build its own distinct culture, it also ensured such horizontal sharing of resources, ideas and best practices through the Knowledge Integration Programme (KIP).

At the heart of such sharing and integration lies the need for creating a trust-based culture within the group. It is this internal trust that provides the ultimate justification for diversification—it allows managers of the different businesses to cooperate in a way that they cannot do through arm's-length market transactions. Internal transparency and openness and a great deal of attention to ensuring fairness and equity in all decisions are the two key requirements for building such a trust-based culture.

The other requirement for horizontal integration is a set of mechanisms and forums through which people can work together. In ABB, a plethora of cross-functional councils, cross-company boards and ad hoc teams drawn from different parts of the organization dot the company. These are not merely talking shops, typically they have specific and challenging tasks to accomplish, with clear deliverables. Not only do these forums facilitate cross-unit sharing of resources, knowledge and competencies, over time they also serve as the main instruments for developing managers who are able to focus on their own businesses while simultaneously being aware of and committed to the overall goals and priorities of the group.

Up to the 1970s, the highly independent Tata companies were held together by the silken threads of several such integrating processes: the leadership of JRD who personified the group's values and carried profound normative authority because of the respect he enjoyed inside the company and outside, the network of common directors supporting the web of intercorporate shareholdings, the lateral moves of TAS managers across the businesses carrying with them both their own networks of personal relationships and their knowledge of business processes and practices in the different companies—all of which contributed to and reinforced the vision of the Tatas as a unified group rather than as a conglomerate of disjointed companies. The organizational and managerial problems the group faced in the 1980s and 1990s arose largely from a crumbling of these mechanisms.

The first sign was the choking off of inter-company flow of knowledge and people. Rivalry among the businesses vitiated the earlier environment of trust and sharing. The flow of TAS executives was increasingly choked by the blockages of personal ego: 'Forget TAS,' Russi Mody was known to have told a new executive posted to Tisco. 'You are now in MAS—Mody Administration Service.' Increasingly rich and resourceful, the different companies no longer felt the need for each others' advice and support. Many entered the same business, competing with each other.

Clear evidence of the collapse of the spirit of integration and sharing came in 1981 when Ratan Tata wanted to establish a strategic planning forum composed of the chief executives of all the major Tata companies.[14] 'I didn't get great enthusiasm from any of my colleagues,' said Ratan Tata, recollecting the experience. 'Some of them were apprehensive that I might use the strategic planning exercise as a guise to build an empire. There was also resistance to openly sharing information with their colleagues from other companies, owing to strains of inter-company rivalry.' Representing the other side of the great divide that the company had become, a senior Tata director said, 'Every one of our companies does continuous strategic planning and there is an advantage in having different, independent, autonomous units loosely tied together by broad policies. Our companies are so diverse, their technologies so different, that centralized planning may lead to disastrous strategic mistakes.' Clearly, the tradition of decentralized entrepreneurship had degenerated into profound political pathologies—as it inevitably does when horizontal sharing and lateral integration are allowed to wither or decay.

The corporate engine: Percy Barnevik, then the company's CEO and now its non-executive chairman, once described ABB as an

---

[14]See the case, 'The Tata Group of Companies', authored by Professor Ashish Nanda of the Harvard Business School.

'overheads company'. He was not referring to administrative overheads—with less than 150 people in the corporate headquarters of a $35-billion company, ABB is one of the leanest companies in the world—but to the hundreds of overhead transparencies that top corporate-level managers of ABB carry with them in their continuous travels to the company's businesses around the world, to reinforce the company's vision, values and polices. 'To decentralize, you have to build a central framework,' says Göran Lindahl, ABB's current CEO. A clear vision of what the company wishes to achieve, a coherent set of values to define what kind of an organization it wants to be and a sense of overall institutional identity constitute this 'framework', the embedding of which ABB's top-level managers see as their central task in order to integrate the company's business and geographic diversity.

The framework defines the boundaries, in terms of both the businesses the company wishes to be in and the internal norms of behaviour within which both decentralized entrepreneurship and cross-unit integration can flourish. It includes clear definitions of the company's strategic aspirations and its performance expectations. Without such a framework, decentralized entrepreneurship soon degenerates into political fiefdoms and incoherent adventurism—the source of the ultimate downfall of many conglomerates over the decades.

As an integral part of building this framework, the selection, development and deployment of key people also become prime corporate responsibilities. Ultimately, a diversified company lives or dies by its ability to develop people who can manage diversity. This does not happen by accident and cannot be left to the exclusive purview of business-level managers. As Jack Welch repeatedly emphasizes, this is the single-most important concern for the corporate management of GE: managing the people 'pipeline' that will create the ongoing leadership of the company.

Ultimately, it was the weakening of the corporate engine

that severely corrupted the integrated network organization that the Tata group once functioned as. It began with the diminishing of an ageing JRD's role within the group. As described by Ratan Tata, JRD's eventual successor:

> As he grew older and his lieutenants stronger, the group started unravelling. JRD would dismiss fears of the group breaking up by saying 'I like to race horses.' But, in my view, this ended up giving even greater endorsement to the independent mindedness of the different companies. I feel a fatal blow to the unity of the group was struck when JRD started stepping down from the chairmanship of different companies, and began to reward the chief executives of these companies with chairmanships. I pleaded with him not to do so, to choose one successor, and step down in favour of that one person only. But he didn't, and I strongly feel this greatly contributed to the diffusion of the group.

MANAGING DIVERSITY AT WIPRO

Far too many Indian business groups are overdiversified. Their management capability is too limited to carry the load of their stretched portfolios. For them, the first step forward is to refocus, to bring down the diversity of their businesses to match their limited organizational and managerial capabilities. It may be tempting to hold on, hoping that they can build up their quality of management to catch up with the complexity of their portfolios, but this is hope overcoming reality.

At the same time, there is no need to fear diversity itself. Focus is not a religion, it is merely the pragmatics of knowing how much complexity you can cope with. There is an enormous window of opportunity now opening up in India and managers need have no fear in exploiting these opportunities as long as they have the resources, competencies and courage to take on the challenge.

But to do so, they have to transform themselves. Most diversified Indian groups are decentralized federations, with autonomous businesses, no cross-business integration, and a weak and ineffective corporate engine. To convert to the integrated network, they have three key tasks.

First, autonomy at the business level must be matched by the quality of business-level managers. In too many cases, the businesses of diversified Indian groups are headed by overpromoted functional mangers, with poor general management skills and even poorer entrepreneurial flair. The first task is to improve the quality of management at the business level because without that, nothing else will work.

Second, they must institutionalize horizontal sharing and integration. This is perhaps the hardest challenge of all, if only because there is typically too little of trust and mutual respect between the management teams of their diverse businesses. While developing trust is a long and slow affair, the process must start with the creation of a set of mechanisms and forums for open sharing, review and challenge at both the general management and the functional levels across the businesses.

Finally, the top-level corporate managers must confront the inadequacies of their own roles and value added within the group. Have they created a 'framework' to act as the glue to integrate the group's diversity? Have they shaped a clear sense of overall purpose and identity? Are they serving as the key catalysts, communicating and reinforcing the group's vision, values and policies across the different businesses and front-line units? Have they developed the mechanisms and processes to manage the people 'pipeline', or are they still focused only on managing financial transfers across the units? Ultimately, they can build the integrated network organization only if they learn to become integrated network managers themselves.

While this transformation challenge will be unique and distinct for each diversified group, dependent not only on the nature of its business portfolio but also on the history of its management practices, a case example may help in stimulating ideas and suggesting actions. We choose the story of Wipro not only because of its remarkable success and visibility but also because, in terms of diversification, it is a pretty extreme case.

In the mid-'90s, Wipro Corporation's activities spanned vanaspati, toilet soaps, toiletries, hydraulic cylinders, computer hardware and software, lighting, financial services, medical systems, diagnostic systems and leather exports. While the various activities were structured into five distinct legal entities, Wipro Corporation, for the purposes of management control, was split into eight separate mini-companies, each with its own separate 'equity'. These were Wipro Consumer Products, Wipro Lighting, Wipro Fluid Power, Wipro Financial Services, the two businesses in the field of information technology, Wipro Infotech and Wipro Systems, and finally the two health care-related businesses, Wipro GE and Wipro Biomed.

As will be manifest, there is not much in common across this porftolio and each business of Wipro is managed with very significant levels of strategic and operational autonomy, 'as a company within a company', in the words of A.V. Sridhar, chief executive of Wipro's network systems business. Yet, the overall group functioned in a manner that Azim Premji, founder and Wipro's chairman, described as 'a diversified integrated corporation'. The integration is achieved through a set of shared beliefs and leadership values; through people; and through a set of well-defined management processes.

Integration through Shared Beliefs and Leadership Values

Premji had, in 1973, 'much before it became fashionable to do so', articulated a set of beliefs that since then have governed the management of Wipro. Premji said, 'The Wipro beliefs give a common cause and a sense of purpose across the businesses making Wipro in essence *one company*. Our beliefs define our basic philosophy of managing business and will remain the spirit and essence of Wipro.'

Wipro Beliefs

1. Respect for the individual. People are our greatest asset.

2. Achieve and maintain a position of leadership in each of the businesses we are in.

3. Pursue all tasks to accomplish them in a superior manner.

4. Govern individual and company relationships with the highest standards of conduct and integrity.

5. Be close to the customer in action, example and spirit, and ensure superior quality products and services.

6. Measure our effectiveness by the long-term profits we achieve for our enterprise.

Premji described the role of these beliefs in the management processes of Wipro:

> Our beliefs are mutually compatible and supportive of one another. All of them have equal priority and need for constant practice. Our goals, objectives, policies and actions flow from our beliefs. Conceptually, our beliefs are at the top of the pyramid (see figure 7.2). From them flow our five-year goals, three-year/annual objectives for the corporation and business units, departmental objectives and individual objectives. To meet the challenges of the future we are prepared to change everything about ourselves except our beliefs, as they alone guide, govern and bind us together as an organization. It is essential that we consciously internalize our beliefs and be fanatical about consistently practising them. If we fail to honour our beliefs, we will lose credibility, not only as individuals, but also as an organization.

These beliefs serve as an effective integration mechanism only because of the complete uniformity and total discipline with which they are implemented in all the different businesses. Premji emphasized this need for rigorous implementation, using the belief about integrity as an example:

At Wipro we walk the talk. For example, we are not flexible about boosting our sales by securing orders the non-Wipro way. If any deal requires practices that compromise our integrity, we will not do it. We have blacklisted a number of customers who seek favours while entering into business deals. I do not think by adopting this stance we are losing market share. The business heads are expected to achieve their targets—despite lack of flexibility over issues of integrity. I expect them to factor this inflexibility in while setting targets. Ultimately I believe any customer seeks good technology, good after-sales service and a competitive price. We offer all of them. We will not compromise on these three critical factors. We can therefore afford to be inflexible on the integrity issue.

Figure 7.2: Pyramid of Wipro's Management Practices

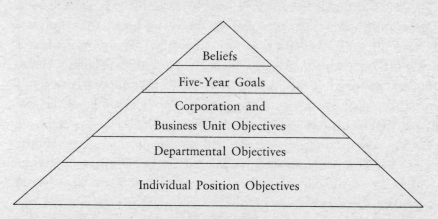

Almost every year Wipro issued thirty to forty notices to the employees who were suspected to be short on the integrity front. And if any inappropriate behaviour could be proved, the employee would be sacked—regardless of his or her position. 'Recently, in 1993, we dismissed the employee union leader at Wipro Fluid Power, when we discovered that he had falsified his travelling expenses. Following the dismissal we had a strike there. We preferred taking a strike, even though the market was just coming out of recession and the customers wanted delivery. We preferred to explain to the customers the principled stand we took,' Premji added.

The Wipro beliefs had not undergone any change since they were first articulated, save for the addition, in 1982, of a sixth belief: 'Being close to the customer'. In 1992, a proposal for dropping the belief 'Measure our effectiveness by the long-term profits we achieve for our enterprise' was once again made (it had earlier been contemplated in 1989). It was argued that enough emphasis had been built into the organization on profits and that it did not merit inclusion in Wipro beliefs, that it would be appropriate to incorporate it as part of the five-year goals. However, the belief was retained.

Wipro believed that leadership played a critical role in embedding a value-based culture that was in consonance with the company's beliefs. As described by P.S. Pai, president of Wipro Consumer Products, 'I lead by example. My staff see me operating without a personal secretary and yet, they know I have all the information at my fingertips. Therefore, when I exhort my team to save on costs, I am credible.' Girish Gaur, corporate head of HR, added, 'At Wipro the prerogative of and the responsibility for providing leadership is not that of the top management alone. All the employees, whether in the field, or on the shop floor or at the top of the business are Wipro leaders.' The company had articulated a set of Wipro Leadership Qualities. All the employees were expected to possess or acquire these qualities.

Integration through People

Though closely held—Premji's family held over 75 per cent of the equity—Wipro had a strong and powerful team of professionals. 'One of Premji's outstanding abilities has been to repeatedly recognize, develop and support highly talented executives,' said Ashok Soota, then president of Wipro Infotech. Almost every one of Wipro's businesses had been built around and in turn built by the people who were heading them.

The culture at Wipro was an open and sharing one. 'I am psychologically incapable of coping with intrigue,' said S.R.

Gopalan, chief executive of Wipro Financial Services. 'I am very uncomfortable operating in environments which are full of politics and where decisions are not taken on grounds of merit. At Wipro, we have independence of work. I do what is essential for the business and not worry about it. If I am fired, I am very sure that if I were sitting in the decision-maker's chair—Premji in this case—I too would arrive at the same decision. I can get fired only for unethical behaviour or non-performance. Not for any other reason.' Soota added, 'We discuss even our "dirty linen" in the open. Sometimes I think we are much too open.'

Discussion of managerial values, business plans, strategies and policies was encouraged. Every year, after the annual planning exercise was completed in March, Premji travelled across the country to the offices of the various businesses and addressed all employees to communicate and share the plan with them and invite their suggestions. While Premji shared the plans for the corporation as a whole, the respective business unit head shared the plans for the business to which the employees belonged. 'This reduces dependence on control mechanisms, improves individual commitment to goals and adoption of sound methods,' Premji said.

Integration through Management Processes

Each of Wipro's businesses enjoyed a wide latitude and operated quite independently. However, approved corporate-wide policies were inviolable, regardless of the circumstances the individual businesses might find themselves in. Premji said, 'Each business exists for the enhancement and betterment of the whole corporation.' Asked whether it would be right to describe him as a hands-off manager, Premji said: 'Yes and no. I spend a lot of time with my people, asking the right kind of questions to find out what is happening in our various businesses. I may not be an operations man. But then, neither am I merely an investor-chairman.' V. Chandrasekharan, chief executive of Wipro Systems, concurred: 'He is a details man. Although he allows us tremendous freedom, he knows exactly what is happening where.'

The Wipro corporate office played an important role in ensuring the 'betterment of the corporation as a whole'. Certain powers and responsibilities were reserved for the Wipro corporate office. These were:

a) *Setting*:
   Beliefs, goals and basic policies
   Select plan drivers and other standards of measurements

b) *Approving*:
   Plans and budgets
   Appointments at middle management and above
   Employee salary structures, benefits and incentive plans
   Appointment of advertising agencies
   Interaction with the government on key policy issues
   Charity and other contributions

c) *Responsibility for*:
   Selecting statutory auditors and counsel
   Corporate audit across the corporation.

The corporate office held the overall responsibility for the corporation's finance; human resource; corporate planning and business development; and government and legal affairs functions. While each of the businesses independently carried out these functions, the heads of these functions had a dotted line relationship with the corporate functional heads.

The annual planning exercise was the key operational management process by which the integration was sought to be achieved. Each business prepared its own business plans for the year. As described by Vinod Wahi, chief executive of Wipro Biomed, 'In addition to our open culture, one of our strengths is our very strong planning and review culture. We document not only our plans but also have a rigorous system of preparing minutes of our review meetings. We have monthly reviews with the chairman and quarterly reviews with the CEC (Corporate Executive Council).'

Each business was required to define its key result objectives for the year. The number of variables for which the objectives were required to be defined was restricted to six. In 1994, the corporate office defined four of the variables, with the definition of the other two being left to the discretion of the individual businesses with only a stipulation that the variables defined by them be measurable. Two of the variables defined by the corporate office were Speed and Customer Satisfaction and were to be valid for the next five years. Each business was expected to reduce all current cycle times by 20 per cent each year and increase by 5 points each year the percentage of customers who rated Wipro 'overall' a 5 and 4 in a 1 to 5-point scale. The other two variables stipulated by the corporate office for which the individual businesses had to define their objectives were Financial and Employee Morale. The measurement criteria for the Employee Morale objective was through an annual Employee Perception Survey, attrition rates and internal growth. The financial objectives were to necessarily cover objectives on (a) Sales, sales growth and market share; (b) Profit before tax; (c) Profit after tax; (d) Cash flow; (e) Return on average equity; and (f) Return on capital employed.

The corporate office also informed the individual businesses of the norms for approval of investments. In 1994, these were 29 per cent return on average equity and a minimum 22 per cent return on capital employed. All investment proposals had to meet these criteria for approval. Only in exceptional cases, where the proposal came from the newer businesses and the considerations were strategic, did proposals which did not meet these criteria get approved. Additionally, a debt-equity norm was specified. 'We specify the debt-equity norm as each business unit organizes its own debt funds,' said Gopalan. 'We believe in adhering to strict self-imposed norms. At WFS, for instance, we maintain debt to equity ratio at 6:1 even though the company is entitled to go up to 10:1.'

The annual plans were approved by the CEC comprising Premji, the presidents of the various businesses, and the corporate heads of finance and human resources. CEC was the apex policy-making body at Wipro. Apart from articulating the vision for Wipro Corporation as a whole, it was the final arbiter of policies for the whole organization. While the corporate office monitored the performance of the businesses on a monthly basis, the CEC met every quarter to assess, comprehensively, the performance of the individual units and the corporation as a whole. The CEC also approved of extra-plan corporate initiatives (strategic thrusts) and other corporate-wide programmes. 'CEC enables the chairman to manage the diversity,' said Gopalan.

In 1994, apart from the CEC, there were two other councils which were fora for discussing common issues across the various businesses and to initiate and implement corporation-wide strategic thrusts. These were the Wipro Finance Council (FC) and the Wipro Human Resource Council (HRC). The formation of two other councils, the Materials Council, which would focus on supplier management, and the Marketing Council, which would focus on the marketing dimension, was being debated by the CEC.

The FC was headed by the corporate vice-president (finance) and had the chief financial officers of all the businesses as members. In 1994, the FC had embarked on an extra-plan initiative of achieving a corporate-wide savings/earnings to the tune of Rs 2.5 crore through adoption of superior financial practices. The HRC was headed by the corporate vice-president for human resources and had the chiefs of this function in all the businesses as members. In 1994, the HRC was the prime driver of the PRIDE programme which aimed to bring about a mindset change within the various businesses. Girish Gaur, the chief of the HR council, explained, 'PRIDE, which stands for Productivity improvements, a Responsive organization, and Involved People, by Driving Change and Empowering them, is a method of problem resolution. It involved setting up of cross-functional teams, each comprising five to seven members, who are then given the mandate to find solutions to specific problems.' In 1994, twenty-nine cross-functional teams were functioning at Wipro, and the number was expected to go up to 130. Premji said, 'We need to shake people up to rethink the business. A business-as-usual attitude will not succeed in the drastically changing environment.'

Leveraging Opportunities

The attitude to diversification opportunities varies from management to management. At Hindustan Lever, the entry into the flour and ice-cream businesses are like small skunk projects: both businesses are expected to become big in the future but currently require limited financial and human resources. At Zee and Reliance, the entry into new satellite and refinery businesses dwarfs the original businesses. Yet at the same time all companies which diversify successfully take care to protect their core businesses. At Hindustan Lever, soaps and detergents, and beverages—which are its two main businesses and contribute 56 per cent of net sales—are growing at a clipping rate. Between 1989 and 1999, HLL energetically introduced sixty-four product innovations (forty-four new launches and twenty relaunches) and over 50 per cent of growth during this period came from these launches. At Zee, the parent company, Zee Telefilms, is earning more revenue from advertising than it has ever done and has added Rs 1560 crore to its market value in 1998-99 (a 631 per cent increase over the previous year). In the case of Reliance, Jamnagar will supply raw materials to Hazira and Patalganga at costs lower than they were earlier paying.

In their bid for fast-paced expansion through diversification, these companies have neither lost focus nor their appetite for organic growth. There is a lesson here for family groups. In extensively diversified family groups, splits and divorces automatically brought in focus. In an earlier, more leisurely and sympathetic era, a business dynasty could afford to relook at its growth patterns once every generation. But no longer.

8

GOING GLOBAL

Many Indian managers aspire to internationalize their companies. But without powerful brands or proprietary technology, how realistic are these aspirations? Given their relatively small size in typically stable and mature industries, can they ever develop strong profitable positions in international markets? More generally, in a world of competitive consolidation and market globalization, how can small companies—particularly those from non-OECD countries like India—compete against the established and increasingly concentrated global giants? Too often their stories are like Arvind Mills', once the superstar of the Indian textile industry for having achieved tremendous success supplying denim and other articles of clothing to leading western companies. As overseas sales grew, Arvind's stock soared on the Mumbai Stock Exchange and Sanjay Lalbhai, its CEO, declared that the company was well on its way to globalization. Within two years, however, the bubble had burst, a victim of the fickle demands of the global fashion business and cut-throat competition among offshore apparel makers battling for the shrinking US jeans market.

Stories such as Arvind's have been told hundreds, even

thousands of times, with the concluding moral often being drawn around the inherent risk of global markets, and the competitive disadvantages of smaller, less experienced companies located outside the triad markets of the United States, Europe and Japan. And there is much that is true in this inference: going global is an extremely difficult and challenging process for such companies. Yet, what this inference ignores is the counterpoint and the counter-examples: while difficult and challenging, it is not impossible for small companies from developing economies to succeed in tough global markets.

Acer grew from a tiny start-up electronics consulting company in Tawain to become the world's number two personal computer manufacturer. Brazil's Weg has emerged as the fifth largest producer of electric motors in the world, with operations in fifty-five countries spanning every major continent in the world. Mexico's Cemex has successfully challenged the global dominance of Germany's Holderbank and France's Lafarge in the cement business. Jollybee Corporation, a Philippines-based fast food chain, has successfully defended its domestic position against the onslaught of McDonald's, and—stimulated by that challenge—has expanded abroad not only within Asia but also in the United States. In India, Ranbaxy, Sundram Fasteners and Infosys, among others, have demonstrated the same counter-case. While by no means are these companies 'global', they have established a viable and sustainable process for getting there.

Despite the diversity of their industries and national backgrounds, the globalization strategies of these companies share one common characteristic: they have seen globalization not only in terms of expanding their markets, but also—and more so—as a learning opportunity that would improve their overall competitiveness by moving them up the value curve.

In international markets, an Indian product or an Indian company continues to be associated with the expectations of low cost, low price and low margins. Despite being capable of providing quality and value comparable to those of their Western competitors, Indian companies in fields as diverse as pharmaceuticals, textiles, software services and engineering are unable to raise their margins because of these expectations. As a result, they are unable to invest in new resources and competencies that are necessary to protect and enhance their competitiveness. This is precisely the situation Japanese companies faced and overcame in the 1960s. Unless Indian companies can overcome this liability, they will be locked in the lower decks of international business.

This is the key challenge for all Indian managers who would like to see their companies become fully paid-up members of the multinational club. They have to find ways to move up in the value curves of their businesses. Some companies— Ranbaxy in pharmaceuticals and Infosys in IT services are good examples—have recognized this challenge and are taking determined steps to respond to it. There is much that other Indian companies can learn from the efforts and experiences of these pioneers.

Moving up the Value Curve

The value curve is a simple but powerful concept that has broad application across a variety of industries. Almost any business consists of a hierarchy of product-market segments, each of which generates profits roughly in proportion to the technical and/or marketing complexity of the segment. Early stage multinational companies, particularly those from developing countries, often enter the global market place by competing in the lower margin segments—even when their internal capabilities exceed the demands of that segment. It is as if they feel obliged to fulfil the expectation that companies of their status produce the low-cost undifferentiated products that characterize the low end of the value curve.

Such was the case of Ranbaxy, when it first broke into the global market place by producing and selling the bulk substances and intermediates that defined the bottom end of the pharmaceutical value curve (see figure 8.1). With gross margins of 5-10 per cent, the additional production economies generated by this business did not even offset the added costs of international sales and distribution. The management's only way to justify the negative impact on return on capital employed was to focus on the prestige associated with being an Indian multinational and to make vague promises about using its overseas contacts and experience to upgrade the business.

Figure 8.1: The Pharmaceutical Value Curve

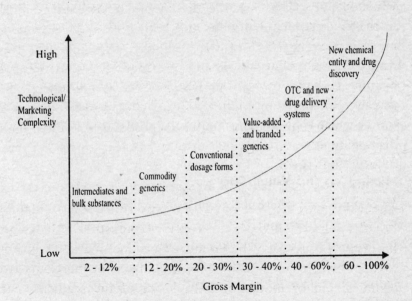

Over the years, this is indeed what the company was able to do. It first made the leap to commodity generics, then branded generics, both much tougher global businesses that required the development of new customer relationships, different distribution channels, and eventually, a strong brand image. By using its international experience to develop these new resources and capabilities, Ranbaxy was able to establish a profitable generics business in China, South Africa, Europe, and, finally, North America.

The company's ambition, however, is far more aggressive. It aspires to be a 'research-based international pharmaceuticals company'. What this means is that it wishes to move up to the highest part of the curve—discovering new drugs—where margins of 100 per cent or more are available. This is the territory of giants like Merck, Glaxo-Wellcome, Pfizer and Eli Lilly. Not content to serve these masters with low-cost intermediates, Ranbaxy is taking determined action to become their equal, albeit in miniature scale to begin with, by creating its own chemical entity. This was the dream of Dr Parvinder Singh, Ranbaxy's erstwhile chairman, and both he and Mr Devinder Brar, the current CEO of the company, have pursued this dream with complete commitment over many years, investing 4 to 6 per cent of revenues in R&D. Once it gets there, the company can begin to enjoy the fruits of a positive feedback cycle in which high margins from new products will allow high investments in research, which in turn will lead to further new products, and so on.

The same phenomenon of a value curve also exists in the IT services industry where the recent success of Indian companies like Infosys, Wipro and TCS will be short-lived unless they too, like Ranbaxy, make determined efforts to climb to higher levels. Historically most of these companies created their toeholds in international markets essentially through body shopping. By now, some of them have moved up a step by doing more and more work in their back offices located in India. But, they are still locked in a cost-based model, where they respond to customer requests for specific services and are paid based on estimates of hours of work required on a cost-plus basis. Intense competition among themselves has only helped in reducing the 'plus' element of this calculation.

At the same time, as we described in chapter 5, the salaries of software professionals in India are rising annually by about

25 per cent. Other costs, such as international travel, are also going up at an alarming rate. To maintain and enhance their margins—without which they cannot invest for further growth nor maintain their share prices—these companies need to move up to a value-based model of business in which customers pay for products and services based on perceived or realized value, and not on the costs that are incurred. This is the model in which their international counterparts like Cambridge Technology Partners operate, with revenues in excess of $200,000 per employee. It is only if they can transition to this high-value business that companies like Infosys, Wipro and TCS can maintain the expectations and momentum they have generated.

Such a climb up the value curve can be done, as is manifest in the amazing twenty-year success story of Acer. Throughout its short history, founder and CEO Stan Shih has focused his organization on continually increasing the value added of its products, particularly in the international markets where they always faced powerful established competitors. In the early days of supplying components, he pushed his engineers to develop exciting and different new PC products; when Acer began supplying these as an original equipment manufacturer (OEM) to established companies like Unisys and ICL to sell under their own names, Shih became determined to establish the Acer brand; and as the PC industry became more commoditized, he challenged his organization to develop new capabilities in software and solutions. 'If there is one lesson you learn from competing in the global market,' said Shih, 'it is that you must use it to continually upgrade your skills and adapt your business.'

Moving up the value curve is easier said than done. It is a marathon that needs to be run in a never-ending sequence of 100-metre dashes. The process is both tough and risky and needs enormous amounts of managerial vision, courage and grit. The experiences of companies like Acer, Weg, Sundram Fasteners, Ranbaxy and Infosys suggest that Indian companies desiring to run this marathon face three core challenges:

- First, they have to overcome the liabilities of their Indianness.
- Second, they have to develop or capture a range of new competencies that are vital for international success.
- Third, they have to protect their past while building their future.

Overcoming the Liabilities of Indianness

One day, one hopes, the label 'made in India' or 'made by an Indian company' will be a symbol of high quality and value, but today is not that day. Just as companies like Sony, Toyota and NEC transformed the image of Japanese products, Indian companies that desire to move up the value curve will be the pioneers who will create such high-quality images for products and services originating in India. But, for themselves, they will have to overcome the liabilities of their Indianness. Indeed, this is a common challenge for all intending multinationals from emerging countries—to successfully internationalize, they have to overcome the liabilities of their origin.

This liability has many different dimensions. First, there is the constraint of ingrained customer expectations. Through either ignorance or experience, most international customers expect the products of unknown companies from emerging countries to be inferior. And it is extremely hard to change this perception.

Less than a decade ago, Samsung, the giant Korean chaebol, still suffered from this liability. Yet, because its products were so well regarded at home, most Samsung managers remained unaware or simply denied the existence of negative customer perceptions abroad. To force the company to deal with the problem, Kun-Hee Lee, chairman of Samsung, flew his hundred seniormost managers to the United States, to see for themselves how their products were treated in the local stores. Prominently displayed in the front of the stores were Sony, Bang and

Olufsen and other prestige brands. Lined up behind them were brands such as Philips, Thompson, Toshiba and Hitachi. At the back of the stores, with big 'bargain sales' stickers on them, stood the Samsung TVs and VCRs, sometimes with a thin layer of dust dulling the high-quality finish that the company had invested very significant resources to achieve. Technologically, the Samsung products were often at par with or better than the best alternatives. But, as the close-to-tears executives learnt first-hand, while joining their chairman in dusting their products with their pocket handkerchiefs, they had much work to do to overcome the liability of their origin.

It is this same liability of customer expectations that affects the international expansion of most Indian companies. The Calcutta-based Usha Martin group has world-class skills for production of wire ropes. Yet, foreign customers are unwilling to source sophisticated products for demanding applications such as bridge building from them. Despite the worldwide acclaim for India's software skills, Infosys, Wipro and other Indian software services companies still find it very hard to be considered for the big and complex jobs that lie at the top end of the IT services value curve. For years, GM restricted its purchases from Sundram Fasteners to only the simplest products and that too only for models it was phasing out.

A second liability of origin is the prison of local standards. Consider the case of Thermax, the Pune-based engineering company that, like Ranbaxy, is committed to becoming an international player. It does have a core strength in the area of small boilers in which it is one of the top six producers in the world. In international markets, a radical reduction in the size of boilers would clearly lead to a higher value position. Through determined investment in technology and an extremely innovative R&D team, Thermax has developed a new shell-type boiler, based on very high fluid velocity, that would reduce size by a third.

Clearly, the new product can be a winner in the Indian

market. But, for that, the boiler has to be designed to the standards laid down in the Indian Boiler Regulations (IBR) which are very different from both the British Standards (BS) and the US Standards (ASME). Besides, in global markets, packaged solutions are desired, requiring minimal site work. With low labour costs, Indian customers are willing to put in the site work to avoid the higher costs of a packaged solution.

Thermax is faced with a dilemma. Designing the boiler for international markets would make the product unsuitable for the Indian market—which accounts for over three-fourths of the company's total revenues and over 100 per cent of profits. Designing it for India would make it unattractive abroad, depriving it of its one good shot at breaking through in both Europe and North America. And designing it for all markets would meet the needs of no one. To move up the value curve internationally, Thermax has to, at least initially, sacrifice the domestic opportunities.

A different facet of the prison of local standards, and attributable to the same differences in technical or market needs, is the luxury of local opportunities. This has been the historical constraint for Bajaj Auto—the third largest two-wheeler company in the world and the second largest producer of scooters—preventing it from leveraging its enormous strengths in India into a successful operation abroad.

Almost from the day he joined Bajaj Auto, Rahul Bajaj has dreamt of making the Indian company the world's leading manufacturer of two-wheelers. This was when Bajaj Auto had only one product, that too a Piaggio lookalike, and there was a ten-year waiting list. Yet, in every interview he gave, Bajaj would talk about internationalization, about the need to become world-class, and so on. Asked once to spell out what he meant by 'world-class', he had said, 'The day 20 per cent of my production is exported, I will say I am world-class.'

Yet, in 1990, exports accounted for only 1 per cent of Bajaj's sales, and even in 1998, they were less than 5 per cent.

The company claimed that it had captured 65 per cent of Colombia's scooter market, 30 per cent of Uruguay's motorcycle market and 95 per cent of Bangladesh's three-wheeler market. But, as Rahul Bajaj candidly admits, 'There's not much point in saying that we have a major presence internationally when we export 40,000 vehicles to fifty countries and, of these, 30,000 go to just five relatively small markets.'

The problem has historically been a combination of the attractiveness of the Indian market, and Bajaj's dominant strengths in that market. Even looking to the future, the Indian market would remain highly attractive. Penetration rates continue to be much lower in India compared to other developing countries: 26 per 1000 households for motorcycles, 51 for scooters and 30 for mopeds in 1998. As a result, the overall two- and three-wheeler industry is likely to grow at about 16 per cent per annum over the next four or five years. While this continuing attractiveness of the market is a key barrier to internationalization, the problem is made worse by the very cost efficiency of the Indian operation that has been the bedrock of the company's historical success: 'Scale has made us extremely cost competitive in the market place,' said Rahul Bajaj. 'Size has also allowed us to offer a full range of products and bolstered our financial strength. But no foreign market can provide me the volumes I can command in India.'

Finally, perhaps the most constraining liability of origin lies in the minds of senior corporate managers. Deep in their hearts, most of them simply do not believe that they can succeed abroad, particularly in developed markets. This lack of belief acts as a self-fulfilling prophecy: half-hearted measures are quickly seen by both insiders and outsiders to be what they are, leading to a negative spiral of ineffective small steps. As a result, they either dip their toes in a few markets abroad, and pull out as soon as the temperature rises, or they thrash about in the water with no systematic progress in building their competencies.

There is no quick solution to this liability of origin and, in the absence of a revolutionary technological breakthrough that few non-OECD companies can realistically aspire to, the only way to overcome this liability is through determined and patient efforts over long periods of time. However, to even start on this journey, companies need to create two strong forces— one to pull them from abroad, and the other to push them out from home.

Pulling from abroad: While they claim to be committed to an internationalization strategy, many Indian companies dedicate a few relatively junior managers to drive the initiative. With no linkages to the web of personalized relationships among senior managers, these executives find it very hard to even access, far less influence, the corporate decision-making processes. Besides, their inexperience also leads to a host of administrative, financial and marketing problems that only help to strengthen the ambivalence of corporate managers about the possibility of international success.

In contrast, Ranbaxy divided up the world into four regions, of which India was one, and posted equally strong managers to head each region even when the Indian operation was four times larger than the other three put together. All four regional managers were treated as equals and each had a seat in the key decision-making committees. As a result, international operations ceased to be a peripheral appendage to a dominant domestic business and could continuously influence resource allocation decisions.

Such a pull from abroad inevitably implies significant investment of resources, both financial and human, in foreign markets well ahead of demand. Although the size of Ranbaxy's European operation could not justify it, Dr Parvinder Singh hired a senior British executive from a leading pharmaceutical multinational to head the region. It was the stature of the individual, as well as his manifest knowledge of the business, that persuaded middle and senior corporate managers back in

Delhi to support his cause. At the same time, his background and seniority in the industry was an enormous source of credibility and confidence for Ranbaxy's international customers, and his wide connections provided access to their key decision makers. Above all else, his 'weight' strengthened top management's courage to persist in the enormously difficult task of establishing a position in the sophisticated and highly competitive pharmaceutical markets of the UK, France, Ireland and Germany.

Pushing from home: Just a pull from the organizational periphery, however, is unlikely to create and sustain a strong enough force for internationalization unless it is complemented by an equally strong push from the corporate centre.

Until the positive reinforcement of international success begins to kick in with full force, persistence in the path of internationalization is an act of faith, and like all matters of faith, it requires a visible symbol for overcoming the moments of doubt and, at times, even ignoring the voice of reason. It is not reasonable for Ranbaxy to expect that it can create a new chemical entity, given its puny size and meagre R&D resources, nor is it reasonable for the company to invest in a 200-people organization in China when the same resources could augment its Indian sales force many times over, with much quicker effects on revenues and profits. In every company that has succeeded in internationalizing its operations, without exception, top management has embodied this symbol and has acted as the personal carriers of this faith. They have pushed the organization out, adding to the pull of the international managers.

With a Ph.D. in pharmacology from Michigan, Dr Parvinder Singh had always been a scientist at heart. 'To become a research-based international pharmaceutical company' was his personal dream and he consistently symbolized this dream for every employee of Ranbaxy. Every time financial constraints demanded cost savings, he protected the R&D budget. Every time urgent domestic needs appeared to overwhelm R&D priorities, he protected the programmes that would support foreign markets and those that searched either for a new drug or for a new drug delivery system. Whenever the established intermediates business appeared to monopolize the time and energy of international managers, he reminded that the ultimate purpose was to move up the value curve and that the intermediates business was a means, not an end.

But, beyond specific actions, he protected the faith. Just like the ancient temples in rural India, where nothing much happens throughout the day but which influence the lives of every member of the village all the time by simply being there, he was there for internationalization. To respect him always meant that one must respect his dream, and that—more than perhaps anything else—pushed the senior managers of the company to persist with international initiatives, even when the costs appeared to be too high.

Beyond a powerful symbol, the push from the centre also needs clear operating processes and support. Perhaps the key to such support lies in separating the corporate centre from the domestic operation—clearly and, if possible, physically, as Ranbaxy did when it established the regional structure—to ensure that corporate resources are used to support worldwide operations, not just the one that is geographically and emotionally the most proximate. Perhaps the most important of these resources is senior management time—while Dr Singh supported research and the spirit of internationalization at Ranbaxy, it was D.S. Brar, till recently the company's chief operating officer and now its CEO, who constantly travelled around the world to support local operations, solve local problems and provide high-level customer contacts in local markets. He created forums for the international managers to meet, among themselves and with key corporate staff groups, and followed up on the promises and commitments that these meetings elicited.

Developing New Competencies

As we described in chapter 5, for moving up the value curve, the new buzzword in Infosys is 'value-based selling'. To achieve this goal, Infosys' key challenges are to develop and strengthen a set of resources and competencies that are crucial to the value-based segment of the IT services business. The most crucial new competencies required are, first, to build international brand strength and, secondly, to build location-wise domain knowledge within the home countries of the customers, together with the ability to develop and maintain close customer relationships.

The need to build new resources and capabilities is a common challenge for any company that wishes to internationalize its operations, whether from a developed or a developing economy. This challenge is particularly acute for Indian companies since most of them start on the internationalization journey on the strength of low-cost labour-based manufacturing, and lack both the upstream capabilities of technology development and design, and the downstream strengths in brand marketing and distribution. To succeed in this journey, they have to develop an urgency about building new competencies or acquiring control over missing capabilities to allow them to move up the value curve. This requires management to adopt the explicit objective that its motivation for expanding abroad is not just to capture incremental sales but also to develop world-class skills and capabilities. Indeed, the second of these objectives may well need to be the primary motivation for many emerging Indian multinationals.

Companies can pursue this goal in two ways: they can develop new core competencies internally; or they can choose to gain control over new capabilities through alliances, partnerships, or acquisitions. Most, however, may require a combination of both approaches.

Building new competencies: Building entirely new core competencies—or even radically overhauling existing ones—is an incredibly challenging task for any company, but it is the price of admission for those companies that want to move up the value curve. Fortunately, the global market place is an excellent classroom and international competitors are demanding teachers for those willing to learn the lessons.

The most common challenge for aspiring multinationals is to build new competencies in the downstream part of the value-added chain, learning how to master the differences in distribution, sales and marketing that are key to cracking overseas markets. The simplest solution is to find a local distributor—as many Indian companies choose to do, particularly in complex and challenging markets like the United States, Europe and Japan, or indeed as several US companies have done in India. While having the advantage of being a quick and efficient solution involving low investments, this often tends to be a temporary step rather than a durable basis for building a sustainable presence in international markets.

A few companies, on the other hand, have chosen a seemingly slower route. Infosys is developing downstream capabilities by creating a set of Proximity Development Centres (PDCs) in key cities around the world. It has recognized that it cannot succeed globally unless it can develop insider positions within the networks of business relationships in the local markets. More than 20 per cent of its business activities need to be near the customer, e.g., requirements definition, presentation, sign off, installation, training, and so on. To effectively manage these activities and to build true customer intimacy, Infosys' PDCs would be staffed predominantly by local people in an attempt to provide the image of a local company—American in America, German in Germany and Chinese in China. Its first PDC was opened in Boston in 1999, managed by a local manager who was acclimatized physically and socially to the environment, with a high awareness of the culture and personal roots in the local community.

Developing such downstream resources often requires

relatively large initial investments that take time to generate positive returns. Worse still, half-hearted measures rarely work. This is why most companies shy away from making such investments and even those who dip their toes withdraw rapidly when their over-optimistic projections fail to materialize. Yet, in the long run, these investments prove to be the most vital for building a sustainable process of internationalization. Also, while expensive to start with, once such facilities take root in the local market, they become incredibly valuable. Ranbaxy has invested patiently over the years in building up its local unit in Shanghai. But, over time, the unit has not only become a very powerful vehicle for the company to develop its branded generics business in China—one of Ranbaxy's brands now features among the top thirty pharmaceutical brands in the country—it routinely receives very large offers from multinationals who would love to acquire the fruits of Ranbaxy's patient efforts.

While building downstream capabilities is difficult, moving upstream in the value-added chain is often an even more difficult task, but companies that view their international expansion as an opportunity to learn find it is perfectly feasible to do so. This was clearly the strategy behind Ranbaxy's commitment to move its international business out of the bulk intermediates sales where it got its start.

Ranbaxy's research capability was born of necessity when its long-term distributor agreement for an Italian pharmaceutical company was cancelled. Forced to manufacture its own products, the company soon developed the processing expertise in manufacturing sophisticated chemical entities. Under Indian law, this capability allowed Ranbaxy to produce existing drugs, even those under patent, as long as a novel production process was employed.

When price controls in India limited growth and profit opportunities at home, the company began expanding abroad during the 1980s. It was not until 1993, however, that Dr

Parvinder Singh committed to making Ranbaxy a truly international research-based pharmaceutical company with revenues of $1 billion and the development of one new chemical entity (NCE). The latter objective would be particularly challenging, since Dr Singh was determined to achieve it with less than $100 million of investment rather than the $300 million or more typically spent in the development of a new drug.

By the late 1990s, Ranbaxy's commitment was evident in the first-rate R&D lab the company had built, the 250 scientists it had employed, and the 4 to 6 per cent of sales it was investing in research. Internationally, its business shifted from supplying bulk chemicals to selling formulated products, often adapted to local markets. Dr Singh believed that experience gained in drug formulation, registration, manufacturing and marketing would build the capabilities for the NCE with $400 to $500 million sales potential beyond 2003.

Capturing others' capabilities: Sometimes companies have neither the need nor the means to build new competencies internally, yet they lack some vital capability to move up the value curve. But one of the great benefits of international expansion is the exposure it gives management to different companies with complementary capabilities and a mutual interest in cooperation.

The simplest—though not always the most economic—way to capture others' expertise is to acquire it. This strategy is particularly appropriate when an internationalizing company wants to gain a quick entry into a market and create a capability base on which to build. One of Infosys' stated objectives for listing on the NASDAQ is to raise resources for acquiring a few small and specialized companies abroad. Ranbaxy has already made a number of such acquisitions including that of Ohm Labs, a US-based generics company with strong formulation capability and FDA approval experience that would be vital to its American business. Tata Tea is clearly following this strategy, and on a bigger scale than any other

Indian company, through its acquisition of Tetley.

Frequently, however, Indian companies are capital constrained, particularly if they are expanding into multiple new markets simultaneously. Alliances and partnerships can provide these companies with the means to leverage their own resources and core competencies while capturing the supplemental resources and capabilities the partners bring. The key, however, is to ensure that the partnerships are built on genuine mutuality rather than a one-way dependence that results in an obsoleting bargain.

This is one area where Indian companies appear to face some particular difficulties. Their experience with joint ventures within India have been relatively disappointing. Abroad, they have fared even worse. Very few Indian companies seem to have been able to effectively use the alliance route for developing resources and capabilities abroad.

Ranbaxy, for example, had set up a high-profile alliance with Eli Lilly in the United States. Ranbaxy had devised a new low-cost process for manufacturing Cefaclor, Lilly's best-selling antibiotic. The promise of the alliance was that Ranbaxy's competencies in low-cost production through process innovation would allow Lilly to compete in the genericized Cefaclor market in the US, after expiry of the drug's patents. In return, Lilly would use its enormous distribution and marketing muscle in the US to help Ranbaxy access the market for its other products. While this alliance has been of some initial usefulness for Ranbaxy, it has not substantially supported its marketing efforts in the US, in part because of Lilly's growing disaffection with the generics business.

International experience suggests that Indian companies should be able to do a lot more through alliances. Perhaps there is something in the psyche of Indian management that hinders their ability to work horizontally, in a partnership mode, with foreign firms. The ability to form, sustain and learn from alliances may well be a core competency that intending multinationals from India will have to acquire or develop.

The power of an alliance-based strategy of internationalization is manifest in the experience of Acer, the Taiwanese computer company. As we described in the introductory section, Acer has grown from a local supplier of IT services in Taiwan to a major global PC manufacturer in less than two decades. Stan Shih, Acer's founder and CEO, based his company's overseas expansion on extensive use of partnerships and alliances, even making this approach a part of the company's cultural norms. Believing that his upstart company could never follow the approach of the resource-rich established multinationals—'the nobility' in his words—he adopted an expansion strategy that deliberately aligned his company with other 'commoners'—mass-market customers, supplier-partners, owner-employees and local shareholders. In Acer's multinational expansion, this 'commoner's culture' manifests itself in a philosophy he described as 'global brand, local touch', with the second part of the motto being implemented as a series of national distribution companies with local majority shareholding. Believing that such an organization brought huge resource leverage, Shih's objective was '21 in 21'—to have Acer evolve into a worldwide federation of twenty-one publicly listed companies by the twenty-first century.

Protecting the Past, Building the Future

It takes enormous commitment—both human and financial—for smaller companies in the backwashes of the global economy to launch an attack on overseas markets. And it takes even more determination to use that initiative to build sustainable advantage by moving up the value curve.

There are two types of traps aspiring multinationals can fall into during this process. The first, and by far the most common, is the timidity trap. As was the case with Bajaj Auto, even the most successful domestic companies often fail to push their competitive base beyond their home market. With the luxury of local opportunities as their security blanket, managers in such companies ignore, postpone or underinvest in their commitment to leveraging and expanding their competitive advantage in foreign markets. But, as so many have subsequently learned at great cost, if you don't seek out the global competitive environment, it will soon enough seek you. Today Bajaj Auto is competing against every major two-wheeler manufacturer in the world in its own home market.

Yet there is another risk for internationalizing companies that lies at the other end of the spectrum—one we might call the macho trap. These are the companies that become so seduced by the huge opportunities they see abroad and so mesmerized by the chance to move up the value curve that they ignore or even destroy their foundation to build their new overseas business. Such an approach quickly becomes a blueprint for building castles in the air. In many ways, this is precisely what happened with ITC, in its heady days of trying to become an Indian multinational, and, to a lesser extent, in the case of Arvind Mills.

The challenge for those who plan to scale the value curve as they internationalize is to keep a balance between building on and protecting their historical assets and resources while using the overseas expansion to leverage and expand them for the future. This means supporting existing businesses in the home market and harnessing them for the resources to build higher level business capabilities through offshore forays. In short, management must not only focus on where it is going to, it must recognize where it is coming from. It must maintain a strict discipline of building the future on the solid foundations of protecting the past.

This task is greatly facilitated by two powerful management decisions. Most successful value curve migrators create separate but linked organizational units to manage the capability upgrading triggered by their international expansion. And they also bring in or assign strong managers to head these new entities and become the engines driving the company's ascent up the value curve.

New tasks, new units: Typically the market structures and consumer needs in international markets differ significantly from those of the home model. And, if a company is open to using its overseas expansion to build new competitive capabilities, it will find that the drivers of success for businesses at different points of the value curve are quite different. Not surprisingly, therefore, companies moving up the international value curve often find themselves constrained by their traditional organizational units built to develop and deliver their historically successful business models.

The most common first response to this situation is to create a separate geographically-based organization form that frees up those exploring new markets to adapt and respond to those differences. This was the approach taken by Ranbaxy as it established its region-based structure. Eventually, however, companies must ensure that such organizational units do not become isolated, cut off or compartmentalized. If international's role is not only to provide incremental sales and profits, but also to access the information, knowledge and capabilities needed to move up the value curve, then management must ensure it is closely linked with the base business.

The most effective solution is to create an organization model that allows the geographically separated units to be overlaid with structures and processes that allow each business to be managed on an integrated worldwide basis, including the home market. This is the type of organization Acer decided to implement in what CEO Stan Shih described as his 'client-server' organization model. With the underpinnings of his philosophy of 'global brand, local touch' and building on the local partnerships Acer had formed worldwide, Shih created an organization built on four major Strategic Business Units (SBUs) and four key Regional Business Units (RBUs). Each of the SBUs was held responsible for managing one of Acer's core businesses worldwide (peripherals, semiconductors, etc.) while RBUs managed all businesses in their region (Europe, North America, or elsewhere).

Infosys has created a similar worldwide alignment of its different businesses through its SBU structure. Its eight strategic business units each focuses on specific industry segments, so as to build and exploit 'domain knowledge', i.e., knowledge about the clients' businesses—and skills—related to the unique demands of those businesses. On the other axis of the organization, eight departments provide functional support to the board, to the company, and to operations. Linkages across the SBUs and client needs in different markets are maintained both through fluid movement of people across the different organizational units and also through institutionalized mechanisms such as an intranet-based 'Body of Knowledge' database that allows everyone in the organization to access information acquired by the company on different customers, technologies, methodologies and projects.

Matrix organizations such as these are notoriously difficult to manage, and like most companies, Acer and Infosys have faced their share of integrative difficulties. But living in a world of complex and contradictory product and market imperatives, and operating with a strategy that requires managing increasingly sophisticated business models, from generics to patented drugs or from computer components to integrated systems, companies have little choice but to learn to meet these challenges.

New roles, new skills: But structure alone won't solve the problem of building for the future on the solid foundation of the past. One key reason why companies find it so hard to move up the value curve is that they cannot overcome the biases of those who grew up managing their traditional business model or offset the power base they acquired in doing so.

To represent the diverse needs of foreign markets and to develop strategies appropriate for businesses further up the value curve, new managers are often needed. These managers must not be captives of the conventional wisdom that often dominates a company's way of doing things. And they must be strong enough to represent the different point of view that will emerge as they learn to serve new product segments in new geographic markets.

For many companies, this has meant bringing in strong outsiders who brought with them the knowledge of the new businesses further up the value curve. This was Ranbaxy's motive in hiring the experienced pharmaceutical executive to head its European division. This is also why Infosys is recruiting strong local managers to manage its Proximity Development Centres.

There is another vital qualification, however. Because they sit at the intersection between the new business and the old, these key individuals must be accommodative team players. They must have the credibility to capture resources from the core and invest them profitably in the periphery. And they must have the skill to take the knowledge and experience accumulated in the new business and transfer the learning to the old.

III

REVITALIZING PEOPLE, ORGANIZATION AND RELATIONSHIPS

9

CHANGING THE SMELL OF THE PLACE

Trinidad, April 1989. A little-known Indian company assumed control of a Caribbean steel mill which was losing $1 million a day. A year later, the company had been turned around. Earnings in 1997 were $49 million. Before Lakshmi Niwas Mittal took over the management of the government-owned company, it was being run by American consultants and German managers drawn from top-notch companies. Mittal sacked the Americans and the Germans. Instead of inundating the company with new planning techniques and more stringent control systems, he focused on something even more basic. 'The most important thing was to change the way people thought and acted,' recalled Mittal, reflecting on the dramatic turnaround of Iscoot in Trinidad that, in turn, earned him the opportunity to acquire and transform Imexsa in Mexico—the story we told in chapter 6.

Back home in India, another steel company was just beginning to understand how critical was the need to change people's behaviour if it were to survive in a newly liberalized environment. Since its inception, the government had kept SAIL in a warm protective cradle, shielding it from the chilly winds of competition. Import duties were high, steel production was controlled, as was distribution and price. All that disappeared in 1991. There was decontrol down the line, of prices, production and distribution.

'For years we had lived by a philosophy where we produced what we wanted and the market would absorb it. Suddenly we found we had to produce to market needs,' recalled M.R.R. Nair, chairman and managing director of SAIL. 'We realized we had to improve customer satisfaction; we had to become internationally competitive; and we had to improve our operational efficiency.' All these, as Nair explained, required a fundamental change in the behaviour of people.

Moving the organization from a totally regulated environment to a competitive buyer's market was the best thing that could have happened to SAIL. In the three years between 1993 and '96, SAIL's production climbed 20 per cent, sales by 48 per cent, capacity utilization by 11 per cent. Net profit increased by 317 per cent and only a small part of that increase came through price adjustment. The rest came by increased productivity and value-added production. Net profit to sales ratio improved by 116 per cent, cost reduction by 2 per cent every year. SAIL reduced its manpower by 60,000 people in six years 'without any noise, without any protest from anyone', said Nair. He attributed this radical improvement in performance, above all, to the revitalization of people stimulated by a very different set of people processes the company had adopted.

In 1997 Nair left SAIL to join Mittal's Ispat group.

REVITALIZING PEOPLE

Both at Caribbean Ispat and at SAIL, success depended on people's ability to change. You cannot renew a business without changing behaviour. No company can achieve radical improvement in business performance without revitalizing people.

Put that way, most managers will readily accept this assertion. In fact, most will see it as a motherhood. But what does 'revitalizing people' really mean? Most will interpret this as an attitudinal change. There is a new word every time this topic comes up and the new word now is 'mindset change'. In recent years, company after company in India and abroad has launched an expensive, large-scale culture change programme with this objective.

But then you ask: how likely is that? Can you change people's attitudes? Can you really teach old dogs new tricks? The answer is unambiguous: very unlikely. Generally, adults do not change their fundamental attitudes. Well, occasionally they do, but only in response to a profound personal tragedy, such as the death of a spouse or a child. Otherwise, things happening in their professional lives do not change attitudes—not of adults.

Now we have a dilemma. Renewing businesses requires revitalizing people, that is, changing people's mindsets. But, if you cannot teach old dogs new tricks, where does that leave us?

Resolution of the dilemma lies in the recognition that revitalizing people is not about changing their fundamental attitudes. The same individual, with the same attitude and personality traits, can behave very differently in different contexts. It is possible to change behaviour without necessarily having to change basic attitudes. The challenge of changing behaviour at work, then, is much more about changing the context that managers create around their people. Every company has an internal behavioural context that shapes how people within the company think, feel and act. To change behaviour, that context has to be changed. The responsibility for creating the behavioural context lies at the level of senior managers. Therefore, senior managers must change their views about management and their actions in the workplace—for only then will the people lower down change their own behaviour.

As Ranbaxy's Parvinder Singh once said, 'We are recruiting

well and take on good people. Somehow our environment does not allow them to remain good and they become sub-optimized'. By 'our environment', he was referring to Ranbaxy's internal behavioural context, and he was emphasizing that having good people was not enough, a company needs to create the context in which good people can become the best they can be and perform at the highest level.

What does the term 'behavioural context' mean? Perhaps the best way we can explain the term is by relating it to a personal experience that most readers can readily empathize with.

For many years, one of us—Sumantra—taught at INSEAD, a business school in France, and lived in Fontainebleau, a chic little town about forty miles south of Paris. But Sumantra's hometown is Calcutta. So, every year he used to visit Calcutta in the summer, typically in the month of July. Why July? Because that was the only time when his children had a long enough break from school.

Calcutta is a wonderful city—at least to every Bengali, including him—but not in the month of July when the temperature hovers around 104°F and the humidity is over 95 per cent. In downtown Calcutta in July, he felt tired most of the time. Exhausted by the heat and the humidity, he spent all his time indoors, and a lot of it in bed.

In Fontainebleau, however, he felt and acted very differently. Beyond being a beautiful little town, what made Fontainebleau a wonderful place to live in was the magnificent forest that surrounded it. It was one of the prettiest forests in all of Europe. In the spring, he would go to the forest for a leisurely walk but would soon find himself jogging, jumping up to catch a branch, throwing stones—doing something more active and more spirited. The beauty of the forest in spring, the fresh smell of the trees and the crispness of the air would be too energizing, too invigorating to just have a leisurely walk.

Herein, we believe, lies the essence of the issue of revitalizing people. Most large companies in India and abroad end up creating the environment of downtown Calcutta in summer inside themselves. It is the enervating context that saps away all the energy and creativity of their people. The challenge for managers of these companies is to transform this behavioural context into one that is as invigorating as the Fontainebleau forest in spring.

Downtown Calcutta in Summer

Think about the behavioural context as 'the smell of the place'. We intellectualize a lot in management. The reality is that you can walk into a sales office, a factory, a head office and in the first 15 to 20 minutes, you will get a smell. You will get a smell in the quality of the hum. You will get a smell in the look in people's eyes. You will get a smell in how they walk about. What is the smell of the place in the front-line units of most Indian companies? Typically their internal contexts suffer from four debilitating characteristics (see figure 9.1).

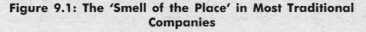

Figure 9.1: The 'Smell of the Place' in Most Traditional Companies

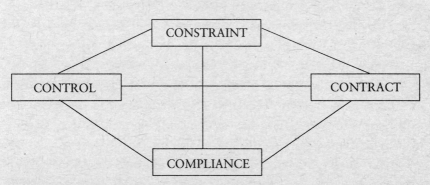

The first characteristic is *constraint*. Top-level managers of the companies take all the decisions, make all the choices. They are very wise, they have lots of information, they have very good staff. So, by products, by customers, by markets they create wonderful strategies. They also work very hard, twelve hours a day, fourteen hours a day, so as to be able to tell everyone exactly what needs to be done. But what does all that they do mean for the people working in the sales office, in the factory, eight levels below them? What does all that hard work of theirs, all those decisions, all those strategies, boil down to for the people in the shop floor? Constraints. That is how they feel about the stuff that comes down from the top—constraints on how they can use their own initiative, creativity and thinking; constraints on the choices they can make; constraints on the joy and excitement they can derive from acting on their own steam.

The second characteristic is *compliance*. Top managers create all kinds of systems—human resource systems, planning systems, budgeting systems. Each system by itself is totally justified. However, collectively, what feelings do they create for the employees down in the factory floor? Compliance. All those systems hang like a black cloud over them that must be complied with.

Another pervasive aspect of the context within most large companies is *control*. Why does the boss exist? Not just the direct boss, why does the entire management infrastructure exist? As far as the humble employees eight levels below the top can tell, they exist for one reason and one reason alone—to control them. To ensure that they do not do the wrong things.

Finally *contract*. We are increasingly using the word in every aspect of business, certainly in the West, but increasingly in India. The job is a contract. The budget is a personal contract. Transfer prices are contracts. Relationships between colleagues and departments and divisions are all contracts.

That is the internal environment, defined by constraint, compliance, control, contract. That is the smell of the place in the front-line units of many Indian companies. And yet what is the behaviour that companies want from their people? They want employees to take initiative. They want their people to learn continuously and bring the benefits of that learning to the company, to support its success. They want people to collaborate, to share, to help each other. They want their people to feel a sense of commitment to the company. How can managers elicit these responses if they create a context defined by constraint, compliances, control and contract around their people?

Fontainebleau Forest in Spring

In our research, we found a few companies both in India and abroad who have been able to create an invigorating internal environment and have been able to achieve very high performance levels on the strength of the behaviour of their people. Abroad, we smelled the Fontainbleau forest in spring in Intel and at 3M, in ABB and at Imexsa; in India, we found the same smell of an energizing work environment in Infosys and at HDFC. In all these companies, the internal behavioural context was characterized by four very different attributes: constraint had been transformed to stretch; compliance to discipline, control to support, and contract to trust (see figure 9.2).

Figure 9.2: The 'Smell of the Place' for Organization Renewal

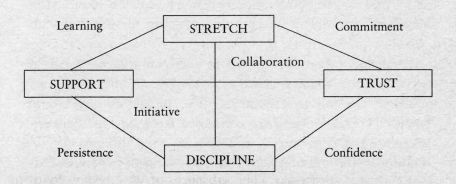

What is *stretch*? As we described in chapter 1, large companies often fall victim to the disease of 'satisfactory underperformance'. By the time the company falls into a crisis, change becomes easy. The real problem is not when the company is in crisis. The real problem is often the long period before the crisis hits, when the company coasts along in this mode of satisfactory underperformance. Everyone within the company knows that, given the company's resources, brands, quality, technology, people and so on, it is not doing as well as it could. But, as opposed to confronting that reality, people create rationalizations on the one hand and they bring down the level of aspirations on the other, so as to remain satisfied with that underperformance.

Stretch is the antithesis of satisfactory underperformance. Stretch means that every individual, in whatever he or she is doing, is trying to do more, rather than less. In that process, each individual is continuously pushing himself or herself. But with that, all of them are also pushing everyone around them, pushing the management, pushing the company, to do more, to do better.

As Lakshmi Niwas Mittal emphasizes, 'Today most of my companies are the lowest cost producers in their fields because of the people. If people are motivated, if they think like I do, they come up with plans to drive costs lower and lower. They come up with ideas to implement those plans. This is the secret of our low-cost products and our leadership in certain product segments.'

The first change in context is from constraint to stretch. The second change is from compliance to *discipline*. The difference between compliance and discipline is subtle but profound. People comply with something that is external, outside of themselves. Discipline, in contrast, is internal, ingrained in the day-to-day behaviour of individuals and in all management processes. The absence of the heavy load of compliance does not imply a free-for-all chaos. Nor does it mean that a company cannot have systems. 3M has rigorous systems. ABB has rigorous systems. Intel has very rigorous systems. The issue is not whether a company has systems or not, but what management does with the systems. Does it use the systems to impose compliance or does it use the systems to instil self-discipline into people's day-to-day behaviour?

Discipline is management by commitment. It implies that everyone does what is promised. If someone promises a 14 per cent reduction in inventory, he or she will do everything possible to keep that promise. But it is more than just numbers. Self-discipline in people means that if there is a meeting at nine, everybody is in the room at nine. Self-discipline means that even if the management team takes a decision that one particular member of the team disagreed with or argued against, he or she will fully commit to the decision once it is made.

Intel has a norm it calls constructive confrontation. The company rules are clear: not only is each employee, irrespective of rank, allowed to talk on any topic that affects her, she is obliged to express her views and argue for them as strongly as she can. What this well-entrenched norm leads to is vigorous, table-thumping, head-butting debate for which 'constructive confrontation' is an extremely polite label. At the same time, Intel also has the norm that says 'at the end of any meeting, a decision will be taken and, at that point of time, agree or disagree, but commit'. That is the context of discipline.

Third, the behavioural context of high-performance companies replaces control with the norm of *support*. As opposed to the perception that bosses exist to control, to ensure that people do not do the wrong things, you achieve a genuine change in behaviour when people at the coalface really believe that their bosses exist for one reason and one reason alone: to help them win. To help them win by personal coaching, guidance, mentoring; to help them win by helping them gain access to the resources of the rest of the organization that they themselves may not have access to, but, ultimately, to help them win. That creates the context of support.

SAIL's Nair emphasized this support role of management when he made a programme for helping people develop new knowledge and competencies a central platform of the company's revitalization process. 'It has to be the responsibility of top management to ensure that people can learn new competencies,' he said. 'People have to be first prepared before the changes can be brought about.' In essence Nair created a support infrastructure, including training sessions involving over 500 officers, that allowed these officers to learn new skills and then use that knowledge to draw up detailed action plans for improving the company's performance.

While the workshops and the frequent reviews provided support, they also helped improve discipline. Intense and frequent peer-based reviews of commitments led to candour and honesty in interactions and, ultimately, helped people develop a sense of accountability.

Finally, there is the shift from contract to *trust*. Not just as the contractual, instrumental version of trust that says: 'If you and I come to a deal, I trust you that you will keep your side of the deal.' A real feeling of trust is much more than that; it says: 'You know, we are a part of the same organization and I trust you. I trust you as a starting condition, and till you prove untrustworthy, and not the other way round.'

From Context to Behaviour

Most companies have recognized the need for front-line initiative to build competitiveness and drive growth in a liberalized economy. But, how do you get such decentralized entrepreneurship? How do you get employees—sales people, factory workers, office staff—to take initiative within their own work areas?

We believe it is the combination of stretch, on the one hand, and discipline, on the other, that creates the basis for such distributed entrepreneurship. Just stretch without discipline—a great ambitious vision of the future without the capacity for efficient, methodical execution in the present—can be very dangerous. It can make management float out into the sky, like a hot-air balloon, never to land back into reality again.

Many companies have paid dearly for such daydreaming ambition that is not counterbalanced by a sharp sense of discipline. Similarly, discipline, without stretch, can be corrosive. Over time, it can destroy all sense of excitement within the company, all sense of fun and joy. But combine the two—the yang of stretch and the yin of discipline—and then, out of the tension between the two, arise individual initiative and a fundamental spirit of entrepreneurship at all levels of the company.

Every company we know is trying to get more collaboration, from cross-functional teams, working at the plant level, all the way to collaboration across divisional presidents in the corporate executive committee. And most are finding it very hard to achieve the kind of spontaneous and voluntary collaboration they need. Dr Yoshio Maruta, CEO of Japan's Kao Corporation, describes such collaboration as biological self-control: if your finger gets cut, every organ in your body that can provide any support to it would automatically do so, immediately. That is what is needed in an organization. Whenever one unit or an individual faces an opportunity, a problem or an issue, anybody in the company who can help must do so without having to be asked.

How do you get that quality of collaboration in a large, complex organization? By combining support and trust. How do you get learning? It is the tension between stretch and support. One could go on for each of the different behaviours shown in figure 9.2, but that is not necessary. Overall, the point is simple: if you wish to see initiative, collaboration, commitment and learning, the challenge is to create a 'smell of the place' built on the norms of stretch, discipline, trust and support.

But, this is very hard to do, even for the best of managements. At Ranbaxy, for example, the need for a new way of working was clear but the company's legacy of a hierarchical, top-down management style proved to be very hard to shake off. Senior leaders found it very difficult to delegate responsibility and accountability till they had the confidence that those they would delegate to had both the competence and the commitment to take the company forward. At the heart of their hesitance was a profound loyalty to the company and a great deal of pride in how they had struggled to grow the small pharmaceutical distributor into one of the most admired companies in India. They could not conceive of any action that might jeopardize the company's position and reputation. Ranbaxy was their life, and they found it hard to trust anyone else with their legacy.

Many Indian companies, particularly family-managed business houses, suffer from precisely this problem. They recognize the need to change from a top-down hierarchical organization to a more open, entrepreneurial and professional orientation, but find themselves in a catch-22 position. Top-level managers cannot let go till they feel that people are ready; people find it hard to be ready till the leadership is able to let go.

However, in our research, we also found a few companies that had been able to create invigorating behavioural contexts within themselves, and had been able to achieve very high performance levels on the strength of the behaviour of their people. Infosys is one clear example, but it had the advantage of being in an industry where such a context may be relatively easier to create. So, we highlight here the story of another company—the Housing Development Finance Corporation, HDFC—where the achievement is all the more credible precisely because of the ordinariness of its businesses, customers, depositors and employees.

An Invigorating Forest in Mumbai

An extraordinary company, run for ordinary Indians by ordinary Indians—that is HDFC, India's premier housing finance company and one of the most successful, most admired and most competitive institutions in the country.

The usual customer of HDFC is a very average person. In 1997, the average cost of a flat or house financed by the company was Rs 398,000, and its size was a mere 76 sq. metres, or about 800 sq. ft. The average size of a loan was Rs 199,000—roughly 50 per cent of the cost of the unit—with an average payback period of 11.21 years. This average customer was 38 years old and had a monthly household income of Rs 10,800 only—neither the elite at the top of the pyramid in Indian society, nor the very poor at the bottom, but squarely in the middle. This average Indian, however, was an extraordinarily reliable borrower, as evidenced by HDFC having had to charge off a mere Rs 0.8 crore as bad debt since its inception—against a total loan disbursement of Rs 11,200 crore.

Equally ordinary were a vast majority of the one million depositors who provided a bulk of the funds that HDFC disbursed to its borrowers. Attracted by the company's courteous and efficient service—the investors received their certificate of deposit on the spot and the interest payments reached them exactly on the due date—they entrusted the company with their savings, eschewing potentially higher returns offered by many other institutions.

The employees of the company were of a very similar profile. The culture and hiring practices of HDFC discouraged 'stars'. As a matter of policy, the company did not recruit fresh MBAs from the top-rated schools, the favourite hunting ground for most financial services companies in India. Management recognized and accepted that it could be giving up an opportunity to hire the best raw material. But, in doing so, it was also avoiding the baggage that typically came along—prima donna antics, jealousies, and an aggressively competitive environment. HDFC hired people from the next-tier institutions who tended to have more subdued personalities and were able to work jointly with others.

The only thing not ordinary about the company has been its

performance. In a poll conducted by *Euromoney* in 1998, HDFC had been voted as the most competitive company in India. For two years in a row, it was also ranked as the best managed company in the country. Despite enjoying a dominant 58 per cent share of the housing finance market, the company was growing at about 33 per cent per year—improving its share by about 3 per cent each year in a rapidly growing market. It had a very strong balance sheet, with a capital to risk-adjusted asset ratio of 18.5 per cent, against the norm of 8 per cent minimum set by the National Housing Bank. As a result, it was the only AAA rated financial services company in the country. Its financial and capital market performance were stellar and it was consistently highlighted by the World Bank as a model private sector housing finance agency for developing nations.

But, perhaps the company's greatest achievement of all lies in the enormous contribution it has made to Indian society. It has pioneered the housing finance market and has, in essence, created the opportunity for middle-class Indians to own a home. At the same time, it has demonstrated that a wholesome business, meeting an important social need, can also be extremely profitable.

At the heart of this outstanding performance has been the HDFC management's ability to create the kind of behavioural context that we have described as the Fontainebleau forest in spring. The context will be manifest to anyone who walks into an HDFC office—whether a small branch in a rural market or its spartan head office in Mumbai. This invigorating context has, in turn, led to precisely the kind of behaviour we have highlighted in the preceding section.

Voluntary initiative and commitment? HDFC had a major fire in the company's main office in Mumbai. The ground floor was gutted and it was impossible to serve customers in the office. Employee response? While some people sacrificed their personal time to regroup and re-equip the office, others took the office to the pavement outside the building and handled customer enquiries on the road side.

Stretch and discipline? Consider how HDFC reduced the cycle time for loan approval from four weeks to a point where the decision could be made and communicated across the table. In reflecting on this story, keep in mind that this was done in an environment wherein HDFC was the best service provider and much better than its nearest competitor.

Initially, all loan applications were reviewed and approved at the head office and, typically, it took four weeks to approve a loan. Clients were so happy to get the money that they did not worry too much about the delay. However, its management felt that four weeks was too long and hired Dr S. Mahesh, a professor of service management at the University of Buckingham, UK, to work with the company to start collapsing the cycle time.

This process was started in 1989 with a workshop attended by all the branch managers in each region. It kicked off with an overview of service management and then proceeded to identify specific bottlenecks in HDFC's loan approval processes. Cross-functional groups were established to investigate each bottleneck and recommend solutions. A 'champion' was identified for the most vexing issues (20 per cent) and the participants agreed to develop a solution within a tight time-frame. At the end of the prescribed period, the various groups came back with their proposals and the company had the basis to reduce the cycle time from 15 to 45 days (average four weeks) to 2 to 5 days, once all the recommended changes were implemented.

The next stage came in 1994, when customers started noticing the 2 to 5 days cycle time and started seeing it as a delay. The company went back to the 1989 formula and ran another set of workshops. The managers found they had various unnecessary manual operations around the approval process and this resulted in needless delays. The non-essential items including manual filing were eliminated and a new set of standardized procedures were put onto the computer. This called for a team of two people to prepare each application and another two to check and approve the loan. Once implemented, this resulted in the capability to approve applications across the table.

What is it about HDFC that stimulates such behaviour in its people? Why is it that despite a booming market for finance personnel, it has consistently enjoyed extremely low employee turnover and no senior manager has left the company in many years?

· The wellspring of such behaviour lies in the company's deep commitment to its customers. The company came into being as a product of the dogged determination of one man, H.T. Parekh, who had sensed a strong need for housing finance in India, and had staked his formidable professional reputation on building an institution that would meet this need. Beyond the business possibilities, Parekh was motivated by a social cause. Until then, middle-class Indians had almost no opportunities for purchasing a home except a lucky few who could do so at the fag end of their lives by encashing their pensions, gratuity and all other savings. Parekh wanted to change this situation and solving the housing problem in India was, for him, a matter of deep personal passion.

He embodied this passion in a statement that defines the purpose of the company: 'To HDFC, business is not merely about earning profits, but a way through which we provide essential and valuable service to society.' Undoubtedly, this spirit was motivated by Parekh's long stint in the quasi-public sector ICICI, which had shaped his belief that it was possible to combine commercial success with social commitment. Through his own behaviour and actions and through constant exhortation to all his people, he established customer service as the core mission of HDFC.

This compelling and motivating sense of purpose was further supported by a set of values that Parekh built as the core of HDFC's institutional identity. As the company's 1996-97 annual report highlighted:

> This year for the annual report, we have chosen to underline some key principles HDFC has adopted and maintained for nearly two decades of its existence. They constitute the 'core values' we hold dear—values that are not subject to compromise and reinterpretation as the environment changes around us. They are immutable and true through time and circumstances . . .
>
> Core values are the basis of a vision, they do not constitute it . . . Visions can be wrong, hopelessly off the mark if they are not born from strong values . . .
>
> Values without principles are hollow . . . Principles form the immutable and unchangeable core of right action. HDFC from its very first day of operation, has built a principle-centred organization. By this we mean . . . an organization that has been built on the basis of fairness, kindness, efficiency and effectiveness.

This ability to create a sense of purpose—an exciting goal that people can relate to, as well as a set of values that people find satisfying—is a common element in every company that has been able to create an invigorating behavioural context. But, just articulating an overall mission is not enough; a management must also put in enormous efforts to bring that sense of mission down to the level of each employee. Creation of this sense of purpose and its linkage to each employee's work is the fundamental prerequisite for establishing the smell of the Fontainebleau forest in spring in the front-line units of large companies.

Beyond creating a sense of purpose, it is also important to establish some fundamental people processes to support the kind of individual behaviour we saw in HDFC. It is these concrete processes that transform a purpose from an empty rhetoric to tangible reality for people. This became manifest to us in our discussions with a cross-section of HDFC officers and staff. 'Why did you join HDFC?' we asked. 'Why do you stay?

Why do you think, feel and act as you do?' The responses yielded the following answers about HDFC's organizational and people practices, that supported its internal behavioural context.

- Informal atmosphere

This was carefully cultivated by senior management including the chairman who frequently walked through the offices in shirtsleeves and willingly answered a ringing phone in an empty office (typically, he left a message for the person concerned). H.T. Parekh was credited with creating the informal atmosphere, and Deepak Parekh for maintaining it.

- Concern for people

The company worked with an open-door policy. With virtually no turnover, everyone knew everyone else and they could walk into the office of the MD, the executive director or a general manager (even the chairman if he was in) to raise their concerns and have them addressed. Tenure was given a lot of respect in the company. When HDFC Bank shares were being distributed at par to employees, the allocation formula recognized seniority in terms of position, but more weightage was given to tenure.

- Large responsibilities

HDFC was a merit-oriented organization and it did not hire laterals (with very rare exceptions). There was a shared belief that lateral hires might not fit as well into the culture of the company. As the business was growing at over 25 per cent per annum, there were significant advancement opportunities for most employees. The company had an appraisal process wherein employees were kept fully informed of their performance.

- Equity

Information was shared freely through a regular and active communication programme. There were few status symbols accorded to senior managers. They drove fairly ordinary cars and were not particularly well paid by industry standards. So, there was no real We–They distancing between the seniors and the others. There were many internal communication organs and better still, the full-time directors made it a point to address all employees at the various locations of the company on a regular basis.

• Ownership

The people who worked at HDFC did not see themselves as employees or the company as an employer. The company belonged to them as much as they belonged to the company. This was an extended family. The management had a no-firing policy except in cases of fraud/deception, etc. This sense of belonging and security resulted in a very high level of both loyalty and commitment. One manifestation of this sense of ownership: there was no union at any location of the company.

• Personal development

The management had set-up a specialized housing finance training centre at Lonavala. All employees rotated through the training centre on a regular basis and had ample opportunities for personal development. In addition, the company reimbursed each employee for the cost of two professional qualifications. This process of training and development along with a commitment to merit and a reluctance to hire laterals had created some unique opportunities. For example, the Manager (Deposits) in the head office had joined the company as a Stenographer (Typist) in 1981. In India, very few other companies would have offered this possibility.

• No politics

The 'no-star' policy of the company described earlier had led to a very open environment, with very little overt politicking.

EXTRAORDINARY RESULTS THROUGH ORDINARY PEOPLE

In India, a number of companies in a variety of businesses— from consumer electronics and domestic appliances to automobiles and light engineering—are caught in an intensifying spiral of competition (figure 9.3). Excess capacity and a proliferation of new entrants have depressed prices and profit margins. To restore profitability and stem market share losses, they have restructured, cut costs, reengineered and improved internal operations to reduce inventory and cycle time. For some, these actions have led to some temporary respite but soon others have caught up, leading all of them back to the starting position. Efforts to get a technological edge have often gone the same way, with competitors copying or obtaining the same technology, restoring the original condition. With all companies doing practically the same things, they have collectively drawn themselves lower and lower into an abyss.

Figure 9.3: The Intensifying Spiral of Competition

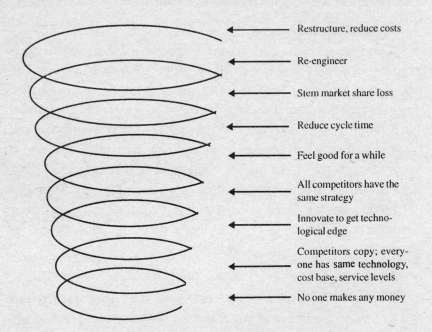

Restructure, reduce costs

Re-engineer

Stem market share loss

Reduce cycle time

Feel good for a while

All competitors have the same strategy

Innovate to get techno-logical edge

Competitors copy; every-one has same technology, cost base, service levels

No one makes any money

In this process, these companies have become addicts of new tools and fads. Walk into these companies and you will see a plethora of 'change initiatives', under fashionable terms like 'learning organization', 'visioning', 'speed', 'globalization' and so on, and, of course, 'total quality'. Employees deep down the organization are frustrated and fatigued by this 'initiativitis'—and have learnt to keep their heads down, as another new slogan makes its way through the company, knowing that it will soon pass, to be replaced by another, newer slogan.

To break out of the negative spiral and to overcome employee cynicism, frustration and exhaustion that have become all too common in their organizations, managers need to recognize that while corporate renewal may be initiated by strategic, structural, technological or operational changes, it endures only if it is supported by fundamental changes in people's behaviour. Their role, therefore, is not only to reframe the configuration of organizational assets and resources, but also to redefine the behavioural context that shapes how people in the company think and act.

In a regulated economy in which capital and licences were the scarce resources, a company's employees were managed as if they were just another set of inputs: factors of production to be deployed and controlled to achieve maximum utilization. The work environment was often deliberately designed to ensure that employees' behaviour was as predictable and controllable as the machines they worked on. A behavioural context of compliance, control, contract and constraint ensured that employees operated within clearly defined boundaries and they did things the way the management mandated.

In a liberalized economy, the fundamental basis of competition changes. Instead of capital or licences, people become the scarce resource and the primary source of competitive advantage. No company of any size can expect to recruit and retain only geniuses. The competitive challenge then becomes one of creating an internal context in which ordinary people can produce extraordinary results. Building a behavioural context of stretch, discipline, trust and support is an essential prerequisite for responding to this challenge.

While most companies in India still suffer from the

downtown-Calcutta-in-summer syndrome, there are a few who have succeeded in creating an energizing and motivating context to take advantage of each employee's unique knowledge and personal initiative. We have described the case of HDFC in this chapter. But we have seen the Fontainebleau forest in many other places in India—at Hastings Jute in Calcutta, a story we will tell in chapter 13; within Infosys in Bangalore, as we will describe in chapter 10; in Kevincare in Chennai; and in the factory of Hero Honda near Delhi. They prove that it is possible to create an exciting, motivating and liberating work environment in almost any kind of company, in any kind of business, in any part of India, and that the efforts required to create such a context are inevitably rewarded through outstanding performance.

However, as we will elaborate in the concluding chapter of this book, the shaping of such a behavioural context requires a fundamental shift in a company's management beliefs. Rather than managing through the abstractions of plans, budgets and controls, top-level managers must recognize that their key task in building competitive advantage lies in stimulating the company's most valuable resource—its people—to be more motivated, creative and entrepreneurial than the employees of its competitors. Only when they liberate and challenge their people to develop and leverage their knowledge, skills, imagination and courage will they have created a dynamic, self-renewing company.

10

THE COMPANY AS A UNIVERSITY

D r Yoshio Maruta introduced himself as a Buddhist scholar first, and as the president of the Kao Corporation second. The order was significant, for it revealed the philosophy behind Kao and its phenomenal success in Japan. Kao was a company that not only learned, but 'learned how to learn'. It was, in Dr Maruta's words, 'an educational institution in which everyone is a potential teacher'.

Under Maruta's direction, the scholar's dedication to learning had metamorphosed into a competitive weapon that, in the 1990s, had elevated Kao to one of the most admired companies in Japan, regularly rated by *Nikkei Business* ahead of well-known names like Canon and Toyota in terms of corporate originality, innovativeness and creativity. The company's success lay not only in its mastery of technologies or its efficient marketing and information systems, but in its ability to integrate and enhance these capabilities through continuous learning. As a result, Kao had come up with a stream of new products ahead of its local competitors such as Lion and also foreign rivals such as Procter and Gamble and Unilever, to emerge as the largest branded and packaged goods company in Japan and the country's second largest cosmetics company.

Maruta's reframing of Kao, not as a soap and detergents company but as an educational institution, tapped into a fundamental reality of human nature. People are innately curious and, as social animals, are naturally motivated to interact and learn from one another. Over thousands of years, families, clans and broader social groups have evolved as teaching and learning communities, with individuals sharing information and synthesizing knowledge as a key engine of their individual as well as collective progress. Yet, somehow, most companies are constructed in a way that kills this natural instinct in people.

To achieve sustained, superior performance, managers have to counteract this trend. They have to open up their organizations and their people to the invigorating force of continuous learning. Like Maruta, they have to think of their organizations not just as a portfolio of businesses, their people not as mere factors of production; they have to view the company as an educational institution and recognize that competitive advantage flows from people's ability to constantly enhance their knowledge and skills. Formal classroom education is only a part of the continuing learning process, albeit an important one. The more difficult part of redesigning a company as a learning centre is to reshape its work methods, information flows and management processes to create continuous self-development opportunities for people within their daily routines.

Continuing Education

Intel Corporation, the world's largest and most profitable semiconductor company, has a relatively young workforce. However, most of the technologies used in Intel's Pentium chip did not exist when its scientists finished their graduate studies. Without very large investments in continuing education—Intel has its own university with a plethora of courses that employees can self-nominate themselves to, it participates in a large variety of external courses offered by universities and consultants, and offers a sabbatical scheme so that people can take from a few months to a year off to go back to school, either as a faculty or as a student—Intel simply could not survive in its business. Continuous skill updating of its employees is not a 'feel good' factor for Intel's management; it is a prerequisite for the company's competitiveness.

In most Indian companies, continuing education is still treated as a luxury and a diversion. Senior managers are occasionally sent off to a course in a hill station while junior employees ritualistically attend in-house training programmes that have little relevance to their tasks and have undergone little change in a decade. Top management tolerates the expense as a symbol of the company's modernity while employees treat the programmes as the next best thing to a paid vacation. With no skin in the game from either side, the activity becomes totally peripheral to the business.

In contrast, continuing education is one of the few things that are mandated by the corporate top management in Motorola, and is carefully monitored and controlled throughout the company. Every employee, including the chief executive, has to undergo forty hours of formal course work at the minimum each year. While the company delegates almost all activities including R&D to its different business divisions, education is managed by the corporate head office in Chicago through its large and well-funded Motorola University that has branches all over the world.

Courses are tailormade to respond to current business needs and include not just discussions on state-of-the-art management concepts and practices but also extensive involvement of senior managers and actual work on specific and important business problems. A vast range of short seminars on specific topics allow Motorola employees around the world to fill in specific gaps in their knowledge and skills. It is this commitment to education that allowed Motorola to launch and implement its much-imitated 'six sigma' total quality programme. At the same time, the reputation of Motorola University has increasingly become a key source of the company's competitive advantage in recruiting and retaining the best graduates from the leading schools in every country in which it operates.

While still the exception, there are companies in India that can boast of a similar commitment to continuing education, and of similar success from that commitment. Hindustan Lever, for example, has not only implemented locally the educational philosophy of Unilever, its Anglo-Dutch parent company, but has emerged as a global centre of excellence, providing training to Unilever managers from around the world. Gulita, Hindustan Lever's spacious training centre in Bombay, hosts courses attended by participants from forty countries that are taught by the most renowned experts not only in India but also from the best business schools in Europe and the United States.

As an example of the company's commitment to education and development, consider the initial socialization process each of Hindustan Lever's management trainees goes through. All non-MBAs start with a two-and-a-half-week special course at IIM Ahmedabad. This is interspersed with stints in the field, in different functions, that expose the young graduates to various aspects of the company's front-line operations. They start with shadowing a salesman for a week, and then for four weeks they actually work as salesmen. After that, they shadow a sales officer for a week before spending another four weeks as field sales officers. This is followed by a week at a branch office and a month on a special assignment. The next stage is a six-week stay at the Integrated Rural Development Centre at Etah, where each trainee lives with a village elder (female trainees are accommodated in a guest house) and works on projects such as building roads, developing smokeless cooking stoves, negotiating with government officers for development assistance, and so on. This experience plays a vital role in exposing the trainees, who are typically from urban backgrounds, to the reality of rural life in India and helps them develop the perspective they need for creating new products, delivery systems and marketing programmes aimed at India's large rural markets.

After this first phase of training, the new recruits are moved into open positions in a specific functional area such as manufacturing, supply chain management, marketing or sales, and are given subordinate charge for a twelve-month period. This is their opportunity to learn the basics of leadership. During this period they are closely counselled by a senior officer. At the end of this phase, subject to satisfactory performance in a confirmation interview, they are absorbed in the ranks of Hindustan Lever's management.

This is just the beginning. Once accepted, Hindustan Lever executives receive regular guidance from seniors on the job and are regularly nominated to attend relevant management programmes in India and abroad as an integral part of their careers in the company. This large investment in education has made Hindustan Lever a hothouse of management talent, allowing it to adapt and prosper not only in good times, like now, but also in bad times, such as the decades of the 1960s and 1970s, when local subsidiaries of multinational companies were on the retreat all over India. At the same time, the same structured educational process has also served as a glue, bonding its people to the company and to one another, making it one of the most cohesive business organizations in the country. The people themselves have also prospered, both within the company and outside. Hindustan Lever has not only grown in-house all its top managers but has also been a major supplier of chief executives both to Unilever subsidiaries outside India and to a number of large private and public sector companies in India, making it one of the most attractive employers in the country.

Reliance is another company that pays a great deal of attention to formal training. IIT Powai has a basic engineering course for Reliance employees with mechanical, electrical and instrumentation modules designed by the IIT faculty in collaboration with department heads at Reliance. IIM Bangalore has developed a special four-month residential course for improving the general management skills of Reliance engineers. At the Jamnagar refinery complex, just in front of the temple is the Learning Centre, a cluster of small, well-equipped classrooms and library. At all locations, there are regular screenings of videos of well-executed projects and rousing speeches by Dhirubhai exhorting the 'Reliance family' to be entrepreneurial. Truck drivers—they are not employed by Reliance but by the company's contractors—who come to pick up and drop raw material at the Jamnagar refinery for the first time have to attend a formal training session on the best way to load their trucks. A refresher session is organized for each individual every three months. 'There is a lot of difference between saying "I think so" and "I know so",' says Anil. 'We pay attention to that difference.'

There is a large retraining programme in place at Reliance. There are structured programmes for mechanics and operators. Groups of engineers are frequently sent abroad for training in plants selected by companies who provide technologies to Reliance. 'This ensures that technology transfer and operations take place without any loss of time,' explains one engineer. 'The basic objective of our training programmes is to assist employees at all levels to improve their skills and knowledge and develop an attitude that in a fast-growing organization, consensus building is essential for achieving targets,' says Mukesh. For the future, Reliance believes 'company-grown MBAs' are probably the best-equipped to take over the reins. The idea is to gradually reduce the company's dependence on the Ambani family members alone for the magic of breathtaking ambition that has made it the number one private sector firm in the country. Similarly, as managers of Reliance almost universally affirm, working for the company has become the best management education that money can't buy in India.

There are two aspects of the educational processes in companies like Intel, Motorola, Reliance and Hindustan Lever that differentiate them from the many others, including most public sector companies in India, who also invest significant amounts of money and time on this activity.

First, education is structured as a continuing process, not as an event or a series of unrelated events. The process is also built around people, not programmes. Every manager—and all these companies are now extending the process to cover all employees, not just the managers—goes through a predetermined sequence of courses, at specific career stages, and the primary objective is to both deepen their skills in their areas of specialization and also to broaden their perspectives and overall managerial capability. At its very best, such as in Andersen Consulting, the world's largest consulting company, the training inputs are also synchronized with job assignments and career paths, so that the supply and demand of skills are closely matched.

Second, while aimed at individual development, the process is also focused on organization development by explicitly linking the content with the company's business and strategy. Off-the-shelf lectures on general topics is the exception rather than the rule. Instead of patching together a string of generic presentations from the training manager's favourite lectures, courses are designed around specific business situations and needs, and they continuously change to reflect changing business demands. Company cases and project assignments tighten this link between employee education and individual development, on the one hand, and corporate competitiveness and organization development, on the other.

Redesigning Work

In traditional organizations, work is structured to maximize predictability and control. However, such a structure of work inevitably leads to deskilling of employees. Predictability and control in work is possible only when tasks are defined specifically and narrowly. Ultimately, the logic of such structuring of work is based on the insights of Adam Smith and Frederick Taylor: that the benefits of large organizations derive from economies of specialization and, therefore, the best way to run such organizations is to subdivide activities into routine tasks that can be easily measured and controlled. But to stay with Adam Smith's famous example, after years of making pinheads an employee loses all abilities other than those required for making pinheads, and the company loses all flexibility and can only remain a pin factory.

While both the company's and the individual's losses from such deskilling have been widely recognized, some managers believe these to be the unavoidable costs for achieving efficiency and productivity. These managers may find the following example of some interest.

Rockwell Golde Gilfhorn is a small German subsidiary of Rockwell Corporation, a large, highly diversified American multinational. Located in Gilfhorn, seventeen kilometres from Volkswagen's factory in Wolfsburg, the subsidiary supplies about 3000 sunroof systems a day on just-in-time basis for fitting into Volkswagen's Golf model of cars. As a highly automated assembly-line operation, the factory represents a classic prototype of the dehumanizing and deskilling production technology that Charlie Chaplin depicted in *Modern Times*.

For Günter Kraft, the manager of the factory, protecting the motivation and commitment of his relatively young and mobile workforce has been a major concern. 'Total education' is his solution to the problem. To achieve this strategy, he has designed what is now known within the company as 'the Pathfinder' system. Its purpose is 'to get every worker to become a passionate collector of skills and qualifications, as a way to reduce his boredom and to enhance his employment security'.

The pathfinder lists the specific skills that are associated with each of the different jobs in the factory. At the same time, it structures these skills in a set of hierarchies—the paths—with each preceding skill facilitating a worker's ability to acquire the next skill in the path. In consultation with his supervisor, each employee of the company has chosen one of these paths as his personal development goal.

On the days when Volkswagen's demand for sunroofs is relatively high, each worker takes his position on the job in which he is most proficient, thereby maximizing the factory's output. But, on days when Volkswagen's demands are lower, workers move to the jobs that correspond to the next set of skills they should acquire. The entire process of switching between a production factory and a learning factory is self-regulating and results in a multi-skilled workforce that makes the company not only one of the lowest cost, highest quality suppliers of sunroofs in the world—as certified by Volkswagen—but also one of the most profitable subsidiaries of Rockwell, with the lowest employee turnover rate in its industry in Germany.

Once again, such a philosophy of work design is not a total novelty in India. Some leading edge companies here have adopted a similar approach, with similarly satisfying results. Sundram Fasteners, for example, has split its earlier integrated manufacturing system into smaller production modules, what the company calls the 'zones of autonomous production' or ZAPs, with the same objective of enhancing workers' skills on the one hand, and the company's flexibility on the other. And, as has been the case with Rockwell Golde Gilfhorn, Sundram Fasteners has benefited from not only a very low rate of labour turnover, despite the manifest enhancement of the market value of its employees, but also one of the best records of employee relationships in the country, not having lost a single man-hour due to industrial disputes since its inception.

Like many infotech companies, HCL rotates employees between on-site (software developed at an overseas customer's site) and off-shore (at the software contractor's site at home) jobs. But HCL's large domestic customer base offers more opportunities. A typical HCL engineer steadily travels up the learning curve—she begins with a domestic project, works her way up and gets posted on an on-site assigment and then returns and does the same work at home and builds up the knowledge base of the company.

Ultimately, work itself is the most important source of learning that a company can offer to its people. Therefore, redesigning work with learning potential as an important concern is a central requirement for developing a company as an educational institution. Such a redesign is possible, irrespective of a company's business or its production technology, as long as its management has the commitment and the imagination to reshape the company as a learning institution.

Perhaps the strongest evidence for this claim is provided by the International Service System or ISS—the world's largest cleaning service company, based in Denmark. The company cleans offices, from large establishments like Heathrow airport in London to small factories like a printing press in Brazil. Few businesses can offer lesser employee development opportunities than that of cleaning floors. Yet, ISS spends a significant part of its worldwide earnings on training, with courses for cleaning crews and their supervisors not only on new cleaning products and technologies but also on financial planning and leadership. Not only that, it has also redesigned the work of each cleaning group to include responsibilities for soliciting business, customer service, profit planning, and process innovation. While this has increased ISS's costs to levels slightly above those of its smaller competitors, the benefits in terms of new business, improved customer relationships and a more skilled and committed workforce have far exceeded those costs.

Democratizing Information

Dr Maruta described learning as 'a frame of mind, a daily matter' in which truth had to be sought through discussions, by testing and investigating concrete business ideas until something was learned, often without the learner realizing it.

The primary raw material for this learning process is information. Maruta regarded information not as something lifeless to be stored, but as knowledge to be shared and exploited to the utmost. He repeatedly reminded his managers that 'in today's business world, information is the only source of competitive advantage. The company that develops a monopoly on information, and has the ability to learn from it continuously, is the company that will win, irrespective of its business.'

However, a vital requirement for information to be used in this way is its democratization. 'In order to make it effective to discuss subjects freely, it is necessary to share all information,' said Maruta. 'If someone has special and crucial information that others don't have, that is against human equality, and will deprive us and the organization of real creativity.'

In Kao, every manager and most workmen had fax machines in their homes to receive results and news, and a bi-weekly newspaper kept them informed of competitors' moves, new product launches, overseas developments and outcomes of key meetings. As a senior manager told us, 'In Kao, the "classified" stamp does not exist.' Terminals installed throughout the company ensured that any employee could, if they wished, retrieve data on sales records of any product for any of the company's numerous outlets, or product development at their own or other branches. The latest findings from each of Kao's research laboratories were available for all to see, as were the details of the previous day's production and inventory of every Kao plant. 'They can even check up on the president's expense account,' said Maruta without any trace of exaggeration. He believed that the improvement of learning and creativity that resulted from this open sharing of all information far outweighed the risk of leaks. In any case, in an environment of *omnes flux*, things moved so rapidly that 'leaked information instantly became obsolete'.

For a host of historical and cultural reasons and also because of a pervasive history of unethical practices, most Indian companies suffer from a profound problem of information blockages. A deeply entrenched hierarchical mindset makes managers hoard information as a key source of power and influence. Despite sincere efforts, companies have found it very hard to democratize information. For example, even in a company as well-managed and as successful as Ranbaxy, Dr Parvinder Singh found it very hard to improve internal sharing of information and knowledge. The company's attempt to introduce e-mail is a case in point. Many senior managers resisted the change. Some insisted on having their full designation added to their e-mail ids—making it impossible to standardize addresses. As a frustrated Ranbaxy manager commented, 'The biggest bottlenecks come from people not letting go of power.'

The challenge of democratizing information is not one of installing an IT infrastructure, it is above all else a matter of changing corporate culture. An environment of trust and support, as we emphasized in the preceding chapter, is a vital prerequisite for creating willingness and ability to share information freely. And it is the creation of such an environment that defines the most crucial challenge of reshaping a company as a learning institution. It is precisely these attributes of its culture that have led to the much greater benefits that Hindustan Lever has received from its investments in creating an IT platform for sharing and integrating information than many other companies whose similar investments have floundered on the rocks of their unchanging management mindsets.

Senior Managers As Faculty

While day-to-day tasks need to be redesigned to provide opportunities for deepening the operational skills of employees, it is equally necessary to reshape the broader strategic and administrative processes of a company so as to broaden people's analytical and conceptual skills, and to enhance their quality of thinking and judgement. Less tangible and concrete, these latter sets of skills and capabilities are perhaps the more crucial for enabling them to take responsibility for the company's competitiveness. At the same time, widening employee access to these skills requires radical changes in a company's core management processes, a far more daunting task than re-engineering day-to-day operations.

In most companies, strategic thinking and qualitative judgement are seen as the preserves of top management and it is only those who are part of it who have the opportunity to develop and deploy these capabilities. To move up to them the relevant information that typically resides at the operating levels, companies create elaborate systems of planning, communication and control. Junior employees provide the information in a variety of scheduled and unscheduled reports, often in standardized formats, and these reports are processed through complex systems to yield consolidated inputs for decision making. Such a formal, systems-driven management process is often viewed as the essence of professional management, with the elaborateness of the systems as the measure of the company's managerial sophistication.

Such systems, however, act as a shield, preventing people below from participating in the strategic debates and thereby insulating them from the learning potential of such debates. Because of their position and their accumulated experience, top managers develop broader perspectives and sharper intuitions which are perhaps the greatest gifts they can give to those lower down in the organization. However, it is only through constant interaction that these capabilities can be passed on.

To create opportunities for such direct interaction, companies need to fundamentally reshape their management processes, cutting out much of the elaborate infrastructure of information, planning and control systems they have built, so that information can flow through direct relationships, strategy can be framed through shared debate and implementation can be guided through personal mentoring and coaching.

As an illustration of such a direct, face-to-face management process, consider Dr Maruta's description of how decisions were made at Kao. 'We view work as something fluid and flexible, like the functions of the human body,' he said. '. . . [T]herefore, the organization has to be designed to run as a flowing system which would stimulate interaction and the spread of ideas in every direction and at every level.' To demonstrate that hierarchy was merely an expedient and should not become a constraint for teaching and learning, he had abolished organizational boundaries and titles.

'At Kao, no one owns an idea,' said a senior manager. 'Ideas are to be shared in order to enhance their value and achieve enlightenment in order to make the right decision. By inviting all the relevant actors to join in with forging the task, we achieve *zoawase*—a common perspective or view.' This, according to him, was a vital requirement for people to learn and for senior management to play their role as teachers.

The physical layout of the Kao building was designed to support this joint teaching and learning process. On the tenth floor, known as the top management floor, sat the chairman, the president, four executive vice-presidents and a pool of secretaries. A large part of the floor was open space, with one large conference table and two smaller ones, with chairs, blackboards and overhead projectors strewn around. This was known as the 'Decision Space', where all discussions with and among the top management took place. Anyone passing, including Maruta, could sit down and join in any discussion on any topic, however briefly. And they often did, consciously using the opportunity for passing on their accumulated knowledge and wisdom to people at operating levels.

Picture this layout, this decision process, and the role that senior managers play in this process. Contrast this picture now with the top-management floor in most Indian public and private sector companies—large, well-decorated, dead spaces with closed doors, cold silence or hushed whispers, designed to be remote and awe-inspiring—a courtroom in which senior managers act as judges rather than teachers, passing sentences instead of sharing knowledge and building shared perspectives.

Is Kao a five-legged cow, to be ignored as a quirky and special case? In the best-performing companies around the world we have seen the same transformation taking place, replacing formal and abstract management processes with direct interaction that enables senior managers to play this teaching role.

Nowhere has Jack Welch's transformation of General Electric been more striking than in the arena of strategic planning. GE had invented corporate strategic planning, including some of the key tools and concepts that have since been widely diffused throughout the world. Over the years, it had built up an elaborate planning system driven by a formidable corporate planning staff. Highly detailed and analytical business unit plans were aggregated by sectors and were reviewed by the top management in even higher levels of aggregation by what were called 'arenas'.

While many Indian companies are now installing precisely such a system, Welch has spent the last ten years tearing it out from GE. He has replaced this formal, complex and multi-step planning process with a more personal, informal and intense process of direct 'manager-to-manager' discussions that focus on the key strategic issues faced by each business. The multi-volume planning documents have been replaced by slim 'playbooks' that provide concrete answers to questions about each business's global market dynamics, key competitive activities, major risks, and proposed GE responses. These playbooks become the basis for half-day shirtsleeve reviews in midsummer when business heads and their key people meet with the top management in an open dialogue on core plans and strategies. Beyond reducing the corporate bureaucracy, speeding up decision processes and enhancing the quality of the final decisions, the new process has also become a key instrument for Welch and his colleagues to directly and personally coach managers who are often three or four levels below them.

The so-called professionally managed companies in India, including, specially, the public sector undertakings, often epitomize the bureaucratic, distant and abstract management process that impedes learning in organizations. Not only are their planning and control systems overly formalized, so are most day-to-day interactions with the top management. Quarterly review meetings are typically overstructured, with a series of slide presentations summarizing facts that are already known. Site visits are carefully orchestrated to be as information- and spontaneity-free as possible. As a result, top managers in these companies have few opportunities to coach while junior and middle managers have few opportunities to develop their strategic perspective or their organizational savvy.

In contrast, both the traditional family-managed companies as well as those built more recently by a younger generation of entrepreneurs have a relatively more informal style of management. Instead of deriding their systems as primitive or unprofessional, multinational and public sector managers should consider emulating at least some aspects of their supposedly more ad hoc style.

In Reliance Industries, for example, a host of corporate and functional heads report to the Ambanis. There are no 'span-breaking' managers in the middle, no staff-intermediated processing of written documents. Decisions are taken through direct interaction between the managers and the family entrepreneurs. The company's legendary speed—whether it is in entering new businesses, floating Eurobond issues or rebuilding cyclone-hit plants—is one outcome of this verbal and interactive style of functioning. The hardwaring of the entrepreneurial orientation of Dhirubhai, Anil and Mukesh Ambani among the company's senior managers is another, perhaps equally important, outcome. As we described in chapter 4, through continuous interactions of this kind, the family leadership of the company has fundamentally reshaped the orientation of people up to several levels below them. 'Working with them I have become more ambitious,' says Subhodh P. Sapra, a member of the core management group. 'I believe I can aspire to head a division in ten years' time,' says S.S. Date, a 35-year-old site shift manager at Patalganga.

Developing people and bringing them up to scratch started as a necessity for Reliance. There were simply not enough experienced managers and engineers for Reliance to hire. But the commitment to continuing education stems from a deeper source. The company was founded by the son of a village schoolteacher who could not afford to go to college. He learnt on the job, learnt to use and trust talent wherever he could find it; so helping people to become the best they can be became an act of faith. 'It is necessary to modernize men as well as plant and equipment,' Dhirubhai stressed. 'Ideas are no one's monopoly . . . I do not consider myself cleverer than my colleagues.' In the early 1970s, a professor of accounting joined Reliance as an exports executive. By 1994, he was head of the textile division, graduating thereafter to becoming president of the textile business group.

To build the Hazira and Jamnagar complexes, the company had to identify, recruit, train and develop a large number of people and the whole process had to start from scratch. The strategy was to recruit a core group of experienced senior managers from both India and abroad and simultaneously initiate a programme of recruiting a large number of fresh graduates from engineering, science, management, finance and accounting colleges. 'The core group took on the responsibility of both setting up the business as well as training and developing the younger people,' explained an HRD manager. Mukesh was impatient with those who could not mentor. 'India does not need a tie-wallah golf culture. You don't need leaders who say we will motivate you—and by leaders I am not talking of CEOs but leaders at all levels—but you need ones that drive your company to become a strong knowledge-based achiever.'

HELPING PEOPLE BECOME THE BEST THEY CAN BE

A commitment to redesigning every aspect of the company's work, organization and management processes to improve the learning opportunities for all employees is, in essence, a commitment to helping each individual who joins the company achieve his or her greatest potential. It is a commitment to continuously allow people to add value to themselves. In a globally competitive economy, it is the courage to make and keep such a commitment that will be perhaps the most important source of a company's competitive advantage.

Is it possible to build such a company in India? Yes, it is. We have invested considerable space in this book to Infosys, describing its evolution in chapter 5 and its internationalization in chapter 8. The one core feature of the company, and the key to its outstanding success, according to N.R. Narayana Murthy, its founder-chairman, has been its unwavering commitment to helping people become the best they can be. It is perhaps the most outstanding example in India of a company that views itself quite explicitly as a university.

The Campus in Electronics City

For an outsider, walking into Infosys' head office and software development centre in Bangalore's Electronics City can be an interesting if somewhat unsettling experience. Walking through the reception area would lead the visitor to a bridge over a little stream running through a landscaped garden. Walking over the bridge would lead her to the canteen, the little kiosk which sells cold drinks and snacks, and the basketball court. At any time of the day, individuals or groups can be seen here either deeply involved in some heated debate about the project on which the team is working, or simply lying on the grass and having a quintessential 'chai-break'.

Coffee and tea drinking is an essential feature of the daily life in Infosys, spilling over from the cultures of the engineering colleges where most Infoscians spent their university years. Beverage stations are located in each floor of the office building and dispense almost 2400 cups of tea and coffee a day. As a project manager explained, 'This campus-like workplace is certainly critical as the company mostly recruits freshers from engineering colleges and IITs. This setting helps the transition from a semi-campus to a productive environment.'

As in college, except for scheduled meetings (the equivalent of classes), there are no fixed timings for anything. Infoscians can work the hours that suit them, just as they can play the hours that suit them. Explicitly called 'the campus', the facility offers basketball, volleyball and tennis courts, and people can be found playing these games at any time of the day. For the less competitive, there is the health club, and for the more sedentary, the sauna. The artists display their creations in the 'Galerie d'Art Infosys' while the internet junkies use their breaks at the Cybercafe on the internet or the equally interesting intranet.

This deliberately designed campus environment is reinforced at Infosys by a massive commitment to continuing education. Immediately after joining the company, all professional recruits have to undertake a 105-day training course. Designed to create a standard starting point for technical skills, the quality and intensity of the course is such that any student emerging successfully from this training develops technical skills equivalent to a graduate in the US with a Bachelor's degree in Information Systems. Beyond this initial training, Infoscians take courses continuously, to update their knowledge, to hone up on new technologies and emerging ideas, and to broaden their management skills.

'At Infosys, we recruit on learnability. We define learnability as the ability to derive generic conclusions from specific instances and apply them to new problems. This is the key to our adaptability and a critical competitive advantage in our business. We can thus leverage existing knowledge to develop new, high-impact business solutions. There are specific sections in the recruiting process which assess candidates on their ability to derive generic knowledge from past experience and to apply them to the future. The rigorous selection process at Infosys ensures that all our knowledge professionals possess high learnability,' says K. Dinesh, a founder-director.

Once accepted as Infoscians, instead of being narrowly specialized into particular tasks, the young employees—the average age of all employees at Infosys was 26.5 in 2000—have the option of a variety of projects to choose from. Referred to as 'resources', they are organized essentially in a talent market, building their reputation through peer recognition. Project managers have free access to the overall pool, and can interview anyone who appears to have the right skills package for their team. Conversely, an engineer can market himself or herself, seeking out projects of particular interest.

At the end of every project—and at any given moment of time there are between 600 and 800 ongoing projects—there is a Closure Analysis Report which examines both what was well done and what was not in terms of meeting customer requirements, quality, deliverables and processes. People are encouraged in a constructive manner to learn from their mistakes so as not to repeat them—and they can then select self-improvement courses based on this feedback from middle management. There are company-sponsored workshops on topics as diverse as Java and Japanese. One workshop series on the anvil is based on the Just-in-Time concept, i.e., two- to three-day crash courses for which resources can sign up to quickly upgrade their competencies as projects come up.

In chapter 5, we highlighted the coaching and mentoring role played by Narayana Murthy, but this role is not limited to top management. Indeed, it is formally structured as a key responsibility of every project leader. They have to provide detailed feedback and guidance to each member of the project team twice a year. In addition, each team member receives a comprehensive review at the completion of the project assignment. 'Today 600 people are being retrained for e-commerce. They have been with Infosys for one to seven years. They didn't want to be evaluated but in the end they agreed. The details were sent to their heads—the process was taken very seriously,' revealed Dr S. Yegneshwar, head of education and research.

'All too often, when managers are told they have to attend a course, they read in it an implicit message: it is either as a punishment, a pat on the back, or a way to say "you are on the mend" or "you are on the way up". We, however, see continuing education as a way towards self-realization. Self-realization not in just a philosophical sense but in a business sense. Everyone needs to realize what is competency, where do I add value. To illustrate this point, an elephant is strong but slow. A snake is fast but physically weak. At Infosys, we try to help people balance their nature through continuing education,' says Dinesh. He himself is an example of the benefits constant upgrading of skills and competencies can bring to both the company and the individual.

Currently head of Information Services, Dinesh spent much of life attending night classes. He started his business career at the age of seventeen sorting letters for Indian Railways. Over the next few years, he morphed from telephone operator and bank clerk to computer programmer, before joining hands with Narayana Murthy and others to start Infosys in 1981. Along the way, he handled a variety of jobs, from project management to head of HRD before acquiring a cabin next to the managing director's. 'Without a paranoia for excellence, one cannot succeed,' he says simply.

Infosys generously spends almost 5 per cent of revenues on education, and is perhaps the only Indian company to have appointed a head of education or indeed to have an Education Council. The council consists of ten members—four service providers and six business unit heads, and seniority ranges from

S. Gopalakrishnan (deputy MD and a founder-director on the council) to a project manager. The council meets once a quarter. At the same time, that nothing worthwhile should come free is a lesson Infosys has learnt the hard way.

'We used to send people for higher studies but it was not a successful experience. Like other companies, we thought of tying up with a college or a university to send a regular number of managers every year for a fixed sum. But this institution-to-institution approach is a problem. Managers think they are doing the company a big favour by attending the course. But institution-to-individual works well. We tell people, we'll give you a loan but you must pay your own way. Afterwards, we reimburse them. Then the motivation level is much higher,' explained Yegneshwar. The company has also tied up with the IIMs and IITs for specially designed short courses where the company and the employee split the cost.

'Knowledge management is a funny business. Nobody reads. We have a huge portal where people upload their experiences, but this is static. What does work are our Best Practices Sessions,' said Yegneshwar. Infosys has ten service centres and each centre is required to put forward a minimum of four proposals for a Best Practices Session. Across locations, heads are asked to identify two or three presentations where the learnings were very high and about ten to fifteen are selected. Those selected make their presentations at several locations. A notice that a Best Practices Session is going to be held is tacked on to the bulletin board and people flock to the room. 'The size of the room is the only constraint. People aspire to be selected to make these presentations and they are rewarded. Not financially but with a letter of appreciation and a book.'

The important questions are scale and delivery. In most companies, a few people hog the entire training programme and budget. But at Infosys, at least 3500 of the 5020 employees undertake a minimum of ten days of training. The bulk of this training is in-house, making its coordination a major logistics issue. Under construction is a new library and six large classrooms aimed to cater to 1200 students daily. These will substantially add to the existing infrastructure and the 10,000 books already available to Infoscians.

As for delivery, 65 per cent of the faculty is in-house and full-time while 10 per cent is outsourced. For the rest, line managers come in to take classes. The faculty also spends some time on projects, otherwise they would get outdated. The people in the classroom are not freshers, and so the classes are kept small, rarely more than twenty-five. 'Small is trivial—when we have to design for 5000 people and the number of recruits is pushing up fast every year—that is the challenge. How do you scale up and across locations, how do you know who needs what when everyone is scattered in several countries?' asks Yegneshwar.

Software expertise is highly marketable in India, with a growing shortage of talent and a continuous increase in demand created by the growth of software houses and the influx of multinational companies. The high investment Infosys makes in training, coaching and professional development only increases the marketability of Infoscians. Yet, Infosys' employee turnover is less than half the industry average, proving that a commitment to helping each employee become the best he or she can be only reinforces the bond between the employer and the employee, to the advantage and satisfaction of both. Says Dinesh, 'We tell our resources, yes, you can pull the plug anytime, but *when* you pull the plug is critical. We will help you constantly upgrade your skills and give you so much interesting work that you will not have time to think of quitting.'

If knowledge and information are so valuable, why not hoard them? 'In this business, you cannot stop an idea,' says Dinesh, quoting the example of Pankaj Joshi, a professor who took his sabbatical at Infosys. Teachers are welcomed from all over the world, and there are more cases written on Infosys than any other Indian company. Once they return to their institutions, they teach these cases, in the process spreading the message of the company and helping the recruitment process. Joshi used his time to write *CMM in Practice—Processes For Executing Software Projects at Infosys*. The book's publication generated intense debate internally. A lot of people felt the company had given away knowledge.

Narayana Murthy took the opposite view. If other companies benefited, if it is good for the country, Infosys should not be the speed breaker. 'Soon after knowledge is born, it becomes redundant. We have to keep moving on, to keep reinventing ourselves. The ability of our people to adapt to and assimilate change is our best insurance against obsolescence,' smiled Narayana Murthy. Added Hema Ravichandar, the senior vice-president, HRD, 'Education is a true business partner. By giving high-value training to individuals, by making them management consultants and not just software engineers, we are e-inventing the future.'

11

BUILDING AN ENTREPRENEURIAL ORGANIZATION

B ig organizations look very different from the top and from
the bottom. From the top, the chairman or managing
director sees order, symmetry and uniformity—a logical
instrument for step-by-step decomposition of the company's
activities and tasks. From the bottom hapless front-line employees
see a cloud of controllers—a formless sponge that soaks up all
their energy and time. The result, in the colourful language of
GE's Jack Welch, is a company that has its face toward the
chief executive and its ass toward the customer.

Figure 11.1: Two Views of the Organization

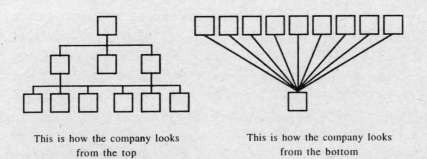

This is how the company looks   This is how the company looks
from the top   from the bottom

Unrecognized perhaps in India, companies here tend to be extremely hierarchical. The public sector undertakings have inherited their hierarchical and bureaucratic orientation from their roots in the government. In family groups, paternalism on the part of the family members and extreme deference toward them on the part of the employees have, with some exceptions, led to the functional equivalent of hierarchy, although without much of the bureaucratic apparatus. Even the multinational subsidiaries in India tend, in general, to be much more hierarchical than the units of the same companies in other countries. There is a widespread belief in India that the entrepreneurial responsibility for creating new opportunities lies with the top management, a belief not entirely inappropriate in an earlier era when both government licences and bank finance had, indeed, to be arranged at the highest level. As a result, most Indian companies lack the entrepreneurial spark and individual initiative in the front lines that are essential in a competitive economy.

Over the last few years, top-level managers in India have increasingly recognized the need for rebuilding initiative in the operating units of their companies. Under the fashionable banner of 'inverting the pyramid', they have invested significant amounts of money and time to cascade the message of empowerment throughout their organizations. In most cases, however, the notion has remained an abstract one, viewed by the rank and file as empty rhetoric, often resulting in little more than additional cynicism at all levels.

Frustrated by this inertia, some managers have come to believe that the barriers to change can be overcome only by replacing people. You can't teach old dogs new tricks, the saying goes, any more than you can teach old managers new ways of behaviour. For those who believe in this statement, the following example should be of interest.

In 1989, when Westinghouse sold a part of its troubled power transmission and distribution business to Asea Brown

Boveri (ABB), the US relays unit was a part of the transaction. Based in Coral Springs, this mature activity was modestly profitable but its ageing product lines offered limited opportunities for growth.

By 1992, under ABB's ownership, the same activity had developed the performance profile of a young growth company. A radical restructuring had doubled operating profits while export sales had increased from 12 to 20 per cent of revenues. At the same time, the unit had developed a significant capability in microprocessor-based relays technology to supplement the traditional electromechanical products, thus laying the foundation for expansion into a major new growth area.

What is remarkable about this story is that Don Jans, the general manager of the unit and the key architect of its turnaround under ABB's ownership, was a thirty-year veteran of Westinghouse, for whom he had been managing the business prior to its divestment. Within a couple of years, an entrepreneur held hostage within a corporate hierarchy had been freed. As described by Jans:

> I am a much broader manager today than I was in Westinghouse. Here we are constantly challenged to look at the world as a market, as a source of expertise, and as a standard of performance. It is tough and demanding, but it can also be invigorating and fun. We feel we are rediscovering management.

What ABB has been able to achieve is not an isolated example. Over the last decade many companies around the world have succeeded in igniting the creative spark of their people, and in protecting and fanning the resulting entrepreneurial flames. In Europe, the traditionally bureaucratic Lufthansa has transformed itself into a highly entrepreneurial federation of disaggregated businesses that include a passenger airline, a cargo operation, a tour company, an engineering and maintenance company and an information technology service provider. In Japan, Toyota has cut out two layers from its organization to create more entrepreneurial space for its front-line managers. In India, this is precisely what Keki Dadiseth has been spearheading in Hindustan Lever, through the Millennium Project. As we compared these companies with the many more whose experiments with empowerment have floundered against unchanging management behaviour, two factors stood out as the main sources of that difference.

First, while recognizing the need for front-line entrepreneurship, most companies attempted to find quick-fit solutions. For example, acknowledging that their mainstream capital budgeting process was slow, cumbersome and inflexible, companies like Kodak and Caterpillar created new 'venture units' to replicate at the periphery of their organizations the greenhouse effect of a venture capital operation. Others, like IBM, spun off independent units to protect specific projects from routine bureaucracy and corporate interventions.

While each of these approaches claimed its initial successes, in very few cases did they provide the broad-based long-term solutions the companies were seeking. The main reason was that the approaches were based on a common principle: rather than attempting to fix the underlying management problems, the objective was to sidestep them. Thus, while IBM was able to create its personal computer in a spun-off independent unit, such a move did little for those still operating within the mainstream structure. Indeed, it did not even resolve the problem of maintaining the unit's entrepreneurial spark once it was reintegrated into the parent organization.

In contrast, companies that have been more successful in truly empowering their people have created an entrepreneurial process at the very core of their organizations, rather than at the periphery. To do so, they have had to make some very fundamental changes in their overall organizational structures and mainstream management processes. In this chapter we will describe these radically different structures and processes which, we believe, are the enabling conditions that allow companies to reignite the spirit of entrepreneurship and opportunity-seeking in the guts of their organizations.

But these organizational changes, by themselves, are not enough. To instil change in the day-to-day behaviour of people, it is also necessary to fundamentally alter the roles and tasks of managers. In most large companies, front-line, middle and top-level managers have long been conditioned to playing certain roles and, in the absence of a clear and well-articulated alternative, these managers have continued to behave as they always have. Even after major organizational changes, top-level managers have continued to see their job as one of setting the corporate strategy and implementing it through their role as the resource allocators. Middle managers too, have remained focused on proper fulfilment of the demands of checks and balances, playing their familiar role of administrative controllers. And swamped by direction and control from above, front-line managers have continued to play the role of operational implementers, responding to the demands of internal organizational processes rather than focusing on external opportunities. This inertia in management patterns of behaviour has, over time, absorbed all the energy from the change process, not because of resistance or sabotage but simply because even the best-intentioned managers have not understood the demands of change on their own activities and tasks.

In contrast, companies with a strong focus on front-line entrepreneurship have created a very different set of roles and tasks for their managers. Instead of being defined by their vertical relationships, these new roles are focused on the very different ways in which each of these management groups can add unique value to the company's entrepreneurial process. In the following section, we will describe and illustrate these new management roles which collectively define what we shall call the entrepreneurial model for managing large organizations.

BUILDING THE ENTREPRENEURIAL PROCESS

While differences in business portfolios and organizational histories affect the management systems of companies, those that succeed in developing an effective entrepreneurial process at the core of their operations share three key organizational characteristics:

- They create small and disaggregated performance units and make them the primary building blocks of their organization.
- They drive performance in these units through a few simple, flexible but highly disciplined planning, control, and resource allocation systems.
- They articulate a clear strategic mission and operationalize it for each unit through unambiguous organizational norms and performance standards.

Disaggregated Performance Units

In the process of building the classic modern corporation, a central objective has been to improve coordination across multiple functional, business, and geographic boundaries. In so doing, small operating units have been 'rolled up' into larger integrated groupings to facilitate the desired cross-unit integration. In this process, however, individual initiative and flexibility that flourished in the smaller units, have usually suffered.

The most basic requirement for building front-line entrepreneurship in a company is to counteract this process—to break down the aggregations that obscure personal responsibility, and to prevent the coordinative pressures from homogenizing individual actions. If the company is to move beyond the stage of creating isolated refuges where endangered entrepreneurs can survive, the management is eventually forced to challenge the overbearing influence of the company's organizational framework—its hierarchic superstructure. This highly developed structural form has become so effective at suppressing individuals under layers of agglomerated units that the senior managers of many companies have lost their ability to see the entrepreneurial trees in the organizational forest.

One of the basic requirements for a company trying to become more entrepreneurial is for its management to fundamentally change the way it looks at the organization. Rather than viewing it primarily in terms of groups or divisions, with operations being run by departments or operating units, it needs to consciously focus on small disaggregated units as the primary elements of the organization. This new perspective will inevitably lead the management to recognize the contribution of the individuals who shape and drive these units.

The Denmark-headquartered International Service Systems (ISS) has built up a $2-billion operation spanning seventeen countries and three continents in the business of daily office cleaning by proliferating small companies—each a separate legal entity with its own profit and loss statement, balance sheet and board of directors. As described by Poul Andreassen, the company's president over the last thirty years, 'The most efficient and profitable way to provide service is through small stand-alone companies led by a local manager who is encouraged to think of the business as his or her own.'

With this philosophy, ISS has created not one national subsidiary in each country but often as many as five different companies, each focused on a distinct business built around a specific customer group. This is also why 3M is organized with the project team as its basic building block. And it was the same belief that led Matsushita to develop the 'one product, one division' structure that resulted in a proliferation of scores of product divisions, each spun off to develop a new product and become self-sufficient.

The point is not that these companies do not have larger aggregated organizational entities, for indeed they do. Rather, the central issue is that the small front-line units are perceived as the basic building blocks—the core element of the organization—instead of being treated as the last points of a command and control chain starting at the top. This simple but profound difference in the perception and treatment of these performance units is what distinguishes them from the departments or profit centres of most large companies. In 3M, for example, it is clear that divisions are simply the organizational form required to manage a particularly successful innovation—not some administrative structure superimposed on businesses deemed to be 'strategically synergistic'. Recognizing that fact, division managers constantly try to seed new projects in the hope of growing them into strong departments, and perhaps even spinning off a new division.

Similarly, in Canon, numerous specialized marketing and production companies have been structured as separate legal entities to reinforce their autonomy even though they are all highly interdependent and do not meet the criterion of functional completeness that was viewed as a prerequisite for structuring SBUs. Some, like Canon sales, have even been partially floated on local stock exchanges. Like most companies developing such performance units, Canon's main objective was to create a work environment in which individuals felt that by taking responsibility they could affect their unit's performance. By reducing the size, scale, and scope of the primary organizational unit with which people identify, Canon and others found that employees became motivated by the knowledge that their actions count, and that their personal contributions to the unit can make a difference.

It is precisely this change, not necessarily in the formal structure of the company but in the perception and treatment of distinct businesses, that Keki Dadiseth has spearheaded within Hindustan Lever. 'How do I retain the aggressiveness and agility of a smaller company as we get much larger?' asks Dadiseth. 'I want to do this by creating smaller profit centres. This will also offer growth opportunities for our key managers.' As a result, from a top-down process of driving the company through the divisions, small businesses within the divisions, headed by 'Virtual CEO's', have increasingly emerged as the focal point of entrepreneurship within Hindustan Lever.

The results have been outstanding. Consider the case of the ice-cream business, in which Hindustan Lever's parent Unilever is a global leader with its strong Walls brand. In India, Hindustan Lever entered the business only in 1994, with the purchase of the Dollops brand from Cadbury. By 1996, with further acquisitions of Kwality, Milkfood, Yankee Doodle, Sub-Zero and other brands, the local ice-cream business had grown into a hodge-podge of forty small factories spread across the country, most of which were both inefficient and unhygienic; nearly 1000 stock carrying units (SKUs), most of which sold in small volumes; and a host of brands with unfocused market positions.

Since then, under the leadership of 'Virtual CEO' K.P. Ponnapa, the business has been fundamentally transformed. Having been given entrepreneurial autonomy within Hindustan Lever's large foods and beverages business, Ponnapa and his team have rationalized production and branding, improved product quality as well as distribution by leveraging Hindustan Lever's technical strengths, and have improved the profit potential of the business by shifting from the low-margin parlour-based products to high-margin impulse purchase stick products.

One of the first actions the new entrepreneurial team took was to establish Kwality Wall's as the new house brand, and bring all products under this brand umbrella. Next, the forty factories were rationalized into sixteen high-quality, well-located facilities. Once the clean-up was completed, they brought in a number of Unilever's global products—Feast, Cornetto, Snacks— as sub-brands to enrich the portfolio.

Looking at the marketing data, they found that their branded pushcarts in Delhi outsold retail stores 3:1 at 2000 to 3000 litres per pushcart per annum. Further, pushcart sales were almost entirely high-margin impulse buys, whereas stores did 50 per cent impulse and 50 per cent bulk sales. Pushcarts were clearly the more effective marketing outlet. The problem, however, was that they were also a high-cost outlet, because of the dry ice they used to maintain their -50°C temperature.

The ice-cream team worked with Hindustan Lever's R&D group to develop liquid pouches that were both reusable and cheaper than dry ice. Moreover, the pouches maintained a temperature of -23°C, which was safer for children. In collaboration with R&D, the ice-cream team also developed a smaller, more compact pushcart with a lower capital cost and a lower carrying capacity of 50 litres instead of the earlier 300 litres. The strategy was to engage pushcart concessionaires, each responsible for managing twenty pushcarts, who would retain a 10 per cent margin. The pushcarts would remain as Hindustan Lever property, and would be issued to the concessionaires against a deposit.

This is but one example of the kind of results that Hindustan Lever is enjoying from its commitment to decentralizing the organization and building it up from distinct, small businesses, led by autonomous virtual CEOs. From being middle managers in a large company, people like Ponnapa are being converted into 'businessmen', acting as the best entrepreneurs do, when they start up and run their own little companies.

Performance-driven Systems

The second vital element for developing an entrepreneurial process is a set of systems that reinforce the focus and accountability of the performance units. In both design and implementation, they stand in stark contrast to the staff-led, document-driven strategic planning exercises, the 'trickle-down economics' of classic resource allocation processes. Rather than being driven by the informational need of top management, the systems in these organizations are designed and managed to be more sensitive to the operating realities facing front-line managers and to maintaining their motivation.

Consider capital allocation systems as an example. Traditionally, in established companies, these processes have been structured for handling large investments, typically after reviewing and evaluating detailed long-range plans and projected returns. In companies with effective entrepreneurial processes, the system needs to be geared to a much more incremental and flexible approach, but one which is still very rigorous.

3M's philosophy of 'make a little, sell a little' which legitimizes multi-stage funding of promising projects is an example of this approach. An entrepreneur's initial idea might secure funding from his or her division to develop the concept further; a new more sophisticated proposal could justify building a prototype; a subsequent report on results might request funding for market and technical testing; and so on. At each stage from the initial idea to eventual product launch, the product champion must review performance against earlier commitments and propose a budget and quantified mileposts to evaluate the next stage of funding. And, as the project evolves in potential and investment needs, the review may be elevated from the division to the group to the corporate level for funding.

In chapter 5, we described the organic growth of Thermax, continuously expanding into new niche businesses based on creative development and application of technology. In a relatively small and resource constrained company, this ability to develop technologies was based not on the strength of large upfront investments in R&D but on the same process of flexible resource allocation, driven by the same 'make a little, sell a little' philosophy.

Thermax's boiler business was supported by its knowledge of heat transfer processes. The director of its small R&D team found that rice and oil mills accumulated a lot of husk, which they then paid to dispose of. With a small investment, he and his team adapted the boiler to use husk as its fuel. The new boiler started selling well, generating revenues and profits. Then the R&D unit used a bit of that profit to adapt the technology so that coal could be used as the fuel. As the businesses grew, the team slowly built a sophisticated and broad capability in the area of fluidized bed combustion systems.

Over a fifteen-year period, such small, multi-staged investments in technology, led by the entrepreneurial instincts of its R&D head, helped Thermax create a whole host of focused and complimentary technologies that undergirded its business evolution (see figure 11.2). From its knowledge of combustion systems, Thermax built niche application technologies in the areas of incineration, drying, cooling and

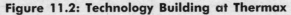

Figure 11.2: Technology Building at Thermax

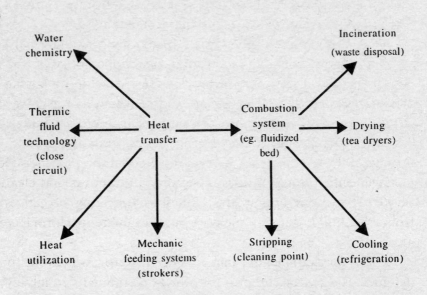

stripping. Heat transfer technologies led to specialized capabilities in water treatment, mechanical feeding systems, thermic fluids and heat utilization. Each step was small, supported by small investments. At each step, the technology was developed to meet a specific customer need, and was converted into a business. And the entire process was led by Thermax's autonomous business managers (see description of Thermax's organizing principles in chapter 5), in partnership with its highly entrepreneurial research director.

Another main pillar of corporate systems is the annual budgeting process, and many companies find that this core system is also too inflexible and impersonal to support the kind of entrepreneurial values they want to cultivate. Desired sales, expense and profit objectives are often agreed at the top and cascaded down, with senior managers cajoling and pressuring unit managers to accept the numbers. Furthermore, the targets are typically set only in financial terms often not fully understood by line managers who pass the management and reporting task off to the financial controller. Lacking credibility, understanding, and commitment, the budget system deteriorates into a mechanical exercise managed by the accountants.

Confronting these problems is difficult, and many are hard to totally overcome. But companies that hope to create an entrepreneurial organizational process must develop budgeting systems that are seen as legitimate, and manage them in a way that is motivating. For most, this approach implies a budget system in which front-line managers not only take more responsibility but are also held more accountable. Corporate management's primary role is to set broad objectives and clear standards to elicit honest and ambitious operating objectives from the units, and to measure and evaluate performance against those objectives.

In ISS, for example, the annual budgeting process is explicitly designed as a bottom-up process, albeit one framed strongly by broad corporate targets. Based on the business plans developed by the small, national companies, the corporate executive group agrees on the company's overall performance targets for the coming year. These broad growth, profit and return targets are then transmitted through the regional divisional offices, ensuring a full discussion between the local managements and their bosses at the divisional level. Andreassen expects his line managers to be deeply involved in the preparation of the budget as well as its tight control. In his view, genuine decentralization implies more, not less, accountability and control since it must create a sense of involvement among those who deliver the final results.

Giving individual units greater voice in their budget goals does not imply, however, that the system used in the entrepreneurial companies is less rigorous. Quite the contrary. ISS's Management Reporting System (MRS) identifies contribution margins at the level of each of the company's tens of thousands of cleaning contracts around the world. Its objective is to give managers at all levels an understanding of the profitability of each job and of the overhead costs associated with each management level. At 3M, similarly, 3900 monthly P&L statements are generated centrally, and these are made available on-line to all operating units. In each of these companies, a simple but rigorous management reporting system has become an essential tool for maintaining operating discipline.

Clear Mission and Standards

Historically, as companies built their increasingly complex hierarchical structures and supported them with ever-more sophisticated formal systems, the role of senior management and their staff often focused on the control activities required to maintain these structures and systems. To overcome the negative organizational impact of this control-driven mentality and the resulting adversarial relationship between headquarters and operating managers, most companies must convert the traditional practices into more support-based roles, as we described in chapter 9, and develop cooperative relations designed to nurture and protect entrepreneurship.

But the limiting factor in senior managers' ability to step back from their traditional role of direction and control is often the extent to which their subordinates have been focused on the company's overall needs and priorities. The reason senior-level

·managers have to be so involved in operations is that those in the front lines of management often take decisions that are not in line with the corporate direction and strategy. But, while the need for corporate guidance is clear, the assumption that this can be achieved only through intervention is not. The alternative, as many corporate leaders have begun to recognize, is to instil clear strategic objectives and unambiguous performance standards within the organization. In doing so, they find that they can greatly reduce the need for the kind of stifling control and overbearing interference that kills front-line initiative.

When James Houghton became CEO of Corning in 1983, the company was struggling to revive its performance in the midst of a major recession. At the same time, the organization was trying to define its long-term strategic direction during a period in which Corning's technology-driven strategy seemed to be pulling in many different directions. For more than a year, Houghton and his senior management worked to define a clear statement of strategy to focus on a set of priorities that would 'create a new balance of corporate perspective and entrepreneurial initiative'. Most important, he got agreement to focus the company's formidable technological capabilities on four clearly defined business segments. Within a few years, the organizational culture that had once been compared to that of a country club became much more focused and energized as managers began to develop a much clearer view of where Corning was headed, and how they could contribute.

Such clarity of strategic objectives is essential for channelling entrepreneurship into cohesive corporate development. Without a clearly defined and broadly communicated strategic mission, front-line managers have no basis for selecting among the diverse opportunities they might confront, and bottom-up entrepreneurship soon degenerates into a frustrating guessing game. Companies should be careful, however, that their strategic statements do not simply define their current situations. The most effective objectives tend to be precise enough to clearly rule out activities that do not support the company's strategic mission, and yet broad enough to prevent undue constraints on the creativity and opportunism of front-line managers.

Entrepreneurship is often mistakenly thought of as the antithesis of operational discipline. In contrast, we found the entrepreneurial companies to have an unusually high level of discipline in their management processes, built through a combination of stretched performance standards and rigorous management reporting. They build a symbiotic relationship between corporate ambition and current results, with each fuelling and stretching the other.

While elaborating Corning's strategic statement, Houghton also let it be known that as the organization drove towards that objective, he would not tolerate the performance levels managers had slipped into as they missed their budgets over the previous six successive years. Setting an objective for Corning's return on assets to be consistently ranked in the top 25 per cent of the Fortune 500, he would simply walk out of presentations that did not measure up to this standard, telling manages to come back when they found ways to meet the target.

One of the reasons that Dadiseth can push for more decentralization and front-line entrepreneurship in Hindustan Lever is precisely because the company has historically developed a profound sense of discipline. As described by Anil Lahiri, its director, HR, 'one of the greatest things about this company is that after the debate, once a decision is taken, everyone falls in line and works to achieve the objective. This happens across the organization and all the way down to the worker on the manufacturing line.' Indeed, for Dadiseth, that discipline is a precondition for empowerment. 'Once they agree on a target, that is a contract,' he said, referring to his expectations about the virtual CEOs.

Ditto at Thermax. In his famous fireside chats—a regular column in Thermax's house journal—Rohinton Aga wrote, 'Honouring a commitment is not a matter of money. It's a matter of culture, of values, of character. If I have made a commitment to do a thing, I take responsibility for it—no delays, no excuses, no alibis. How can we make this an integral part of us?' Indeed, some of the difficulties Thermax has faced in recent years have been due to a slackening in these areas of discipline and performance standards since the untimely demise of Aga.

A PROFOUND SHIFT OF SOCIAL VALUES[15]

Bewildered by the soaring market value of small IT companies like Infosys, challenged by entrepreneurial start-ups like Kevincare, and embarrassed by continuing relegation in the corporate league tables, many established and large Indian companies have recognized that they have to do something to stem the rot. Some of them have also identified their traditional organizational structure and processes as a key constraint, but few have found the courage to make the kind of fundamental change from a bureaucratic to an entrepreneurial model that we have proposed in this chapter. Yet, without such an organizational transformation, they will not have a future.

It is not merely competitive, macroeconomic or technological factors that lie behind the need for change. The closing years of the twentieth century have triggered a fundamental shift in social values, from the bureaucratic to the entrepreneurial ideal. It is not just that large, bureaucratic companies are being replaced by small entrepreneurial firms, although that is happening as well, but that the basic ideologies that underlie these two organizational forms are swapping places. The ideal of bureaucracy has lost its claim as a source of economic progress, just as the entrepreneur is emerging as the hero in the drama of creative destruction.

---

[15]This section draws liberally from the arguments of Donald Sull and Jonathon West in their unpublished article 'From the Old Economy to the New: A Values Shift'.

The bureaucratic model entered the last century as a conquering hero. Its hierarchical structure and rational, impersonal processes provided a powerful basis for achieving efficiency in large-scale collective endeavours. In business, the rise of professional management enshrined this bureaucratic ideal in the practices of admired companies around the world. In their heyday, companies like General Motors, IBM, Philips, Siemens, Mitsubishi, Hitachi and others represented the pinnacle of bureaucracy's advantages of rationality, order, specialization and efficiency. In India, the British ruled the vast and diverse country on the strength of these very attributes of the bureaucractic model and, over time, the model diffused to business organizations that had typically started their lives on the strengths of entrepreneurship and risk-taking.

If bureaucracy entered the last century as a conquering hero, it exited the century as a spent force. Its fundamental strength of depersonalization proved to also be its fatal flaw. While it could maintain the existing order with efficiency, it could not respond to environmental shocks that created the need for a new order. It could rationalize but not revitalize. It could control people but not inspire them.

As the bureaucratic behemoths like GM, IBM and Philips— and their Indian counterparts like the public sector organizations and old family firms—surrendered market share, they also lost their hold on the hearts and minds of employees. An earlier generation of Indians enjoyed the status and legitimacy that came from working with established companies and organizations wore the labels of Tata, Birla, Indian Oil and the IAS as badges of honour. Employees who came of age in the 1990s, however, felt the constraints of being cogs in giant machines. They resented the stifling of their initiative by the need for endless approvals. They were disheartened to see the results of their actions obscured by the company's large size, and politics replace performance as the basis for recognition and reward. By breaking the link between effort and recognition, bureaucracies deprived employees of the opportunity to make a difference and stripped work of its meaning.

While the dry rot had set in a decade or more ago, the final tipping point in the dethroning of bureaucracy came in the late 1990s, with the rise of a new set of institutions, mostly in the IT sector. Companies like Infosys, Satyam Computers, NIIT and others blew the myth that Indian culture cherished hierarchy and paternalism, and that Indian employees preferred to comply than to initiate; to be told rather than to be left free to decide for themselves. These new upstarts not only surprised and shocked the old feudal business maharajas by overtaking their companies' market values and their personal wealth, they also deprived the established bureaucratic organizations of their legitimacy and public respect.

While not all of these new companies may achieve the goal, they have led the transformation in corporate India from the bureaucratic to the entrepreneurial ideal. In a bureaucracy what counts is one's rank in the hierarchy. The key to success is as often the ability to read and rapidly adapt to subtle shifts in the whims of superiors, as it is talent and effort. Personal presentation is critical. In contrast, the new IT companies established transparent links between individual effort and results, by adopting many of the features of the entrepreneurial organization that we have described in this chapter.

To respond to this broad shift in social values, established companies have to adopt the entrepreneurial ethic. They have to commit to entrepreneurial values. The only way they can make this change is through a leap of faith. While making such a leap of faith is always difficult, it is possible, as the experiences of ABB abroad and Hindustan Lever in India clearly show.

Also, they have to go all the way. Half-hearted efforts at 'empowerment' will not do. Committing fully to creating an entrepreneurial process will raise fundamental questions about every aspect of a traditional bureaucracy. How can we break up our enterprise into small performance units? How will we coordinate those units? How can we attract and retain people who are not like us? Managers in most companies try to avoid facing these difficult questions, but the key tests of commitment to entrepreneurial values will come in how managers answer them.

An earlier generation of social leaders gave Indians their political freedom. A current generation of business leaders are extending that freedom into the workplace, by replacing feudalism and the stifling forces of hierarchy with the liberating spirit of entrepreneurship in their organizations. Like Keki Dadiseth, they are liberating the entrepreneurial spirit that had been held hostage in corporate hierarchies. Our advice to others who are still hesitant in making the leap is—don't wait. Once the process of changing social values reaches the tipping point, it moves very, very quickly. Corporate India is experiencing this tipping point. Managers who cannot gather up the courage to rebuild their organizations into the entrepreneurial model may leave their companies stranded on the wrong side of the chasm separating old corporate India and the new, emerging economy.

12

NEW MANAGEMENT ROLES AND TASKS

The changes in organization structure, management systems, and performance standards we have described in the preceding chapter create the context for a less adversarial and more supportive relationship between operating managers and those in corporate or divisional headquarters. But the organization changes are not enough, by themselves, to create the behavioural changes necessary for supporting an entrepreneurial orientation. Ultimately, strategy, structure and systems are abstractions—it is what managers actually do that drives action within companies. To build managerial entrepreneurship, therefore, it is necessary to reinforce these changes in structure and systems with changes in the roles and responsibilities not only of front-line managers, but also those in senior and top-level positions.

In the traditional organizational model (the left-hand side diagram in figure 12.1), the top-level managers sitting at the apex of the corporate hierarchy act as the company's *grand strategists* and resource allocators—they think up the strategy and then drive it down the organization through their control over resource allocation. The front-line managers in the operating

Figure 12.1: Transforming Management Roles

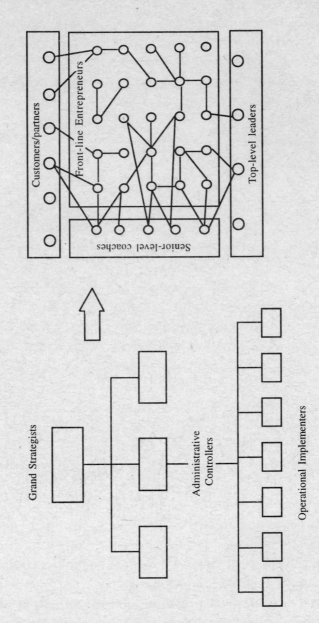

units of the company play the role of *operational implementers*. Their key task is to implement that strategy that comes down to them from the top. Senior managers, located between the top and the front line, play the role of *administrative controllers*, ensuring that the demands of checks and balances are effectively met in the vertical processes of information and resource flows.

In contrast, in the entrepreneurial organization (the right-hand side of figure 12.1) the roles of these managers are radically different.

- Front-line managers, heading small, disaggregated and interdependent units focused on specific opportunities, are the company's entrepreneurs. They are the builders of the company's businesses and they drive the company's performance by continuously strengthening those businesses.
- Like coaches who leverage the strengths of individual players to build a winning team, senior-level managers link these separate businesses into a coherent, winning company. Their value added lies in creating the strategic and organizational framework within which the diverse capabilities of the front-line units can be integrated across businesses, functions, and geographic regions.
- Top management infuses the company with an energizing purpose to develop it as an enduring institution that can outlive its existing operations, opportunities and executives. Like social leaders, they create the challenge and commitment necessary to drive change so that the company can continuously renew itself.

It is through interrelationship and integration of these management roles that the company balances the tensions between short-term and long-term performance; between individual entrepreneurship and collective teamwork; between ambition and discipline; between creating economic value and a sense of emotional fulfilment of its members. Elements of these management roles can be accommodated within the structures of traditional companies. Collectively, however, they represent a radically different way of managing large, complex organizations.

How does one build such an organization? What does it look like in real life? How does it function? One of the companies in the world that has pioneered this new model and also one that is perhaps the most advanced in its implementation is ABB. Let us illustrate the fundamentally different management roles by describing one specific part of ABB that we studied in some detail.

Transformation of Management at ABB

Over the last decade, Percy Barnevik has emerged as one of the more visible corporate revolutionaries. Presiding over the merger between Swedish Asea and Swiss-German Brown Boveri, he has seen the newly-formed ABB grow from $18 billion in revenues in 1988 to $35 billion in 1997, while improving return on capital employed from 13 to 17 per cent. With decentralization of responsibility and individual initiative as the two cornerstones of his management philosophy, the organization Barnevik shaped for ABB has all the features we have described in the earlier chapter as hallmarks of an entrepreneurial company.

Asserting that 'large companies need to organize in clear profit centres with individual accountability as the only way to lift profitability and keep it there', he has built ABB as a federation of 1200 small companies, each employing only 200 people, on average, and generating between $25 million and $200 million in annual revenues. Structured, to the extent possible, as separate legal entities, each company is given responsibility not only for its profit and loss statement but also its complete balance sheet. It is explicit corporate policy to allow each company to retain a third of its net profits, thereby allowing managers to inherit results over the years through changes in their company's equity. The companies, in turn, have created over 4500 profit centres in ABB, each profit centre employing an average of fifty people.

Front-line entrepreneurship is reinforced in ABB by the ultra-lean structure above the company level. There is only one level of management between the corporate executive committee chaired by Barnevik and the heads of the 1200 companies. The corporate headquarters of the $35-billion company has less than 100 people. At the intermediate level, business area managers are supported by a staff of three to five. Barnevik's rule of thumb for restructuring the traditional organizations of the merged or acquired companies from which ABB was formed was to remove 90 per cent of all employees at each level above the operating companies.

At the heart of ABB's management system lies ABACUS— Asea Brown Boveri Accounting and CommUnication System— a highly sophisticated and fully automated information system that interconnects the personal computers in each of the 4500 profit centres in over 120 countries to the company's central mainframes in Vasteras in Sweden and Zurich in Switzerland. Governed by strict rules to ensure consistency in data definition, format and timing of inputs, ABACUS gathers monthly performance data concerning orders received, revenues, gross margins, period costs, net earnings and headcount for each operating company and allows mangers around the world to access that data to generate both standard reports as well as seek answers to specific questions. The effectiveness of ABACUS has allowed the company to implement some empowering and democratic rules such as: people shall not report twice and ABACUS will be the only official reporting channel; no one can ask a company manager to report earlier than the ABACUS deadline or in a different format; and information from the system is to be made available to all managers, irrespective of rank, at the same time.

Both the strategic planning and annual budgeting systems at ABB are designed to involve, motivate and support front-line managers. The strategic plans of each business area are discussed by the concerned manager directly with the group executives and are approved by Barnevik without any involvement of the corporate staff groups. Budgets are set bottom up, based on agreed strategies, and are seen as personal agreements between the head of the operating companies and the top management which the former must fulfil and the latter cannot arbitrarily change.

The entrepreneurial process in ABB is defined within a clearly articulated corporate mission: 'contributing to environmentally sound sustainable growth and making improved living standards a reality for all nations around the world'. The mission has been given more direct managerial relevance by its translation into a set of strategic objectives: 'to increase the value of our products based on continuous technological innovation and on the competence and motivation of our people . . . becoming a global leader—the most competitive, competent, technologically advanced and quality-minded electrical engineering company in our fields of activity'. Barnevik has further operationalized the broad mission by expressing it in terms of financial performance standards: '10 per cent operating profit and 25 per cent return on capital employed.'

Yet, while all these organizational characteristics of the company have received considerable media attention both in India and abroad, what is really remarkable about the company is not just its 1200 separate companies or the ABACUS system. To really understand the transformation that has occurred at ABB, one must understand the radically different roles and tasks it has defined for its front-line, senior and top-level managers to create a symbiosis between those organizational characteristics and its management behaviours.

Front-Line Managers As Entrepreneurs

In chapter 11, we told the story of Don Jans, the head of ABB's relays company in the US, who attributed the remarkable transformation of his business's performance to his own 'rediscovery of management'. Let us return to him to explain how ABB's organizational philosophy fundamentally transformed the role of front-line managers.

In 1989, when ABB acquired a part of Westinghouse's troubled transmission and distribution business, it overlaid its radically decentralized structure on a much more hierarchically controlled management system. Like all his ex-Westinghouse colleagues who now found themselves working for ABB, Don Jans soon discovered he had to make some major changes in his management style. As the head of the US relays business, Jans had become accustomed to the five layers of management between himself and Westinghouse's CEO; in ABB he found only two. In Westinghouse, he had to deal with the bureaucracy imposed by a 3000-strong headquarters; in ABB he had to become more self-sufficient in an organization with only 100 people at corporate; in Westinghouse, decisions had been top-down and shaped by political negotiations; in ABB, his unit was structured as a separate company and was expected to take responsibility for decisions based on data and results.

While the structure and systems defined the framework in which Jans and his colleagues operated, and the senior management groups provided the resources, support and challenge, the remarkable improvement in ABB's fortunes, despite its portfolio of mature electrical equipment businesses in the midst of a global recession, relied on these front-line managers' willingness and ability to drive ongoing business performance. Among the many tasks they undertook, we saw that the most effective focused on three core activities (see table 12.2).

First, these front-line managers worked hard to leverage their local assets and resources. ABB's highly sophisticated and fully automated information and reporting system allowed management to analyse standardized data by aggregating or disaggregating it across any business or geographic dimension. Jans regularly received a detailed product-by-product analysis of his company's performance, not only compared to its past results but also ranged against the performance of other companies in his business area and geographic region. Spurred

Table 12.2: Management Roles and Tasks

	Front-line managers	Senior managers	Top-level managers
Changing role	From operational implementers to aggressive entrepreneurs	From administrative controllers to supportive coaches	From grand strategists to institutional leaders
Primary value added	Driving business performance by focusing on productivity and growth within front-line units	Linking and leveraging resources and capabilities across the organization to bring the large company advantages to bear on the performance of front-line units	Creating and embedding a shared purpose to provide a sense of direction, challenge and commitment to managers of front-line units
Key activities and tasks	Improving the productivity of local resources and assets within the units	Providing guidance and support to front-line managers	Building stretch by articulating an over-arching corporate ambition
	Creating required new resources and competencies locally	Creating mechanisms and forums for transferring and integrating skills and best practices across units	Institutionalizing a set of norms and values to support front-line entrepreneurship and horizontal cooperation
	Identifying and pursuing new growth opportunities for the business	Managing the process of building an overall business strategy within which the mission of each front-line unit is specifically defined	Establishing standards to guide choices and provide discipline in front-line initiatives

on by the stretched performance standards, the simple and clear data, and the sense of internal competition, Jans and his team significantly leveraged the asset utilization of the US-based relays company. Inventory levels were cut, receivables reduced, expenses trimmed and operating efficiency improved. As a result of these efforts, operating profits more than doubled in two years.

'Why did you not do these things in Westinghouse?' we asked Jans. 'After all there you were, if anything, under stronger pressure for cost reduction'. 'The difference,' Jans said, 'was that in ABB, I had the maximum degree of freedom. At Westinghouse, orders would come down from the top: cut workforce by 12 per cent, reduce inventory by 10 per cent, and so on. Here, I get no such instructions. I run the company. I have to deliver performance, but I have complete freedom on how to do so.'

The second set of entrepreneurial activities common to most of these front-line managers was triggered by their clearly delegated responsibility for expanding business opportunities. Driven by stretch targets, backed by corporate investment, and encouraged by senior management support, Jans began to explore ways to expand the relays business that had stagnated for a decade in Westinghouse as that company tried to diversify away from such 'mature' businesses.

Jans's appointment to the advisory boards of ABB's Canadian and Mexican relays companies, as well as senior management's encouragement to focus on Asian countries with similar technical standards, resulted in a rapid expansion in exports from 12 per cent of sales to 20 per cent within three years. Similarly, ABB's willingness to transfer its specialized knowledge and expertise allowed Jans to shift his overdependence on products using the old electro-mechanical technology, and aggressively develop control systems based on microprocessor technology that not only expanded the sales base but also blocked an aggressive competitor who had emerged to exploit the technology gap.

Third, the front-line managers in ABB also played a key

role in building new capabilities. Recognizing that in the mature and highly competitive relays business, efficiency would not be enough to build a sustainable competitive advantage, Jans focused his organization on reducing cycle time in order to improve customer service. These efforts were subsequently expanded into a total quality programme that in turn drove a broad cultural change based on employee involvement and continuous improvement. So successful was this overall programme in dramatically increasing customer service that members of Jans' team were asked to transfer their expertise to other companies in the region and in the worldwide relays business area.

Don Jans's metamorphosis from an operational implementer in Westinghouse to an aggressive entrepreneur in ABB is not an exceptional case. We believe that inside every corporate hierarchy, a number of entrepreneurial hostages like Jans are striving to break free. Like him, they have a reservoir of latent ideas, energy and commitment waiting to be tapped. But, elaborate webs of systems and procedures are smothering their creative ideas; staff-driven corporate superstructures are stiffing their considerable energy; and a remote, internally-focused top management are sapping their deep commitment. As Joe Baker, Jans's boss on the geographic axis of ABB's global matrix and another Westinghouse veteran, recalled about his long career in that company prior to joining ABB: 'In comparison with ABB's approach, it is so clear that Westinghouse was limiting its manager's potential. We recruited first-class people, we did an outstanding job of management development, then we wasted all that investment by constraining them with a highly authoritarian structure.'

The first challenge in redefining management roles is to release the entrepreneurial hostages in the front-line units of the company. The risk, however, is that such a focus on front-line entrepreneurship will not only create the indisciplined expansion experience by the conglomerates of the 1960s, but that it would also localize and fragment the company's resources and capabilities. It is the roles played by senior and top-level managers that prevent such outcomes in companies like ABB.

Senior Managers As Coaches

Historically, senior managers, situated between the front-line operating units and the top management, enjoyed a central position in a company's decision processes because of their intermediary role, disaggregating corporate objectives into business unit targets, and aggregating business unit results for corporate review. They were also the crucial lynchpins in resource flows within the company, since corporate managers relied on their judgement of people and situations for allocation of capital and distribution of rewards. This responsibility provided the basis of their controller role, giving them enormous status within the company. In addition, their role as communicators, broadcasting and amplifying top-management priorities and channelling and translating front-line feedback, gave them power because of their ability to influence the vital information flow across the hierarchy.

Recent complementary trends of 'delayering' the middle levels of the organization, 'empowerment' of front-line positions, and the increasing use of information systems for internal communication have threatened to render obsolete all these traditional roles. As a result, in many companies, senior-level managers in the middle have emerged as the silent resistors whose fine-tuned, invisible yet well-organized subversion have derailed the change efforts. In others, a hard-driving top management has broken through the resistance, bypassing the middle layers and establishing direct contact with the front line. In either case, the irrelevance of managers in the middle has become a self-fulfilling prophecy.

In contrast, as the head of ABB's worldwide relays business area and Jans's boss on the product axis of the company's product–geography matrix, Ulf Gundemark played perhaps the most crucial role in managing the tensions inherent in the company's ambition 'to be global and local, big and small, radically decentralized with central reporting and control'. In resolving these contradictions, he focused on three core tasks. First, he was the business strategist, building the overall strategic and organizational framework within which the mandates of the front-line managers were defined. Second, he was the organizational integrator linking and leveraging the resources and competencies developed in the different front-line units. Finally, he was the key source of support and guidance for the front-line entrepreneurs, helping them not only with personal counselling but also with his broader knowledge of and access to required corporate resources. We describe this senior management role as that of a coach, but this metaphor should not evoke visions of some has-been player calling directions from the sidelines. Rather, the image is that of a seasoned professional who works on developing the players' skills, uses his experience to shape strategy in consultation with the members of his team, has the authority to change players when the need arises, and carries overall responsibility for the team's performance.

ABB formally describes a business area head as 'the business strategist and global optimizer'. This was a particularly challenging task for Gundemark since the relays business was composed of the previously independent and self-sufficient relays operations of four companies—Asea, Brown Boveri, Stromberg and Westinghouse—folded into a single worldwide operation. Yet, in executing the difficult and urgent task of integrating the activities of sixteen national relays companies and providing them with a common strategic agenda, Gundemark shunned the direction-and-control bias of traditional senior-level business managers. Instead, he chose to tap into the organization's network of entrepreneurs by extensive involvement of front-line managers in both the decision making and the execution tasks.

Important long-term decisions affecting the overall business were not taken by Gundemark in the privacy of his office but were hammered out in the business area board, a group chaired by him and composed of the presidents of three key national relays units. The philosophy of inclusion did not stop at this level of company heads—it penetrated deep into the organization. For example, he assembled a nine-person task force from junior executives in six countries to develop a strategic vision for the business area. The team's mandate was to be bold, direct and creative, challenging all existing assumptions and objectives. After inputs from the business area board, the team's report was published and distributed to all employees of the relays business. The objective, as Gundemark explained, was to embed understanding rather than impose direction:

I wanted to sweep aside the old assumptions about strategy we inherited from the 1970s and 1980s—that it was defined primarily by the top management, that it was communicated through numbered confidential copies kept in locked files, and that it was updated annually but usually without questioning the underlying assumptions or objectives. I wanted it to become a process that involved all levels of management, that was widely communicated, and that was constantly open to challenge.

Beyond establishing a shared understanding of and commitment to a worldwide relays strategy, developing the resources and capabilities of his business provided the focus of a second set of Gundemark's tasks. But rather than accumulating those resources in a central location, he saw his challenge as one of building a network, linking the knowledge and expertise that existed in the different national operations, so that the distributed capabilities could be integrated and leveraged on a worldwide basis.

As a first step, he initiated a project to rationalize the overlapping structures and responsibilities that resulted from the merger of the established relays businesses of four competing companies. Even for this task, however, he saw himself as a conductor rather than a soloist. He made the rationalization decisions and the integration task the responsibility of a project team composed of functional experts from each of the involved units. In the end, the team negotiated an agreement and transferred resources and responsibilities in such a way that the Swedish relays unit became ABB's global leader for high-voltage products, the Swiss unit specialized in project and systems deliveries, the Finnish unit took leadership in distribution protection and control products, and the US operation headed by Don Jans became the leading expert on ANSI-standard high-voltage and distribution relays of the businesses.

Again, to protect and build on distributed entrepreneurship, Gundemark created channels of communication and forums of exchange to link and leverage the talents and best practices that existed within the different national units. He formed R&D, total quality and purchasing councils, comprising the specialists in those activities from the leading units, and charged these councils with the responsibility for defining and diffusing best practices in their assigned areas. These horizontal coordination mechanisms across organizational boundaries led to numerous instances of spontaneous transfer of knowledge and expertise that became a valuable capability of the ABB organization. For example, at a meeting of the total quality council in the US, the host unit conducted a plant tour as a side event, explaining its time-based management programme that had not only improved customer service levels but also contributed to a significant reduction in working capital. Without any corporate directive, this programme was transferred to every other major relays unit of ABB within a year, solely at the initiative of the functional managers and their informal networks.

Such attention to developing strategy and integrating capabilities did not mean that Gundemark ignored the traditional divisional management's responsibility for operating performance. But, instead of adopting the staff-supported, systems-driven approach to this task that is so common in companies, he saw his primary role as that of providing front-line entrepreneurs with the counselling and support they needed to achieve their objectives.

For each of the national operating companies, Gundemark

created a steering committee, which acted as a small local board. Board members were drawn from the worldwide relays management (Gundemark or one of his only two staff), the national holding companies (the other arm of ABB's matrix), managers from other ABB businesses with specific knowledge or expertise, and the president of the local relays company. Meeting three or four times a year, these local boards provided a forum for managers like Jans to review their units' performance with their business and geographic bosses, and to obtain quick decisions on proposals such as Jans's plans for building up a microprocessor-based relays capability. For Gundemark, such forums represented a much richer control process, one which allowed him to understand, discuss, suggest and support actions to correct potential problems.

Senior managers in the middle of the corporate hierarchy are increasingly the forgotten and forsaken group in large companies. Amid rounds of delayering, destaffing, and downsizing, many companies have overlooked the fact that the success of small, empowered front-line units depends on the company's ability to bring large company benefits to those units by ensuring that they can access each other's resources, knowledge and capabilities. Companies that dismantle their vertical integration mechanisms without simultaneously creating the horizontal coordination processes quickly lose the benefits of both front-line entrepreneurship and large company power. At the same time, such intense horizontal flows can also paralyse the organization. It is the senior managers in the middle who make 'inverting the pyramid' operational both by developing the front-line entrepreneurs and providing them support so that they are not overwhelmed by the ambiguity, complexity and potential conflicts in such horizontal, networked organizations.

Top-Level Managers As Leaders

Those at the apex of many of today's large, complex organizations find themselves playing out a role that they have inherited from their corporate forebears. When the creation of the divisionalized structure institutionalized a management philosophy based on the delegation of responsibility, those at the top level of the corporation saw their main task as ensuring that their newly decentralized organizations were adequately directed. Their primary roles became defined as the formulators of strategy, the builders of structure and the controllers of systems.

As these three tools became increasingly sophisticated, there was a growing assumption that they could allow organizations to drive purposefully towards their clearly defined goals, largely free from the idiosyncrasies and pathologies of individuals. To some extent the objective has been achieved: most large companies have become highly depersonalized, with individual employees acting as captives of the system.

To free these entrepreneurial hostages requires a roll-back of this dehumanizing management paradigm. To capture the commitment and creativity of their people, top-level managers in the entrepreneurial companies we studied had begun replacing the hard-edged assumptions of the traditional model with a set of corporate-level roles that were far less directive and constraining. From being the formulators of corporate strategy, they had become the shapers of an organizational context in which strategic initiative could emerge. Instead of creating formal structures that gave them control over the firm's financial resources, they devoted most of their efforts to developing the organization's human resources. And, rather than using the management systems to monitor and control operations, they got back in touch with people deep in the organization and began to refocus on the individual as the primary unit of analysis.

As a member of ABB's group executive committee, Göran Lindahl had overall responsibility for the corporation's power transmission business sector, of which Gundemark's relays business was a part, as well as for the operating companies in the Asian region. While delegating the central strategy development tasks to his business area managers, Lindahl focused his energy on creating and managing what he called 'the framework'. This was a set of broad strategic challenges and operating principles that he used to shape the assumptions guiding his managers' decisions, and the norms influencing their actions. At the core of the framework was a shared commitment to achieve unambiguous global leadership in power transmission, an ambition he instilled in his people through constant communication and continual challenging of the organization.

In addition to this binding ambition, the framework also defined four strong values to guide management action: the importance of quality, a commitment to technological excellence, a dedication to productivity and performance, and a strong belief in people. Again, he devoted an enormous amount of time to ensure the institutionalization of these values through intensive communication and by personal example as well as through his human resource decisions. 'In the end,' said Lindahl, 'managers are loyal not to a particular boss or even a company, but to a set of values they believe in and find satisfying.'

Thus, instead of defining detailed strategies that would likely constrain rather than liberate those deeper in the organization, Lindahl's framework was aimed at the higher level of imparting an energizing ambition and a set of guiding values. His objective was not to provide top-down direction but rather to foster the initiative and commitment that generates creative strategy as an output rather than as an input.

Beyond framing the strategic context, Lindahl also devoted far more attention to developing people than to allocating capital. By his own estimate, he spent between 50 per cent and 60 per cent of his time and energy selecting, developing and deploying people throughout his organization. Again his aim was not only to develop their individual capabilities, but also to facilitate a process of organizational learning.

In assuming personal responsibility for selecting the key

managers for his organization, he looked not only for a track record of broad experience and proven performance, but also for personal characteristics (flexibility, integrity, 'statesmanship') that suggested a willingness to learn and operate in new ways. He described his approach as being one designed to create an environment of uncertainty to encourage 'unlearning' of old assumptions and behaviours, then to replace the old ways with the objectives and values that made up 'the framework'. As managers proved their ability, he gradually expanded and loosened the framework to encourage them to grow.

He explicitly saw his primary objective as being first to develop capable mangers, then to let them grow into what he defined as leaders—those who had the personal capabilities and the management skills to set their own objectives and standards, and thus the freedom to become truly entrepreneurial. Lindahl saw his task as being to develop all his managers to this stage, at which time he felt he would have created 'a self-driven, self-renewing organization'.

Finally, Lindahl's personal style was far from the isolationist model that resulted when top management's attention was consumed by systems management and staff reports—'an abstract management approach' as he called it. Instead, he preferred an approach he described as 'fingers in the pie' management. Having internalized a clear purpose and ambition, and challenged and coached his managers to become leaders, Lindahl still believed it was vital for the top management to keep its fingers on the pulse of the business—not to direct or second guess, but to monitor the actions being taken on key issues, and to offer support and advice where needed.

In this process, his actions were typically guided by the early warning signals from the ABACUS system which provided consistent and timely financial performance data on all operations. This data was quickly analysed by one of the handful of people on Lindahl's staff, 'a controller who is sensitive to operations and not just a number cruncher'. When aberrant results appeared or an unexpected trend seemed to be emerging, Lindahl would check in with front-line managers to discuss their diagnosis of the problems and their proposed corrective action. Only if the problems persisted would he intervene to initiate change—'to shake things up and create an environment of learning', as he described it.

Lindahl's approach seemed to reflect the simple belief that his job was not only to manage an economic entity whose activities could be directed through strategic plans, resource allocation processes and management control systems. Equally important was his role as the principal architect of a social institution able to capture the commitment and creativity of those within it by treating them as organizational members, not just as company employees. In addition to managing the strategy and structure, he took the time to develop a corporate purpose and shape the organizational processes. And rather than focusing his attention on the performance of divisions or subsidiaries, his primary unit of analysis was the individual manager.

RETHINKING THE CONCEPT OF AN ORGANIZATION

In the recent past, large companies have been under attack all over the world. Highly publicized problems at companies like IBM, Sears, General Motors and Westinghouse together with the rise of the Silicon Valley start-ups have led many to question the fundamental legitimacy and viability of the corporate model that has been developed and refined over the last half century. In India, the same delegitimization of large companies has followed in the wake of a decline of traditional industry leaders and the emergence of a new breed of entrepreneurs.

Amid the broad change in social values away from the bureaucratic to the entrepreneurial ideal that we described in the preceding chapter, there is a growing belief that true entrepreneurship can only exist in smaller firms. Many critics have charged that successive rounds of vertical integration, diversification and geographic expansion have created companies that are too complex and unfocused to be fast, flexible or creative. The solution, according to these critics, is to break up these behemoths and replace them with an entirely new genetically engineered species seductively named 'the virtual corporation'.

Generating $13.5 billion in sales from a portfolio of 60,000 products sold in fifty-seven countries, 3M is not a small company nor a virtual corporation. Yet, year after year, it has generated 25 per cent of its sales from products introduced in the preceding five years. 'Desi' DeSimone, 3M's CEO, has recently raised the bar, demanding 30 per cent of sales to be generated from products introduced in the preceding four years. If the company has literally 'stumbled' into many of its legendary innovations—from its early developments of 'Wet-or-Dry' waterproof sandpaper and 'Scotch' cellulose tape to its more recent innovations such as 'Post-it' notes and optical fibre splicers—it has done so because of the creative ferment it has fostered among its front-line scientists, engineers and marketers. As the saying goes in 3M, 'you can only stumble if you are in motion'. In our study, we found several other companies, like ISS and Canon, that have, like 3M, been able to sustain a core entrepreneurial process over many decades, using it as their primary source of competitive advantage over their smaller competitors. Clearly, size and diversity, per se, are not the problem. Knowing how to manage them is.

Further, if some companies have been able to protect and institutionalize entrepreneurship over their histories, others have demonstrated the possibility of rebuilding front-line initiative far more rapidly than many had believed possible. In the interest of providing one comprehensive example, we have focused our discussions on ABB. However, as we illustrated in chapter 11, many other companies around the world—including in India—have been able to rekindle the sparks of entrepreneurship in their tired and faltering organizations.

What we have found in common in all these companies is an organizational philosophy that is far less focused on macro-structural elements and top-down control and far more orientated to the roles of managers at different levels, and the relationships that connect those roles. It is a way of managing that is not well captured by the conventional representation of the organization as a neat pyramid of hierarchically arranged boxes. That is why, the representation on the right-hand side of figure 12.1 does not emphasize managers' positions in the hierarchy, but the roles they play to add value to the company.

HCL's Fractal Organization

An Indian example of this new management model in operation? Unfortunately, in our limited exploration of Indian companies, we have not found any case where the management has either articulated a new organizational approach as clearly as ABB, or has gone as far in actually changing management roles within themselves. But there are several companies in India that have committed to elements of the new philosophy and are slowly putting in place both the structural features of the entrepreneurial organization we described in chapter 11, and the associated management roles we have presented in this chapter. We have already described some aspects of Hindustan Lever's transition to the entrepreneurial model. But, of all Indian companies, HCL Corporation provides perhaps the clearest example of achieving outstanding performance through a total commitment to stimulating and leveraging the entreprenuerial talent of its people.

Shiv Nadar, founder and chairman of HCL Corporation—the glue that holds together the HCL group—supports his breathtaking growth ambition with the vision of building what he calls a fractal organization: a company that grows continuously by creating replicas, which then create replicas, and so on ad infinitum. His strategy focuses on spinning off individual businesses as separate companies, to be run autonomously by their CEOs, and then encouraging each of those companies to spin off their outgrowths, in turn. The HCL group has increased turnover tenfold every six years by following this logic of fractal growth, led by front-line entrepreneurs.

Perhaps the most celebrated illustration of this process is NIIT. In 1981, Rajendra Singh Pawar, an HCL employee, had the idea that HCL should get into computer education—then a nascent and highly fragmented activity in India. Shiv Nadar's response: to create NIIT as a separate company, funded by HCL and led by Pawar who would also hold a significant equity stake in the new entity.

Another example of the same organizational philosophy is HCL Comnet. Following his practice of constantly looking for entrepreneurial talent within the company and outside, Nadar identified Vineet Nayar, then a mid-level regional manager in the HCL organization, as a potential spark plug. He pulled Nayar out of the organization, to report directly to him, and set him the challenge of looking for new growth initiatives. After evaluating a number of alternatives, Nayar pushed for networking and telecommunications as presenting the most attractive opportunities. Once again, Nadar responded by setting Nayar up as the CEO of HCL Comnet, to do what he proposed and to reap, both for himself and for HCL, the benefits of his own entrepreneurial zeal. Later, Nayar would, in turn, follow the same fractal principles, creating smaller entrepreneurial units focused more specifically on areas such as networking, satellite-based communication, trunking and radio.

Nadar describes his own role in this front-line entrepreneurship-based fractal organization as 'leading the group, getting them together, and moderating them in their structural decisions'. While the CEOs of the operating companies run their businesses with almost complete autonomy, the leadership team at the apex body of HCL Corporation has the charter of 'setting standards and creating policies across the group'. More specifically, they take responsibility for looking at new business opportunities, bringing in financial and accounting discipline, specifying human resource development practices, and handling corporate communication for the group. While the operating companies retain their pioneering zeal, the corporate leaders lay down common structures and processes and generate and manage the synergies. And perhaps the most important role they play is to identify entrepreneurs like Pawar and Nayar, and create the opportunities for them to spread their wings.

Over the years, the HCL group has developed more than twenty-five CEOs, each responsible for the success or failure of the companies under their leadership. At least ten start-ups have been highly successful. Typically the failures occurred—as in Network Typewriters or HCL Global Alliance—when HCL's top team was too hands-off, though outwardly it seemed as if the mistakes lay in inventory management or somewhere else. 'When dealing with young people, it is important to control enthusiasm, instil self-discipline and teach them how to handle authority. There's a the-future-is-bright syndrome which has to be controlled if margins are to be protected,' says Sujit Bakshi, head of HRD at HCL Technologies. 'On a strategic level, the top has to walk just short of the fine line of control, to be at the point where the numbers are reported regularly but initiative is not stifled. Too much control and the CEOs can declare a unilateral declaration of independence, as indeed one HCL start-up company did.'

To illustrate the interplay between the HCL group and its dozens of start-ups (quite a few of which it took public), Bakshi described early events at HCL Frontline Solutions, a company formed in 1992 to capture the home PC market. Ambitiously, it defined its business as selling multimedia PCs for family computing, with on-line services like bulletin boards, e-mail services and other internet services (in 1994!).

Having spotted this gap in the market, HCL pulled out its best sales and support people from within the group. No one was more than six or seven years out of college because Frontline was to be a small, lean organization and 'we didn't want people who were used to the comforts of a large organization', recalled Bakshi. 'We told all these young people in their late twenties to create this new business. This business needed speed—managers had to take decisions quickly because margins were extremely thin (between 3 and 4 per cent)—and the business was risky. But many joined up.'

They agreed to leave the parent organization for various reasons. Some liked the challenge. HCL's campus recruitment process favoured people who had demonstrated excellent academic performance but who also indulged in extra-curricular activities. Inevitably, after joining a large corporation, some felt bored and suffocated by systems. There was a financial upside also. By joining Frontline, they could possibly earn more. The ratio of fixed:performance pay was changed so that if earlier at HCL they were getting Rs 100 as base salary and Rs 20 as performance pay, at Frontline they would get Rs 70 as fixed and Rs 130 as performance. In sum, their compensation would be higher by Rs 80. To earn this extra Rs 130, they had to meet 75 per cent of their target. The incentive was based both on gross margins as well as sales. A good Frontline salesman would make Rs 200 and an average one, Rs 150.

HCL created four companies: in Delhi, Madras, Bombay and Calcutta. Each Frontline had its own CEO. Delhi had about twenty people, Bombay about fifty. Everyone was given equity and each was expected to go public separately. The investment was low, but the challenge was in managing these companies with those thin margins. Pricing and inventory decisions would impact the company immediately. To help the start-ups, HCL formed a governing body, the Senate, with Nadar, Ajai Chowdhry and Bakshi as members.

Every month, the Senate would review the four Frontlines' performances for a full day, and there would be a quarterly review also. 'The role of the Senate was not just to review performance but also to make the kind of decisions which youngsters cannot take,' explained Bakshi. For example, PCL—a company formed by some ex-HCL managers—once made a huge advertising splash offering low-price machines for the home market combined with a cheap financing package in collaboration with a leading finance company. It generated huge demand, adversely affecting the Frontlines. But the demand generated by the campaign was so high that PCL could not meet it. 'We had over 500 machines in stock and Nadar immediately placed full-page advertisements offering express delivery and captured the excess demand. The youngsters could not have taken that decision.'

The Senate also acted as an information pipeline between the four companies located in India's four corners. It monitored and matched inventory levels, for example, so if stocks were too high in Bombay and too low in Calcutta, the Senate would inform the two companies.

On another level, HCL guided its start-ups by providing coaching and training. Everyone at each Frontline went through a thirty-day programme on products and sales with role plays. A process was set up so that groups of ten salesmen would meet every evening from 6 to 8 p.m. to discuss the events of the day. Annually, everyone had to go through twelve days of training, and a four-week programme was developed with XLRI for field people.

Within two years, the four companies had proved their worth even though they were losing money. They broke even in 1995 and started making a profit in 1998. But by 1995, aggregate sales had risen to Rs 85 crore. At the same time, it was clear that the four companies needed to merge. Frontline was a zero-debt company but it had collected many bad debts. Inventory issues were sapping gross margins and there were synergies to size. So in 1995, the Senate brought them together as HCL Frontline Solutions. One of the CEOs became head of the new combined company, another became COO (later he became part of the HCL group's core strategy team), a third became the head of the largest division and the fourth left the HCL organization.

'This business could not have been conceived within HCL,' says Bakshi. 'Its mindset, attitudes are different. People were working out of their residences to keep costs down.' Its hierarchy was slimmer—compared to HCL's four levels in sales, it had just two. It removed superannuation which in the HCL was 15 per cent of sales, and which the older HCL managers liked but which had no significance to younger Frontline people. The rules and performance policies were more flexible. Its managers had more authority, dealt directly with risky customers and had to think fast on their feet. In a sense, Frontline recreated the original HCL culture.

We believe that managers in many hierarchical, divisonalized corporations recognize the need for such a radical change. Yet, most have shied away from taking the plunge. In a brutally honest self-evaluation, the European CEO of a major American company may have provided the most plausible explanation for this gap between intellectual understanding and commitment to action: 'It is more reassuring for all of us to stay as we are, even though we know that the result will be certain failure, than jump into a new way of working when we cannot be sure it will succeed.'

Simply exhorting front-line managers to feel empowered will not help them break free. If it could, Westinghouse would not have died. Incremental adjustments along the corridors of indifference in organizational politics will not free the hostages either. If it could, General Motors would have turned the corner a long time ago. Side-stepping the problem by creating refuges for radicals at the periphery of the organization will be equally futile in the long run. Otherwise Kodak's market share in the bread-and-butter photofilm business would not continue to erode.

To reignite the spark plugs of managerial entrepreneurship that were the original source of their success, large hierarchical corporations need a fundamental reshaping of their organizational mainstream. And to lead such radical change, top managements have to first reorient how they think about organizations. Just as those who pioneered the divisional organization created enormous opportunity for their companies five decades ago, those who will have the courage to build the entrepreneurial corporation we have described in this and the preceding chapter will enjoy a similar advantage in the decades to come.

13

BUILDING SHARED DESTINY RELATIONSHIPS

Only about 25 per cent of Bajaj Auto's total costs relate to anything the company does in-house; the rest relate to purchased inputs. Therefore, reducing purchase costs by 5 per cent will clearly yield far greater benefits to the company than a comparable cost reduction for any internal activity. Reducing external and internal costs are not mutually exclusive, but the relative shares of the two suggest which one deserves a higher priority. As we described in chapter 2, Bajaj Auto has recognized this priority, and has launched a major initiative to improve its supply chain management.

There are two very different ways in which the company can approach this task, each corresponding to a very different management philosophy (see table 13.1). The first way involves the use of its large buying power and the skills of bargaining. This is the way José Ignacio Lopez reduced General Motor's purchase bill by several billion dollars. The other way involves the creation of shared destiny relationships with its vendors, built on mutual trust and a commitment to mutual interdependence, and requires the skills of joint learning and problem solving. This way too can yield outstanding results, as has been achieved by John Neill in UK's Unipart group of companies. Both methods can be effective in the sense that both can achieve the goal of reducing Bajaj's purchase costs. Therefore, the choice between the two approaches cannot be settled on the basis of which one works. It will have to be settled on the basis of the values and beliefs of the company and its managers. Which way Bajaj Auto goes will be determined by who or what it is or wants to be as a company.

Table 13.1: The Two Kinds of Relationships

Power-based Relationships	Shared Destiny Relationships
Win–lose	Win–Win
Transactional	Relationship based
Short-term	Long term
Your problem	Our problem
My benefit	Our benefit
Maximize autonomy	Maximize interdependence

The Power-based Relationship

José Ignacio Lopez has been one of the most colourful and controversial managers of the 1990s. While his career ended in some disrepute following allegations of stealing secret documents and plans from General Motors when he moved from that organization to Volkswagen, even his worst detractors admit that he played a key role in transforming both companies. According to his own claims, Lopez saved General Motors $10 billion a year in purchase costs. According to General Motors, the figure was closer to $4 billion. Wherever between these extremes may the true figure lie, what is astounding about the case is that he achieved these savings in only ten months which is the total time he spent in Detroit. In a company as large and as complex as General Motors, most managers take that amount of time simply to get to know where the toilets are!

Lopez's methods for achieving such dramatic results in so short a time was very simple. The first step involved centralization of purchase. In General Motors, for example, most items were historically purchased separately by each brand company. As a result, the volumes were distributed. By consolidating all important purchases at the corporate level, he first built his own muscle power vis-à-vis the suppliers.

In the next step, he made all GM suppliers offers they could not refuse. He demanded immediate price cuts of up to 50 per cent. In return, he promised significantly higher volumes. Those who refused the price cuts were struck off the supplier list, their shares being handed over to those who agreed. Creative ways were found to get around any contractual obligations to the contrary.

For most of the suppliers, the options were few. GM tended to be their largest customer. Being blocked out of GM would send them into an immediate tailspin. The very large price cuts, while extremely painful, would at least give them some time to create new options. So, many agreed—yielding an immediate and spectacular improvement in GM's cost position and, therefore, profitability.

This is a simplified and somewhat unkind account of what happened at GM. Lopez offered to help the suppliers reduce their costs by sending in his crack team of specialists. He also offered some educational support. But, at the end of the day, the relationship was based on power. Some motivational sloganeering notwithstanding, it was a win-lose game. GM won by saving a lot of money. While some of the savings came from the economies the suppliers could achieve through higher volume, most of it, at least in the short term, came from their margins. The negotiations were largely transactional, with both GM and the suppliers protecting their autonomy, and each focusing on finding the best arrangement it possibly could, given the circumstances, and solving any of the resulting problems.

It is hard to tell how the relationship would have developed if Lopez had continued in GM. As things unfolded, supplier relationships became a major problem for the company after Lopez's departure. While the savings he had delivered were the anchor for GM's celebrated turnaround, the company spent several years repairing relationships with key vendors. Some of the most innovative had left the company fold to become the preferred suppliers of Ford and Chrysler, and GM had to expend a lot of effort to persuade them to recommit to the company. Overall, the productivity, efficiency and cost of GM's supply chain management improved radically but Chrysler, not GM, came to be cited as the model for managing supplier relationships in the US auto industry.

The Shared Destiny Relationship

The alternative to this power-based relationship is best illustrated by the experiences of Britain's Unipart group of companies. Unipart was born when Margaret Thatcher was finally fed up with the government-owned British Leyland—state subsidies to the company exceeded what it would cost to buy a car for every man, woman and child in the UK—and decided to privatize the company. The relatively good bits of British Leyland found corporate buyers; Jaguar ultimately went to Ford, the truck division was bought by Holland's DAF, Sweden's Volvo purchased the bus business, and UK's British Areospace gobbled up the larger car operation, renaming it as Rover. What was left was the stump of a totally uncompetitive parts business, and a portfolio of units engaged in sourcing and distribution. It was this unpromising residue of British Leyland that, following an investor and employee buyout in 1987, became the Unipart group of companies.

At the time of its founding as an independent company, Unipart suffered a two-to-one handicap in productivity vis-à-vis Japanese auto parts companies and an astonishing hundred-to-one gap in quality, according to a UK Department of Trade and Industry study. It inherited an extremely confrontational work climate, the product of a heavily unionized workforce crossed with a traditional and autocratic management. The company's adversarial relationships extended also to its suppliers and customers.

A decade later, the story had utterly changed. Unipart's turnover had shot up to £1 billion, profits had quadrupled to $32 million and a Department of Trade and Industry study had announced that Unipart was the only UK-based company in its industry to meet world-class standards on quality. It had also emerged as one of the highest performing stocks on the FTSE.

At the heart of the company's transformation was one man, Unipart's CEO John Neill, and his absolute commitment to what he described as building 'shared destiny relationships'. Ascribing the chronic problems of the automotive industry in the UK to its reliance on 'traditional power-based relationships', he saw the need for shared destiny relationships as 'not altruism, but essential for commercial self-interest'.

For Neill, the new relationship was not an empty rhetoric and it was soon converted from philosophical ideal into implementable action for all the company's internal and external constituencies. With regard to suppliers, the translation took the form of the 'Ten(d)-to-Zero' programme. Instead of functioning as a traditional supplier rating system, Ten(d)-to-Zero emphasized the measurement of joint Unipart-supplier performance across ten criteria that ranged from transaction costs and lead time to defect rates and delivery errors. The goal was to continue to bring the scores down to zero in each area (hence Ten(d)-to-Zero), with both Unipart and the supplier equally sharing the benefits of process and quality improvements and cost reduction.

Unipart's relationship with Tungstone, a hundred-year-old UK battery producer, provides a good example of Ten(d)-to-Zero in action. Once enjoying a 25 per cent share of the UK replacement battery market, by 1989 Tungstone had declined to a point where the company was seriously considering the option of closing down the business. Just one symptom of its deeply rooted problems: in 1989, fewer than 50 per cent of its shipments to Unipart, one of its largest customers, met the stipulated lead time of two or three days.

Once Neill convinced Tungstone to join the Ten(d)-to-Zero programme, one joint Unipart–Tungstone employee team was assigned responsibility for each of the ten performance measures, with the goal of ultimately reaching a zero score. Following the procedures carefully laid down, the teams took a systematic approach to analysing the entire production and distribution chain across both Tungstone and Unipart, looking into everything from ordering and manufacturing through to delivery and end-customer installation. Together, the teams developed innovations in such areas as forecasting, electronic data exchange, and production processes. The results were rapid and significant: on-time product availability, for example, improved from 48 per cent in 1989 to 96 per cent two years later.

Such results were not easily achieved, however. They required both parties to share information that neither felt comfortable sharing. The interdependence created through the joint teams also made each more vulnerable to the other. At times, the conversations were difficult since all issues had to be put openly on the table. Yet, over time, as the us–them mindset gave way to one of joint learning and problem solving, breakthrough innovations were achieved that radically reduced the costs of the whole chain, instead of merely passing costs from one party to the other.

A FUNDAMENTAL CHOICE

It is not only with regard to supplier relationships that a company faces a choice between the two fundamentally different approaches we have described. They face the same choice in all their relationships—inside the organization, with employees and trade unions, and outside the firm, with vendors, dealers, customers, regulators, joint venture partners, even competitors. Building shared destiny relationships with suppliers and customers makes intuitive sense; therefore, let us illustrate the possibility for some of the other constituencies.

Consider the case of trade unions. The jute industry in West Bengal represents perhaps the most extreme case of an adversarial power-based relationship between owners and employee unions in India. Beyond the problems of rampant asset stripping, falling market prices and a stagnant technology, it is the sustained conflict between unions and management that has effectively destroyed this business. Yet, as we described in chapter 1, amid the graveyard of closed jute mills around Calcutta, one company—the Hastings Jute Mill—has continued to prosper and grow. At the root of that success lies a very different kind of union-management relationship that the Kajaria brothers, Bjiay, Ajay and Sanjay, have built since they acquired the mill in 1994.

'When we took over the mill, we knew that manufacturing costs had to be brought down,' recalled Sanjay Kajaria. 'In the jute industry, wages are typically 40 per cent of the cost of production. Raw material forms 35 per cent, power accounts for 8 per cent, stores another 7 per cent, while miscellaneous costs make up for the remaining 10 per cent. There have been no improvements in jute technology so savings have to come from reducing the process costs. However the poor IR history in the jute industry over the last two decades had led to rigidity in the mindset of workers. To improve productivity and reduce the processing costs, we needed the cooperation of labour and for this, we had to build a very different mindset.'

The first effort was to convince workers and the company's fourteen trade unions that unless everybody adopted a win-win attitude, the mill would close down. The unions were initially sceptical, but a major breakthrough in trust building occurred when the Kajarias regularized the legal status of some 700 'ghost' workers immediately after taking over the mill. In many jute mills, workers came in to work but their names were not on the official payroll and there were workers on the payroll who did not exist. This practice not only deprived permanent workers of their legal rights but was an indirect way of reducing wages and avoiding the payment of other dues.

The goodwill generated by this gesture brought union leaders to the negotiating table. Regular monthly meetings lasting for about two hours started taking place where each union would send two representatives. To come closer to the workforce, twice a week one of the Kajaria brothers would walk through the plant. The mill dispensary started caring not only for workers and their families but also outsiders in emergency cases. The mill's drinking water tap was opened to local people to supplement municipal supplies. As levels of hostility abated, gradually both sides agreed on enhanced productivity norms and incentive schemes. But the biggest triumph for both management and workers was an imaginative training scheme.

The scheme was born out of necessity. Nearly 200 workers retired every year at Hastings and the gratuity cost to the company was Rs 1 crore annually. 'But we did not earn enough to pay this. So we promised to employ one member of the family of the worker who was retiring,' explained Sanjay Kajaria. 'However, the new worker would come in as a trainee at a lower wage. Hastings pays Rs 48 per day for the new recruits, with a net saving of Rs 150 per worker per day. But the unions accepted this rate because Hastings would train a young member of the retiring employee's family for three years. Also we promised that the new worker will not be a "ghost" worker but will be properly accounted for in the system.'

The feeling of sharing a common destiny didn't come about easily. It took four years, two strikes, a lockout and hundreds of meetings, but the wage cost at Hastings came down from 40 per cent to 33 per cent, from 52 mandays per ton to 42, and a saving of Rs 5 lakh per month. In 1998, the Indian jute industry comprised 73 composite mills of which 22 were 'sick', and 25 per cent of installed capacity of 1.95 million tons was idle. Yet every loom in Hastings Jute Mill was busy and productivity in some parts of the mill was 90 per cent. Sales moved up from Rs 13.1 crore in FY94 to Rs 43 crore in FY95, doubling to Rs 90.7 crore in FY96 and stabilizing thereafter. Profits climbed in tandem, jumping from Rs 0.9 crore in FY94 to Rs 3.46 crore two years later.

On the other hand, Hastings workers can earn Rs 15 a day more than workers at other mills, their jobs and provident funds are assured, and there is a promise for the future. The Kajarias are adding 20 per cent more capacity. It is modest in terms of funding, Rs 15 crore capex in five years, but it is a commitment nonetheless and an act of faith in an otherwise shrinking industry. As Kajaria says, 'One can buy peace for some time but not for always. For long-term benefits, mindsets have to change and be flexible. We could do this because we did not inherit the thinking of the old jute dynasties.'

For an even more extreme case, consider the competitive arena. Perhaps the most implausible arena to build shared destiny relationships is with regard to competitors. 'Do lunch or be lunch' is supposed to be the competitive motto of any dynamic, aggressive management. All our metaphors about competitors relate to war, where the enemy has not only to be defeated, but must be utterly destroyed.

This was indeed the spirit with which Komatsu, the Japanese earthmoving equipment company, took on Caterpillar, its American arch-rival. It's slogan was 'Maru-C'—surround Caterpillar—and this strategic intent was supported by powerful symbols such as a giant Caterpillar bulldozer that Ryoichi Kawai, Komatsu's president, installed on top of the company's headquarters building, to constantly remind all employees of the enemy.

This war-like stance served Komatsu well for a time, as the company grew to become the second largest earthmoving equipment company in the world. However, the competitive obsession became a blinder too, preventing the company from focusing on customers and from looking at its emerging opportunities in related areas. Finally, in the early 1990s, Tetsuya Katada, the new president of Komatsu, abolished the slogan. 'I want everyone to stop concentrating simply on catching up with Caterpillar,' said Katada. 'Managers can no longer operate within the confines of a defined objective. They need to go out and see the needs and opportunities and operate in a creative and innovative way.'

Is it possible to build a shared destiny relationship with competitors? Yes, it is. Yes, in India. In chapter 9, we described the outstanding success of HDFC, and the supportive relationship with employees that undergirded that success. It is not just with employees that HDFC has built such win-win relationships. Indeed, H.T. Parekh had committed the company to 'building long-term, mutually supportive relationships with all its key constituencies: employees, investors, depositors, borrowers and regulators'.

While competitors were not explicitly included in that statement, HDFC has, over the years, nurtured it own competitors. Inspired by HDFC's manifest success, the government had started looking for ways to expand the availability of home loans. The National Housing Bank Act was voted in by Parliament in 1987, and the National Housing Bank (NHB) was established by the government as a subsidiary of the Reserve Bank of India, charged with the responsibility for regulating, promoting and refinancing the housing sector. Following that decision, a number of financial institutions including the State Bank of India, Canara Bank, the General Insurance Corporation as well as the Gujarat state government set up new housing finance companies.

Instead of trying to derail these new entrants to protect its near monopoly position—the normal response of most companies—the HDFC management took a very different view. The company's mission was to contribute to solving the housing problem in India by helping middle-class Indians own their homes. Given the enormously large market, HDFC could not possibly serve all the potential customers and more housing finance companies were necessary for HDFC to achieve its core mission. So, the company kept a small equity position in each of these new entrants and fully supported them on strategy and training, helping them to become stand-alone entities. Each of these companies operated independently in the market and competed for business against HDFC. Over time, while HDFC concentrated its efforts in western India, SBI Home Finance focused on the east and north-east, Canfin in the south and PNB Home Finance, a smaller player, emerged in north India.

HDFC has maintained a similar positive relationship with its regulators too. Meeting an important social need, rather than personal profit, was the key motivator of H.T. Parekh, and he firmly believed in the need for building a symbiotic relationship between the public and the private sectors for achieving economic and social progress in India. As a result, both he—and, after him, his successor, Deepak Parekh—maintained a very strong and close relationship with all related government agencies, and invested significant amounts of time and energy working on government projects and initiatives, many of which were of no direct commercial interest to the company they led.

Another constituency with which management relationships often tend to be adversarial is the company's shareholders. In the past, corporate managements largely ignored the providers of funds. Over the last decade, with the rise of 'shareholder power' all over the world, indifference has given way to open conflict. Institutional investors and corporate managements have been at loggerheads in many companies around the world—from IBM, Digital Equipment Corporation and Compaq to Philips, Daimler-Benz and Credit Lyonnaise. While this shareholder power is still in its infancy in India, recent changes in corporate governance regulations have set the stage for a similar adversarial relationship to soon emerge.

In contrast, many of the companies featured in this book have taken the initiative in forming a far more positive and partnership relationship with the investor community. Reliance's investor relations are legendary, with Anil Ambani personally ensuring a continuous flow of reliable information and projections to the company's equity holders around the world. Similarly, Infosys' soaring market value owes a lot to the rigour and transparency with which it communicates with its investors—not just through its annual reports but also through frequent meetings and special briefings.

At HDFC, Deepak Parekh views himself and other managers as professionals managing the company on behalf of its various shareholders. 'I am merely a professional who happens to be at the helm of affairs of a corporation,' Parekh said in December 1996. 'I have always viewed my role as that of a trustee, who is enjoined with the task of running a business enterprise.'

We have titled this section as a 'matter of choice' but our bias is obvious from the way we have framed the issue. Around the world, the power-based relationship was the dominant choice till the recent past. Strategy was framed in power terms—to decrease the power of customers and suppliers, as Michael Porter asserted—and profits were the outcome of market power. So, companies bought out their competitors, to create monopoly power; employees formed militant unions, to enhance their bargaining power; and customers bought from many sources, so as to retain their purchasing power. In India too, most companies adopted that mode in their relationships with all their internal and external constituencies.

Around the world, this situation is changing. While efficient perhaps in the short term, power-based relationships have proven to be very costly in the long term. Suppliers and customers are a major source of innovative ideas; companies that build power-based relationships deny themselves the benefits of those ideas and fall behind in the innovation game. Motivated, committed employees drive the process of continuous improvement in quality and operations; companies that subdue employees with power sacrifice those benefits. Recognizing these costs, companies around the world are moving toward what we have described as the shared destiny model, not in a spirit of altruism or generosity but simply as a business need for ensuring superior performance. The same, we believe, needs to happen in India.

Is this the stakeholder model? Perhaps it is. But we have deliberately avoided that term because of the historical baggage it carries. Typically positioned as a contrast to the shareholder model, it is often evoked as a justification for poor financial results. The reason for developing shared destiny relationships is exactly the opposite—to continuously and radically improve business performance. It is all about maximizing shareholder value. As people like John Neill and H.T. Parekh understood, long-term, open and trust-based relationships with employees, customers, suppliers and others do not come at a cost to shareholder value; they are the means for achieving that end.

Is it possible to work with such a philosophy within the Indian context? Is it not true that in India, you cannot trust people because if you do, you will be taken advantage of? For those who share these doubts, the following story of Hero Honda will prove instructive.

HERO HONDA MOTORS

When Honda, the world's largest two-wheeler producer, looked for an entry strategy in India in the mid-'80s, they first flirted with Bajaj Auto. When those discussions failed, they shortlisted the Pune-based Firodia group and the Ludhiana-based Hero group as potential partners. Having decided to split scooters and motorcycles in two different joint ventures, they offered the Firodias the first choice. Given the structure of the market as it then was, with scooters accounting for 45 per cent of the Indian two-wheeler market, motorcycles accounting for 30 per cent and mopeds the remaining 25 per cent, the Firodias obviously opted for a scooter collaboration. The Hero group got motorcycles. 'We felt we had a raw deal,' said a senior manager of Hero Honda. 'Motorcycles were perceived then as unsafe machines. We had to work doubly hard to shake off that image.'

By the late 1990s, fifteen years later, the two joint ventures had produced very different outcomes. With revenues of Rs 1160 crore and profits of Rs 95.4 crore, Hero Honda had emerged as the thirty-eighth most valuable company in the country with a market capitalization of Rs 135.5 crore. Affected by continuous disputes between the two partners, Kinetic Honda had delivered consistently poor results leading, ultimately, to Honda divesting its equity in 1998 at Rs 45 per share.

Why the two very different outcomes? While a variety of factors were at play, perhaps the most crucial difference between the Firodias and the Hero group lay in their philosophical approach to strategic alliances. Right from the beginning, the Firodias played a transactional game, hoping to get the best possible deal, and constantly manoeuvring to keep most of the management power within the alliance. In contrast, the Hero group saw the alliance as a partnership. Brijmohan Lall Munjal, chairman of Hero Honda and the guiding spirit of the Munjal family, described his approach as follows: 'For an alliance to work, one must control one's ambitions. It is no different here. Yes, we suffered in Majestic Auto (a wholly owned business of the Hero group) because we gave the best to Hero Honda—best dealers, best managers, best people, my sons. And yes, Honda's financial charges were heavy. But I didn't get too upset because the success of Hero Honda Motors is a feather in my cap.'

The Hero group's relationship with Honda has been no bed of roses. The Japanese company sees India as a key strategic market, and has played a complex game, involving several partners, to leverage its strengths to the greatest effect in what could well become one of their largest volume markets outside Japan. In that process Hero Honda has not always got what it wanted and the long-term future of the joint venture remains uncertain. Yet, there is no denying of the fact that, for the Hero group, this alliance has been a major engine of progress. Irrespective of how the alliance develops in the future, Brijmohan Lall's commitment to a partnership and his willingness to look at the joint benefits of both the partners, instead of constantly focusing on his own gains, has served him far better than the more traditional power-based approach to alliances that the Firodias adopted.

It is not with regard to Honda alone that Brijmohan Lall took this shared destiny approach. Like John Neill, he believed in shared destiny relationships as a core business philosophy. 'We are one of the four partners in this business: the workers, the dealers, the suppliers and the management,' he said.

Take, for example, Hero Honda's links with its dealers, links which go far beyond commercial needs. 'I know every dealer by name, his background, his family structure, his type of organization. It is a bond,' says the company's deputy general manager, sales, V. Uppal. Traditionally the Hero group had taken care to foster these bonds and the Munjal culture was extended to Hero Honda. 'In our group, whenever there is a happy event in the life of any colleague or any dealer, an officer has to be there. But if there is any sadness in their lives, one family member must go,' says Brijmohan Lall Munjal. Such gestures enhanced the social standing of dealers.

The affinity crosses generational barriers. Dealers, particularly from small towns and villages, are encouraged to send their children to good schools, to allow them to attend computer classes and eventually go to engineering colleges. Hero Honda makes no bones about its self-interest in this process. 'If we help them with their succession planning, we will deal with better business managers.'

If a dealer faces a financial crisis, Hero Honda's head of sales is authorized to lend him up to Rs 3 lakh without question. Uppal recounted the story of one of their Pune dealers. 'He was one of our finest dealers but he invested in real estate and other activities. He became so overambitious that he could not even meet his family expenses. We didn't dump him. We gave him vehicles on credit. Still he could not fulfil his obligations. But we knew he was a good guy. We kept supporting him and brought him back on track. He slowly returned the money. Any other company would have dumped him.'

It's not all milk and honey, however, for dealers. There are checks and balances. Any dealer who drops sales even for a month is checked out by the head of sales himself. The company's sales agents travel extensively—as did Brijmohan Lall Munjal and his brothers in their time—visiting dealers, listening to their comments, complaints and concerns, keeping tabs and monitoring competitor activity. Both sales agents and dealers are expected to behave towards customers with humility and act efficiently and promptly.

If a dealer flouts company norms or is found to have misappropriated funds, retribution is swift. 'After all, he is the public face of Hero Honda. People deposit their money with him,' said a manager. Frequent interaction ensured that the company would come to know of any infraction within days. Hero Honda would investigate all complaints and if sustained, dealers would have their dealerships taken away and even be taken to court. Hero Honda also vets its dealers' financial health through the latter's bank managers, and dealers are expected to accept this.

But these clearly established rules of the game do not come in the way of nurturing, which continues at the business level. 'We teach them profitability and to think about the future: that from their earnings, they should reinvest one-third into the business, spend one-third on future growth and enjoy the remaining one-third. And they have prospered with us,' said a manager. Hero Honda dealers have to have 1,600 sq. ft of showroom space when other two-wheeler companies are content with 500 sq. ft 'because we want the outlets to have an imposing identity.' At the same time, the company works on a cash basis and dealers make about Rs 1500 per bike, somewhat more than what Bajaj Auto offers.

Hero Honda's relationship with its dealers is also prompted by the understanding that with increasing competition and a greater variety of model offerings, in future dealers will have a greater role in influencing the customer's purchase decision. Gone are the days when Indian customers just wanted a two-wheeler and were satisfied if the dealer could give them one. Customers have also begun asking for service, both pre-sales and after-sales. Hero Honda maintains about 150 authorized service centres. These dealership-cum-service centres have to have another 1500 sq. ft for the workshop whereas other two-wheeler makers ask for just 250 to 300 sq. ft. However, once again, Hero Honda provides substantial inputs: workshop layouts, supervision of showrooms, and an investment of between Rs 25 and 30 lakh.

Pawan Munjal periodically invites fifty dealers to Honda's plant in Japan. During the ten-day trip, they are exposed to Honda technology, Honda showrooms and Honda dealerships. The Munjals are convinced such trips gave dealers strength and the motivation to invest in Hero Honda. Both Honda and Hero Honda pay for a part of the trip's expenses. 'One of our dealers, a rustic sardar, was so moved by his Japan experience that after coming back, he put in carpets and air-conditioned his showroom,' recalled the company's sales manager. 'While he was in Japan, he always had a paper and pencil. He drew the stands and later he entirely replicated a Honda showroom in Bhatinda.'

'We all want and need respect,' said Brijmohan Lall, explaining his approach towards dealer relationships. 'In the end, what is respect? Best technology, large production, warm relationships, and good quality. For that one must attain and achieve shared objectives and one must control one's ambitions.'

The same philosophy guided the company's relationship with suppliers. Like most joint ventures, the Hero group's collaboration with Honda was governed by government regulations which demanded a high degree of local sourcing of components. But in few joint ventures in India did this localization process work out as spectacularly as it did for Hero Honda. Within five years of start-up, indigenization was 90 per cent, by 1996 it was 95 per cent (85 per cent by cost)—a record for a Honda plant anywhere in the world. In terms of value, whereas a bike had 65,000 yen worth of imported parts in 1985, this was down to 7800 yen by 1994.

Once again, it was the nature of the company's relationship with vendors that lay at the heart of these achievements. The Munjals deliberately promoted members of the family and their friends to become key suppliers. At least six Hero group companies were major vendors for Hero Honda, while another twelve were owned by close family friends.

Most companies in India and abroad avoid this practice of appointing family and friends as vendors because of the possible conflicts of interest. Brijmohan Lall, however, looked upon this practice as a competitive advantage. Turning the relationship back-to-front, he pointed to the high degree of coordination between Hero Honda and its suppliers that this practice ensured, leading to tighter controls on the cost and quality of components as well as on the regularity of supply. As one senior manager of the company told us, 'What's special about Hero Honda is that so many of our vendors are family and friends who have been with us for decades.'

Hero Honda's relationships with Sunbeam Castings illustrates these advantages. Promoted and managed by Ashok Munjal, one of Brijmohan Lall's many nephews, the plant was set up with Honda's help. 'It was a new component which was being made in India for the first time,' recalled Ashok. 'At first Honda hesitated, then it changed its mind. Later, when new models came in, Honda participated fully in helping us develop the nine new dies which were needed. Because of our close relationship, Hero Honda can get all its supply of this component from a single source. Otherwise, it would have had to go to three or four vendors. I want to be India's biggest die-caster, supplying not just to Hero Honda but to everyone in the automobile industry.'

Little slack was permitted in the system, however. This was possible because of a shared philosophy. As Brijmohan Lall explained, 'When we started Hero Honda Motors, school friends from Ludhiana who shared the same philosophy became key suppliers.' The company had established strict norms, applicable to all suppliers, to maintain the highest levels of efficiency.

But, at the same time, the relationships were designed to be personal, with a deep sense of mutual trust and loyalty. 'The family is always friendly when a supplier comes, and don't deny him anything,' said Hero Honda's head of purchasing. 'If he needs a car, they will get one for him. They make him feel at home. And they listen to him. Payment is always on time. All terms are settled on logic, not sentiment. For example, pricing is transparent, and if full details are given to us, we will not misuse that information to exploit him. They are brought in by the Munjals and the personal loyalty is there, but loyalty is not enough. We make sure that vendors make money also.' 'We know the value of our established vendors because we came from the field ourselves,' added Brijmohan Lall.

COMPETING ON RELATIONSHIPS

A very powerful new competitive weapon is still invisible to many Indian companies. For over four decades since independence, Indian companies have competed on the strength of their assets—their plants and equipment and their access to capital. Many have made money by cornering licences. Some have also progressed on the strength of proprietary technology and other competencies acquired from foreign sellers or partners.

In the new millennium they will be judged on their ability to build, maintain and leverage their relationships—a decisive resource in the emerging knowledge- and service-based economy.

Recognition of the enormous value of relationships is creating sweeping change in management priorities around the world. Corporate account management, strategic alliances, relationship marketing, supplier partnerships—these are all manifestations of this recognition. However, to build enduring, valuable relationships for the company, managers have to face some fundamental questions about their management values and philosophy.

Both José Ignacio Lopez and John Neill achieved the goal of radically reducing sourcing costs. Both power-based and shared destiny relationships work, at the least in the short term. So, returning to the example we began this chapter with, Bajaj Auto really has a choice. Irrespective of what its public rhetoric might be, the reality of how it goes about restructuring its supply chain management will reflect one or the other of these two relationships. Deep in their hearts, managers of both Bajaj and its suppliers will know that reality.

The choice will reflect the values and philosophy of the company, the deep-seated assumptions its managers make about the nature of individuals and organizations. If they assume that all individuals act only in their self-interest and that at least some are untrustworthy and they cannot be identified in advance, then they will prefer the power-based relationship which, after all, is the relationship that governs all market transactions. If, in contrast, they believe that individuals behave differently in different situations and tend to reciprocate the behaviour of those they are dealing with, then the company may be tempted to try the shared destiny approach. In all likelihood, there will be an element of self-fulfilling prophecy in the outcome—what they assume may influence what they get.

One very rational response may be to select horses for courses. Bajaj Auto managers may decide to build shared destiny relationships with some suppliers, and power-based relationships with others. This can be done, but only to a limited extent. Both individuals and organizations find it very hard to live by conflicting values; ultimately, their behaviour reflects one or the other as the dominant trait. If the company chooses the power-based relationship for some, that equation will ultimately colour its relationship with the others.

To some managers, the shared destiny relationship may appear to be the more attractive, if only because it sounds nicer. Why be the bad guy if you can get the same results by being the good guy? For these managers, let us sound a note of warning. Shared destiny relationships are very hard to build, and even harder to sustain. They cannot be implemented in part—if you wish to build shared destiny relationships with suppliers, you will also have to live by the same rules with employees and customers. It is not something you can just do; it is something that you have to be.

IV

TRANSFORMING THE CORPORATE
PHILOSOPHY

14

A NEW MANIFESTO FOR LEADERSHIP

After almost a decade since India took the first tentative steps to economic liberalization in 1991, most Indian managers who have survived the traumas of industry overcapacity and restructuring, the onslaught of foreign competition, and the growing sophistication of customers and technologies, will quickly agree that companies all over the country, in all kinds of businesses, are in the midst of radical change. The problems and challenges posed by the new competitive, technological and market demands have created a new industry of analysts and consultants trying to understand the nature of the change: every major international consulting firm has discovered India as a growth market and management related books and articles have proliferated.

As a result, senior managers in Indian companies have been swamped with analysis, speculation and war stories that claim to offer lessons and even provide answers for their myriad problems in this era of discontinuous change. In strategy, they have been taught the intricate moves in a global chess game being played by their multinational rivals, urged to identify and manage their core competencies, and shown how to build competitive advantage on the basis of speed and flexibility. In terms of organization development, they have been exposed to new structural models ranging from multidimensional matrices to inverted pyramids; from lean networks to virtual corporations. And with regard to systems, they have been urged to abandon their most basic tools and familiar methods in favour of radically different ones, from activity-based costing to highly leveraged performance-based incentives.

With a mixture of excitement and exasperation, managers in a wide variety of Indian companies have been struggling to adjust their corporate operations to absorb this mostly sound yet highly disparate advice. But, every change has tended to create as much disruption as relief. The problem has been that while each solution has offered a radical change, it has dealt with only a part of the complex linkage of strategy, structure and systems that most companies have built, elaborated and refined over many decades.

This book is a product of our efforts to understand and analyse these challenges that Indian managers have been experiencing over the last decade. To look for insights, we have focused not so much on those who have stumbled and got left behind, but on those who have prospered and taken leadership positions. Our belief is that managers are the best teachers of managers, and we have tried to understand the lessons offered by people as diverse as Narayana Murthy and Brijmohan Lall Munjal, Sanjay Kajaria and Keki Dadiseth, H.T. Parekh and Azim Premji, Dhirubhai Ambani and Rohinton Aga, Lakshmi Niwas Mittal and Subhash Chandra, Rahul Bajaj and Parvinder Singh, so as to be able to distil their insights and form our own views on what Indian companies and managers need to do to become world-class in their strategy, organization and management.

The results of our journey of discovery into Indian management are the biases that we have presented in the preceding thirteen chapters. As we said in the first chapter, we have deliberately resisted the temptation of building any overall conceptual model or theoretical framework and have offered, instead, a series of ideas on the kinds of actions that companies can take to manage the transition in this period of turbulent change. But now, in this closing chapter, it is time to look beyond these specific proposals to reflect on our own overall learning from this brief but highly stimulating exploration of some outstanding Indian companies. How are they different? What is the essence of that difference? Why is it that they are able to do what others find so difficult?

As we pondered over these questions, the answer was both obvious and abstract; both simple and profound. Companies can perhaps act on any one of the individual proposals we have made within their existing strategic and organizational frameworks. But, actions on individual items will not get them where they need to get to. To respond to the multidimensional changes in their environment, they will need a much more broadly based and more closely integrated systemic change in the way they are organized and run. As we compared companies like Infosys, HDFC, Ranbaxy and Wipro against the more traditional Indian companies, we came to recognize that the Indian corporate sector is experiencing the rise of an entirely new model of management and individual companies will not find satisfactory answers to their questions unless they discard not only their tried and tested solutions but also the old perspectives they bring to define and understand the problems.

In defending the importance of theory for good practice, Lord Keynes once said that every living practitioner is a prisoner of the ideas of a dead theorist. Obsessed as they are with the 'real world' and focused as they are on pragmatism and actions rather than on theory or concepts, managers are actually no exception to Keynes' dictum. There is a dominant theory—a doctrine—that influences the basic perspectives of even the hardest driving of Indian managers. Often they are not consciously aware of this doctrine they conform to; like fish in water, they take it for granted. To the extent conformity is unconscious and the assumptions behind it are untested, the doctrine becomes self-fulfilling and, therefore, self-reinforcing.

The problem is that this doctrine, a product of the Indian business environment for over five decades, has become obsolete in the new era. It has been built on assumptions to which the current business world no longer conforms.

That is why the most important challenge facing Indian managers is also the most abstract: the need to change their basic management philosophy. Yes, they need the kind of specific changes in strategy, organization and individual behaviour that we have described in the preceding chapters. But to make such radical and simultaneous changes across all these different fronts, they have to change the lens through which they view the company and the premises on which they frame their own managerial responsibilities.

BEYOND STRATEGY, STRUCTURE, SYSTEMS TO PURPOSE, PROCESS, PEOPLE

As we described in chapter 12, the current generation of corporate leaders in India have learned to frame their tasks through the viewfinder of the three Ss: crafting *Strategy*, designing the *Structure* to fit, and locking both in place with supporting *Systems*.

This strategy-structure-systems oriented management doctrine came to India from the West. The model had emerged in the United States, through the pioneering experiments of Alfred Sloan at General Motors and, in its time, it was a revolutionary discovery. Based on the delegation of responsibility to a new level of divisional general managers, this new practice was made possible by the development of sophisticated planning and information systems that allowed those at the corporate level to maintain control over their diverse set of decentralized operations. And, for decades it served companies very well. In contrast to the earlier model of a functional organization, this new doctrine and the divisional organization that embodied it, had a much greater carrying capacity of complexity. Its modular design supported vertical and horizontal integration, the wave of conglomerate diversification in the 1960s and the start of globalization in the 1970s and 1980s. To get into a new business, all a company had to do was to add a new division. To go to a new geographic area, ditto.

Stimulated by the enormous success of its pioneers, this strategy-structure-systems doctrine soon spread around the world. It came to India in the 1970s and 1980s, under the garb of 'professional management'. Structure follows strategy, it claimed. And systems support structure. Within two decades, these aphorisms deeply penetrated Indian management thinking.

All over India, business schools taught this model. Look at the curriculum of any MBA programme and you will see the strategy-structure-systems doctrine. Consultants spread it from company to company. And soon, a generation of senior managers came to the fore in corporate India who saw these three powerful tools as the primary levers for establishing the direction and leveraging the performance of their companies. As a result, they defined their own roles as the company's designers of strategy, architects of structure and builders of systems. In a highly restrictive and regulated economy characterized by widespread shortages of most products, the key management task was to allocate the company's limited financial resources among the competing opportunities in different divisions and then monitor the performance of divisional managers against their plans through a tight control system. By providing discipline, focus and control, the strategy-structure-systems management doctrine suited this context very well.

The great power—and fatal flaw—of this doctrine lay in its core objective: to create a management system that would minimize a company's reliance on the idiosyncrasies of individuals. If, from the top, the strategy could be clearly defined and communicated; if a clear structure could be established so that everyone knew who reported to them and who they reported to; and if clear systems could be developed for managing the flows of capital, information and other resources, then complex organizations could be run with people as replaceable parts. It wouldn't matter who was in a particular job; they would all do the same things, anyway. And indeed this is exactly what happened in large Indian companies in both the public and the private sectors. As their size expanded, strategies, structures, and reporting and planning systems became more and more complex, fragmenting and routinizing the daily activities of their employees.

Over the 1990s, however, the Indian economy has undergone some profound changes that have undermined the foundations of this strategy-structure-systems doctrine. Overcapacity and intense competition are the norm in most businesses. The lines separating businesses have blurred as technologies and markets have converged, creating new growth opportunities at the intersection of traditional industries. And, most notably, ideas and knowledge have increasingly replaced capital as the scarce resource and the key source of competitive advantage.

In this new world—a world in which an internet portal constructed by twenty people at a total cost of Rs 30 lakh has a market value greater than all the tea gardens of Assam; in which swirling competition outdates established industry structures overnight; and in which hiring an excellent manager or scientist can often be a far bigger triumph than bagging a big bank loan—the strategy-structure-systems model has become obsolete.

In the emerging knowledge and service-intensive economy, the key challenge is not to establish control over people so as to run a company as if it were a machine; it is to be able to attract, develop and retain the best talent and to link, diffuse and leverage their knowledge, skills and initiative to create innovations and new opportunities. In this economy, the old doctrine, the managerial equivalent to Taylorism, has come to an abrupt dead end.

What is special about companies like Wipro and Ranbaxy; HDFC and Infosys? A different management philosophy. While managers in many Indian companies have recognized the limitations of the strategy-structure-systems doctrine, most have lacked either the imagination or the courage to break free from it. In contrast, these companies have adopted a fundamentally different management approach.

Instead of trying to be the designers of strategy, people like H.T. Parekh and N.R. Narayana Murthy took on the role of establishing a sense of *purpose* within the company, defined in terms of how the company will create value for all its constituents, and strategy emerged within their organizations, from the energy and alignment created by that sense of purpose. As opposed to constantly playing with the boxes and lines that represented their company's formal structure in an organogram, they focused on building core organizational processes that would support the entrepreneurship of front-line managers, integrate the resources and knowledge across the front-line units to develop new capabilities, and create the stretch and sense of challenge that would drive the whole company into continuously striving for renewal through new value creation. And, instead of being the builders of systems, they took on the role of being the developers of *people*, creating a context in which each individual in the company could become the best he or she could be. In essence, they replaced the three S's of Strategy, Structure and Systems with the three P's of Purpose, Process and People, both as the philosophical core of the company and as the key anchors for their own roles and tasks within the organization.

It is important to emphasize that this new philosophy does not imply a complete rejection of the old doctrine. That is why we have titled this section not as 'from' strategy, structure, systems but 'beyond' it, to purpose, process and people. Clearly, as our descriptions of these companies in earlier chapters show, HDFC does have a strategy, Wipro has a clearly defined structure, and Ranbaxy has strong, effective systems. But the vital difference between these companies and many others is that managers like Parekh, Premji and Parvinder Singh have extended their focus beyond the hard-edged tools of strategy, structure and systems to embrace the softer and more dynamic model that we have defined as the purpose-process-people philosophy. It is this fundamental difference in philosophy that defines the essence of what is distinct about these companies, and why they have prospered while many others have stumbled.

In some ways, an Infosys or a Wipro has been lucky. They are relatively new companies and were born with the new doctrine. But not all the companies we have described in this book were so lucky. There were those, like Hindustan Lever, Reliance and Bajaj Auto, who grew up in a different environment, and learnt a different approach to survive and prosper in that environment. What makes them special, perhaps even more special than Infosys or Wipro, is the courage and tenacity with which they are trying to move to the new model.

Although this change in philosophy pervades the entire organization, its starting point rests with top management. It is their managers who have to lead their companies' transition, beyond strategy to purpose, beyond structure to processes, and beyond systems to people.

Beyond Strategy to Purpose

For any chief executive, the idea of being the company's omniscient strategist is hard to resist. Strategy is a very appealing concept, both intellectually and emotionally, and the business press in India and abroad is always full of stories about how exceptional CEO's saved companies through their personal redirection of strategy, constantly reinforcing the heroic image of the CEO as an army general, sitting on the proverbial horse, thinking up great strategies and leading his troop to victory in the battlefield.

When companies were smaller and less diversified and their

operating environment was simpler and more predictable, the ability of those at the top to set a clear strategic agenda was much more feasible. Indeed, in their early days, this is precisely the role that people like Dhirubhai Ambani and Rahul Bajaj played in their then much smaller companies. But as companies grew larger and their operating environment became more complex, senior executives needed elaborate systems and specialized staff to ensure that they could review, influence and approve the plans and proposals of their divisions and business units. Over time, as we saw in a large public sector bank in India, the workings of the increasingly formalized planning processes eclipsed the utility of the plans they produced: sterile generalities to which front-line managers felt little affinity or commitment.

The problem is rarely the CEO personally, but rather the assumption that the CEO should be the chief strategist, assuming full control of setting the company's objectives and determining its priorities. In an operating environment where the fast-changing knowledge and expertise required to make such decisions are usually found on the front lines of each business, this assumption is untenable. Strategic information cannot be relayed to the top without becoming severely diluted, distorted and delayed. And even when it does survive that tortuous journey in some useful form, top-level executives rarely have the current knowledge, the specialized expertise or the fine-grained insight often required to sort out the complex decisions and make the sophisticated judgements implied by the strategic proposals.

Abroad, people like Andy Grove, CEO of Intel, have come to acknowledge this limitation. As Grove honestly admits, for a long time neither he nor the other top managers at his company were willing or able to see how the competitive environment had undermined Intel's strategy of being a major player in both memory chips and microprocessors. Yet for two full years before the top management recognized that the company had to get out of the memory business, various project leaders, marketing managers and plant supervisors were busy refocusing Intel's strategy by shifting resources from memories to microprocessors. As a result, Grove came to the somewhat humbling conclusion that neither he nor any of his top team had the control over strategy they thought they had. He recalled the period:

> We were fooled by our strategic rhetoric. But those on the front lines could see that we had to retreat from memory chips . . . People formulate strategy with their fingertips. Our most significant strategic decision was made not in response to some clear-sighted corporate plan but by the marketing and investment decisions of front-line managers who really knew what was going on.

As Grove reflected on the lessons of the most important strategic decision in Intel's history being recognized and initiated by people deep in the organization, he acknowledged the need for top management to adjust its thinking about how it influcnced corporate direction. Instead of concentrating their attention on refining the tools to allow them to develop strategy more precisely at the top, corporate leaders needed to spend more time framing the environment that allowed more strategic initiative and debate to emerge from below. Anticipating the need for future strategic shifts as dramatic as the exit from memories, he said:

> The more successful we are as a microprocessor company, the more difficult it will be for us to become something else . . . We need to soften the strategic focus at the top so we can generate new possibilities from within the organization.

Most top-level managers find this notion of 'softening the strategic focus at the top' very hard to accept. They fear that it would make them appear indecisive or even incompetent. They fear that unless they provide a clear strategic direction, they may lose the respect and admiration of employees. So they continue their efforts to play the role of the strategic guru, adopting sterile planning and control processes and mechanical, simple-minded incentive systems to drive strategy top-down, further eroding the motivation of their people.

In such an environment, in which people no longer know—or even care—what or why their companies are, leaders cannot afford to focus only on refinements to the analytic logic that frames the strategic processes. Strategies can engender strong, enduring emotional attachments only when they are part of a broader organizational purpose. Today, the corporate leader's greatest challenge is to create a sense of meaning with which the company's employees can identify and in which they share a feeling of pride.

What does it take to create a sense of purpose? One key element is to establish a shared ambition or vision. Recall our discussions in chapter 4 about the competition for dreams, and the example we provided of how Dhirubhai's breathtaking ambition drove the whole Reliance organization by creating an enormous sense of pride and excitement in anyone who came in touch with that vision. But growth is not the only form of shared ambition. Recall also our discussion of HDFC in chapter 9: H.T. Parekh never once asserted any need for HDFC to become the biggest. He established a profound sense of purpose by focusing everyone's attention on an important social need—to solve the crippling housing problem in India. Helping middle-class Indians own a home was innately a wholesome goal, one to which employees could relate with a sense of pride and satisfaction. Parekh tapped this sense of mission in every individual, and built up HDFC's famous customer service orientation on the strength of this link between the company's ambition and each individual's need for meaning in his or her work.

But just a vision, a shared ambition, is not enough to create a sense of purpose. It is not enough to define what the company aims to achieve. To create purpose, it is equally important to also shape and embed in the company a set of shared values, a description of what kind of company it wants to be.

'Objectives and strategies don't get you there, values and people do,' says GE's Jack Welch. 'We defined a set of values and those values then determined who would be in the management team. Anyone who could not conform to those values . . . had to go.' Göran Lindhal, the CEO of ABB agrees: 'People are not loyal to a company or to an individual,' he said, as we quoted in chapter 12. 'They are loyal to a set of values they believe in and find satisfying.'

Recall our discussion in chapter 7 about Azim Premji's absolute commitment to Wipro's values and beliefs. Once again, we repeat to emphasize: 'These beliefs and values give a common cause and a sense of purpose across the businesses making Wipro in essence one company. They define the spirit of Wipro . . . To meet the challenges of the future, we are prepared to change everything about ourselves except our beliefs, as they alone guide, govern and bind us together as an organization.'

For many Indian companies, values are the Achilles heel. Stimulated by an environment that was simultaneously inefficient and corrupt, they have developed terrible values that are now deeply entrenched in the psyche of their people. What one does outside inevitably reflects inside: arrogance, cutting corners, 'managing the environment', lack of respect for individual dignity, one's own and others'—a large number of Indian companies are still ridden with the bad habits of yesteryears. They cannot establish a sense of purpose, irrespective of how exciting and well crafted their vision statement might be, unless they take determined action to purge themselves of those debilitating values.

Finally, for the purpose to become an active management process at all levels of the company, it is necessary to bring the vision and the values down to the level of each individual. They have to be translated so that, to quote an old saying, each stonecutter can see his or her job as part of the building of a temple. As we emphasized in chapter 9, it is through such translation to the individual level that a corporate purpose becomes the source of personal identity and meaning for employees, and the basis for the kind of behaviour and actions that we have advocated in the earlier chapters.

Beyond Structure to Processes

Perhaps even more than strategy, structure is a highly seductive lever for top-level managers, and most of them see their control over the company's structural configuration as a powerful tool to shape the broad direction of the organization and to influence the actions of managers lower down the hierarchy. As companies become larger, this top-level preoccupation with structure inevitably leads to complex organizations with multiple layers and increasingly bewildering management processes.

This is precisely what happened to large companies all over the world, as the strategy-structure-systems doctrine diffused from the United States to Europe, then to Asia and other continents. By the mid-'80s, they all started confronting severe problems caused by the weight and elaborateness of their complex structures.

Over the 1980s, big companies around the world started falling off the precipice—IBM, Kodak, General Motors and Sears in the US; Philips, Siemens, ICI and Daimler-Benz in Europe; Matsushita, Hitachi, Mitsubishi and the Industrial Bank of Japan in Japan, and so on. In each case, one could find an explanation for their stumbling in some specific technological or market factors, but the underlying causes were the same across the board. They had all fallen victim to the problems of strategic stagnation and managerial myopia caused by their increasingly complex organizations. Stifling bureaucracy at the corporate level had crushed their entrepreneurial spirit, fragmentation and compartmentalization of the divisions inhibited knowledge diffusion and organizational learning across them, and the hierarchical relationships that were designed to achieve order, efficiency and control had destroyed their capacity for change and renewal. No one put the problem in clearer terms than Jack Welch, in his assessment of the much admired and frequently emulated structure his predecessors had built in GE:

> We had constructed over the years, a management approach that was right for its time, and the toast of business schools. Divisions, strategic business units, groups, sectors—all were designed to make meticulous, calculated decisions, and move them smoothly forward and upward. The system produced highly polished work. It was right for the 1970s, a growing handicap in the 1980s and would have been a ticket to the boneyard in the 1990s.

It is this recognition of the limitations and constraints of the structural solution that has triggered the decade-long flurry of delayering, destaffing and downsizing in companies around the world, to dismantle their bloated and overly complex structures. And, as they have simplified their organizations, managers have found a completely different way to think about their companies, in terms of processes rather than structures.

The shift from structure to processes as the primary organizing device was initially built around agendas such as TQM, time to market, and supply chain management, which all focused on horizontal processes cutting across the organization rather than the vertical processes of command and control that lay at the heart of structural thinking. The gradual shift finally became a tidal wave as the process re-engineering movement swept through the corporate world in the mid-'90s.

In India, however, the trend has largely been the opposite. While Jack Welch was tearing out the old structure in GE, Indian business schools were teaching the outdated GE cases to MBA students and executive programme participants, extolling the value of precisely the same organizational characteristics that Welch described as 'a ticket to the boneyard in the 1990s'.

In several companies, we found consulting reports suggesting elaborate structural solutions to their strategic problems—the creation of a strong corporate head office to improve the quality of strategic thinking and analysis, the establishment of a new regional structure to enhance strategic coordination and integration, and the addition of new management levels within the divisions to augment strategic direction and control. Influenced by these ideas and inputs, many Indian companies have now adopted the same structural thinking that companies around the world have learnt to move beyond.

And this is again where companies like Hindustan Lever, HCL, Infosys, and Ispat have been blazing a different trail. Like the best companies abroad, they too have been focused on developing processes rather than elaborating structures, to concentrate on how the organization would create value instead of how top management could enforce control. This focus on processes is manifest in these companies at many different levels. All of them have significantly improved their operational processes—how to pay bills, for example, or how to assemble a part in the factory—by redesigning the work flow, often with support from new IT-mediated methods. One level above, they have reshaped their strategic processes, such as new product introduction, the logistics chain or the customer engagement process, by questioning and changing some fundamental aspects of their historical ways of working. And, one level above still, they have built their overall organizations on three core processes: an *entrepreneurial process* to drive the externally oriented opportunity-seeking behaviour of their companies; an *integration process* to link and leverage their diverse resources and competencies lodged in different business, regional or functional areas, and a *renewal process* to constantly challenge the existing ways, to prevent past success formulae from ossifying into a recipe for future disaster.

In chapter 11, we have described how Keki Dadiseth was trying to reshape the perennially successful Hindustan Lever away from a structural to a process-oriented mindset. In chapter 12, we illustrated the same focus on entrepreneurship, integration and renewal in HCL, driven by Shiv Nadar.

A company's belief in these processes has some self-fulfilling characteristics. A belief in the entrepreneurial process assumes that individuals lower down the organization can take initiatives, and it creates the context and the mechanisms that encourage and enable them to do so. The integration process both assumes and shapes an environment of collaborative behaviour, based on trust and a sense of support. And the renewal process capitalizes on the natural human motivation to learn and to stretch themselves, and creates the resources and tools that people need to engage these inclinations and capabilities.

This broadening focus, beyond structure to processes, is accompanied by a changing concept of what an organization is. A focus on structure is built around the concept of an organization as a portfolio of activities and tasks. Organizing then becomes all about breaking up the activities into sub-activities, and then reconnecting them—a very engineering mindset. In contrast, a focus on the entrepreneurial, integration and renewal processes leads managers to view an organization not just as a portfolio of activities but as a social system built on the roles people play, and the relationships that connect them. As we described in chapter 11, in companies like Hindustan Lever, the focus on processes has been shaped by a fundamental redefinition of management roles within the company.

Such a process-based organization is built on the strength of a close interplay among three management roles we described in chapter 12. The front-line managers' roles are transformed from that of operational implementers to entrepreneurial spark plugs: they spearhead the entrepreneurial process, supported by the coaching role of senior managers and the framework building role of top-level managers. Beyond this support role in the entrepreneurial process, the senior managers in the middle act as the lynchpins in the integration process, linking the front-line initiatives into coherent strategic thrusts and leveraging the company's competencies by transferring best practices and sharing and coordinating the use of resources. Finally, the corporate leaders drive the renewal process, establishing stretch goals and performance standards, shaping the vision and values of the company, and constantly challenging the organization to prevent ossification and to maintain the performance momentum.

Beyond Systems to People

In chapter 12, we described Percy Barnevik's radical makeover of ABB into a fundamentally different organizational model. What motivated the change? What was the theory of the case? Here is what Barnevik said right at the beginning, as his justification for ABB's radical overhaul:

> Our organizations are constructed so that most of our employees are asked to use only 5 to 10 per cent of their capacity at work. It is only when those same individuals go home that they can engage the other 90 to 95 per cent—to run their households, lead a boy scout troop, or build a summer home. We have to be able to recognize and employ that untapped ability that each individual brings to work every day.

Harold Geneen, quintessential practitioner of the strategy-structure-systems philosophy and the legendary CEO of ITT, famously said, 'I am building a system that a monkey can run when I am gone.' Contrast that statement, and the management perspective that underlies it, with Barnevik's beliefs, and you will understand what the shift beyond systems to people really means.

We have argued that the whole strategy-structure-systems doctrine was developed to free a company from the uncertainties of human idiosyncracy—to make people like replaceable parts. Of all the three elements of this doctrine, it is systems that played the most important role in making people's behaviour as routinized as the machines they worked on.

While top-level managers see systems—planning systems, budgeting systems, control systems, and so on—as the lifelines that provide their information link to the operations, to people in the operating units the same systems feel like ropes that bind them, chains that tug them to heel when problems arise, and as puppet strings that control their actions from above. As a result, of the three S's, it is systems that have perhaps made the greatest contribution in creating in the front-line units of large companies an internal context that we described in chapter 9 as akin to the environment of downtown Calcutta in summer.

Besides this consequence of demotivating and disempowering people, the elaborate infrastructures of systems have led to another set of debilitating problems in large companies. First, there is the enormous cost of preparing, transmitting, consolidating and reviewing a growing array of reports in each of the scores of systems most companies have developed. This has been largely responsible for the expanding bureaucracy companies have suffered from. Equally important, the timelines of most reporting systems are increasingly out of touch with the needs of the businesses. Plans and reports prepared on annual, quarterly, or even monthly basis are of limited value in monitoring the activities of a business where important strategic events and operating developments often occur weekly or even daily. To be effective, systems need a relatively stable environment and they become not only valueless but counterproductive in a world of rapid changes in competitive, technological and market conditions.

These limitations of a systems-orientated model have led to one of the most widespread management fads of the 1990s—employee empowerment. Promoted by management gurus and packaged by consultants, this term has come to encompass anything from simple introduction of an employee suggestion scheme to the implementation of a radical restructuring of the organization around self-managed teams. While some of these initiatives have been carefully constructed so as to respond to the new realities, many more have paid mere lip service to this deceptively simple and appealing notion. To many overloaded senior managers, struggling with issues and challenges they could not fully grasp, the idea of pushing the backlog of problems back down into the organization had great appeal. Under the sanctioned umbrella of 'empowerment', many have handed over responsibilities and delegated decisions so broadly, so quickly, and with so little support that the process can be better described as 'abandonment'.

Once again, in companies like Infosys, Ranbaxy, Reliance, HDFC, Hindustan Lever and Hero Honda, we found a philosophy very similar to Barnevik's. As opposed to relying on formalized strategic planning systems, Brijmohan Lall and H.T. Parekh influenced their organization's direction through the development and deployment of key people. Instead of imposing elaborate and strict control systems to ensure compliance, Dhirubhai Ambani and Narayana Murthy—both in their own different ways—used interpersonal relationships and direct interactions to shape people's behaviour. And, rather than relying on abstract and aggregated information systems, Keki Dadiseth and Azim Premji developed alignment through rich and intense personal communication with those who have access to vital intelligence and expertise. In none of these companies was empowerment confused with abdication—in each company, the senior management worked hard to delegate authority but also to provide support; they kept their 'fingers in the pie', like Göran Lindhal of ABB; and they matched their demands on people with investments on them, to build their capabilities.

In conversations with each of these managers, the one message that came out most strongly was their firm faith in people as the most important source of competitive advantage. While we heard this rhetoric in almost all companies, what made this commitment real in these companies was their concrete people practices. In chapter 5, we have described the obsessions in Reliance, Hindustan Lever and Infosys for recruiting the best available talent, and the extreme lengths each goes to for meeting this objective. In chapter 10, we have illustrated their commitment to training, their focus on development and their philosophy of helping each individual become the best they can be.

Their actions, and the outstanding performance those actions have stimulated, demolishes the core tenet of the strategy-structure-systems doctrine which instructs managers to minimize risk by controlling the idiosyncracies of individuals. In the new management model emerging in India, chief executives recognize that the diversity of human skills and the unpredictability of the human spirit make initiative, creativity and entrepreneurship possible. The most basic task of corporate leaders is to recapture these valuable human attributes and to do so, they need to abandon the constraining strategy-structure-systems doctrine and embrace the liberating philosophy of purpose, processes and people.

CREATING VALUE FOR SOCIETY

Neither Narayana Murthy nor H.T. Parekh started out with the desire to build a company around the purpose, processes and people philosophy. These are our words; our interpretations of what they have done, based on our looking back over the histories of the companies they have built.

But what *did* they start off with? What is it about them that led them to this very different management approach? They did not emulate Andy Grove, Jack Welch or Percy Barnevik—none of these corporate leaders had yet become famous when Narayana Murthy started Infosys or Parekh established HDFC. They did not copy anyone; their beliefs and practices came from within themselves. What was it within them that manifested itself in this very different corporate philosophy?

The ultimate source of this new doctrine, we believe, lay in their very different assumptions about business, and about what a company is supposed to be. The strategy-structure-systems doctrine is based on a narrow economic view of companies and an instrumental perspective on companies' roles within the broader society. Narayana Murthy and Parekh, in contrast, had a much broader view, grounded in a more moral and institutional perspective.

The concept of strategy, for example, is built on the premise that corporate management's primary objective is to appropriate value for itself. Nowhere is this premise stated more clearly than in Michael Porter's theory of competitive strategy that has had such profound influence on management thinking around the world, including in India. Companies are seen by Porter as positioned in the middle of a set of competitive forces that pit them against all others. Companies strive to keep as much as possible of the value embodied in their products and services for themselves, and allow as little as possible to fall into the hands of employees, customers, suppliers and direct or potential competitors, who are all trying to do the same. In short, strategy is about preventing others from eating your lunch.

The difficulty is that in this view, the interests of the company are fundamentally incompatible with those of society at large. For society, the freer the competition among companies the better. But, for individual firms, the purpose of strategy is precisely to restrict the play of competition to keep maximum value for themselves. To do their job of increasing corporate profits, managers must prevent free competition, at the cost of social welfare. The destruction of social welfare is not just a consequence of strategy, it is the fundamental objective of profit-seeking firms and, therefore, of their managers.

This view of the interests of a company and those of the broader society being fundamentally in conflict simply does not square with the reality of modern economies. The last hundred years have seen an uninterrupted and unprecedented improvement in the quality of human life, due in a large measure to the ability of companies to continuously improve their productivity and their talent for innovating new products and services. Most of the economic value in both developed and developing economies is created not through the economists' ideal of highly fragmented, pure competition in a completely free market, but within efficient, well-functioning organizations involving teams of people acting collectively, coordinated by the broader purpose of the total organization.

Most companies that prosper do not do so by merely appropriating value, at the cost of social welfare. Rather, in healthy economies, vigorous companies coexist with intensely competitive markets in a state of creative tension with one another, each contributing to economic progress, but in different ways. Companies create new value for society by continuously creating new products and services, by finding better ways to make and offer existing ones; markets, on the other hand, relentlessly force the same companies to surrender, over time, most of the value to others. In this symbiotic coexistence, companies and markets jointly drive the process of creative destruction that Joseph Schumpeter, the Austrian economist, showed to be the engine of economic progress.

The problem with the strategy-structure-systems doctrine is that it focuses management attention on static rather than dynamic efficiencies. Static efficiency is all about exploiting available economic options as efficiently as possible—making the existing system more efficient. Dynamic efficiency comes from innovations and improvements that create new options altogether—moving the system to a higher level. When the source of value is taken as given—the basis of Porter's theory of competitive strategy—any consideration of 'who gets what?' must necessarily become a zero-sum game in which profits can only come at the cost of someone. In sharp contrast, Schumpeter's very different view of the role of companies focuses on the dynamics of how the pie gets bigger in a positive sum game in which there is more for all to share. In this view, instead of merely appropriating value, companies serve as society's main engine of discovery; they progress by continuously creating new value out of the society's resource endowments, thus stimulating both social and economic progress.

It is precisely this belief about business that stimulated Narayana Murthy, then an employee of Patni computers, to start Infosys. In his heart a diehard socialist with strong leanings to the left, Narayana Murthy had come to the realization that distribution of wealth must be preceded by the creation of wealth. This was the goal behind his founding the new company with six other Patni computer colleagues—to create one hundred rupee millionaires in India, via the establishment of an ethical business firm based on a highly competent and skilled workforce in the area of software development technology. By making Indians rich, he would make India rich.

Similarly, as we described in chapter 12, H.T. Parekh believed that business must serve the interest of society, and that a wholesome business, meeting an important social need, could also be highly profitable. 'Solving India's housing problem' was not a PR slogan for him; it was the key rationale for not enjoying the luxury of a well-earned retirement, and the motivation for starting up a fledgling company, against all odds, after a highly successful career as the chairman of ICICI.

Neither of them engaged in the old and tired debate about the social responsibility of business, which frames social responsibility as something outside of business. Instead, they put value creation for society at the heart of their business. Out of this conviction about the role of companies emerged the very different management philosophy that has powered their companies not only to the prosperity they now enjoy, but also to the prestige and legitimacy that the country accords to them.

Regaining Corporate Legitimacy

And it is on this issue of the legitimacy of business that we wish to draw this chapter, and this book, to a closure.

Over the twentieth century, companies have earned enormous amount of social legitimacy, which has been both a cause and a consequence of their collective success. Amid a general decline of other institutions—think of the state, political parties, organized religion, even the family—the business firm has emerged as perhaps the most influential institution of modern society.

Yet, in the closing decades of the century, companies and their managers suffer from a profound social ambivalence. Hero-worshipped by the few, they are deeply distrusted by the many. In movies and TV serials in every language in India, a businessmen or a manager rarely appears except in the villain's role. When asked by pollsters to rank professionals by their standing in society, people consistently rank managers the lowest of the low—below even politicians and journalists.

Given the powerful and largely positive role companies have played in India, this perception is unfair. Yet, the perception exists, and a few visible misdeeds of some companies and individuals serve to give this perception its ascendancy and to make it potentially one of the greatest risks that companies face today. There is a clear lesson from history—institutions decline when they lose their social legitimacy. This is what happened to the zamindars, and this is what will happen to companies unless managers accord the same priority to the collective task of rebuilding the credibility and legitimacy of their institutions as they do to the individual task of enhancing their company's economic performance.

Far from thinking of their companies as agents for destroying social welfare, most Indian managers believe that their primary role is to create value. Their guilt lies in their unwillingness to confront explicitly the role their companies play in society or to articulate a moral philosophy for their own profession. Through this act of omission, they have left others—economists, politicians, journalists and others—to define the normative order that shapes public perceptions about themselves and their institutions. Those perceptions, in turn, have seduced many managers into thinking about their companies in very narrow terms and, in the process, have made them unconscious victims of the value appropriation logic and weakened their ability to create new value for society.

This is why we believe that individuals like H.T. Parekh, Narayana Murthy, Azim Premji and others we have described in this book will earn their places in Indian's business history. Not because of the economic performance of their firms while they were in the saddle, because hundreds of managers achieve that routinely, but because they have wrested back the initiative to define a new corporate philosophy that explicitly articulates a view of companies as value-creating institutions of society. In that process, they have also contributed to reestablishing the legitimacy of the management profession as key contributor to a country's economic and social progress. Collectively, they are India's role models demonstrating the spirit, passion and moral commitment of which entrepreneurs and managers are capable, and which the strategy-structure-systems doctrine has all but destroyed.

Ideas matter. In a practical discipline like management, they matter even more. The philosophical vacuum of the strategy-structure-systems doctrine has caused managers to subvert their own practice, trapping them in a vicious circle. But, there is a choice. When the solution to a recurring problem is always 'try harder', there is usually something wrong with the terms, not the execution. So, our final advice to Indian managers—when in a hole, the first thing to do is to stop digging. The outlines are emerging in India of a very different management philosophy, based on a better understanding of both individual and corporate motivation. The time has now come to throw out the old paradigm of management, and to make a jump to the new one. Otherwise, the fatal gap between companies' economic power and their social legitimacy will continue to grow, stunting the growth potential of Indians, Indian companies, and India.

INDEX